The Sounds of My Life

The World is Talking…
Are You Listening?

Cinco Cocke

I don't need you to worry for me 'cause I'm all right. I don't want you to tell me it's time to come home. **Billy Joel.**

Therefore, we must pay greater attention to what we have heard, so that we do not drift away from it. Hebrews 2:1

Breathe In, Breathe Out, Move On. **Jimmy Buffett.**

Be yourself, everyone else is already taken. **Oscar Wilde.**

You know what the happiest animal on Earth is? It's a goldfish. Y'know why? It's got a 10-second memory. Be a goldfish. **Ted Lasso.**

Slow & steady wins the race. **Cinco Cocke** *(at least, I think I said it first)*

Dedication

This book is dedicated to my parents, Joy and Jimmy Cocke. You set the bar very high.

Acknowledgments

The genesis of this book started many years ago, and I want to thank all the people who encouraged me to write it.

To the many friends I have enjoyed over the years, thank you for being such a big part of my life. I wish I could name all of you individually, but especially some of my best friends from high school: Mike Biesiada, Kim Nelson, Beth Ferris, Chip Glispin, Shawn Swanson, Jerry Trevino, Annette Shepherd, Wynn Searle, Joe Elliff, and Chad Reininger.

To my ninth-grade English teacher, Ms. Salinas, who saw something in me and encouraged me to try public speaking. The confidence I gained from that experience had a big impact on me.

To the wonderful guys at the Beta Mu chapter of Pi Kappa Alpha, I hope you got as much from it as I did.

To Libby, who taught me truly how to love.

To my sisters, who mentored me about life and the female point of view.

And most of all, to Marshall and Savannah: you made my life whole when you came into the world.

Contents

About the Author

Cinco Cocke grew up in South Texas as the fifth of five children. He lost his older brother to a drunk driver when he was 14 years old and writes poetically about that experience and its impact on his life. A lifelong resident of Texas, Mr. Cocke has traveled extensively around the world and weaves the people and places from those travels, including 9/11, Covid 19, the Navy Blue Angels, Alaska, and South Africa, into this historical retrospective of his life.

Prologue

7:00 AM on a Sunday, the morning comes very early for a fourteen-year-old boy. Even more so when your parents are standing beside your bed with news that will change your life forever. "He's gone," they said. My sleepiness vanished in an instant. And so did a good part of my innocence. A drunk driver killed my twenty-two-year-old brother early that morning on a country road. He and his buddy, Billy, had parked on the shoulder of a two-lane farm-to-market road so Billy could walk to the tree line and pee. My brother—we called him "State," which was short for "Staton"—was getting out of his 1974 VW Beetle on the driver's side when a passing car hit him. Billy was 30 feet away and witnessed the whole thing. He told us that State died instantly. It was the only "good" part of the tragedy, and I knew it comforted my Mom to know that her firstborn son didn't suffer.

Thinking back on my life, this was the first time my world voice spoke to me. And it was talking very loudly. I had no choice but to listen; it was sort of forced on me. But I was only a young boy, not yet equipped with coping skills and maturity honed over years of life. The timeline for growing up accelerated in a huge way. Anyone who has lost a parent or sibling at a young age can relate. So, our family pulled together, grieved openly, and did our best to celebrate his life. State was a dynamic guy who oozed charisma from every pore. We knew he would want us to focus on the positives of his life and the wonderful, cherished memories we had created. So, he was speaking to me, too. And I listened.

There are many cliches about grief and tough times – we've all heard them. I chose to focus on the future and how I might take this message, this loss, and channel it into being a better human, a better son, brother, father, and a more empathetic friend. Perspective is a powerful thing, and I wanted to feel powerful, not weak. You can decide for yourself, after reading this book, if I made it. Thanks for listening.

Part One:
Growing up in South Texas

Chapter 1: This Is Our Playground

South Texas was a great place to grow up. And I do mean South. As in the most southern county in the State, right on the border with Mexico. South Padre Island is only about 45 minutes away. My hometown was a city of roughly 65,000 people called "Harlingen."

The "Rio Grande Valley" stretches for almost seventy miles along the U.S./Mexico border; it's a vibrant and growing area today with a population of over 1.2 million. There's another 1 million on the Mexico side, and we spent a ton of time in all of it growing up there. The area is flat with very fertile soil, so agriculture is a big part of the economy. Growing up, the Valley was covered with orange groves and grapefruit orchards. Tall Washingtonian Palm trees lined both sides of the rural roads as we drove from Harlingen to the "upper Valley" area of Mission. It was very scenic, and in the fall, we had fresh fruit from the orchards surrounding our house in the country for several months. Mom planted some of her own citrus trees on our four acres surrounding the house, including papaya and limes.

Because of the nice year-round weather (it rarely got below freezing), we were outdoors a lot. Bird hunting in northern Mexico; fishing the bay at South Padre; quail and deer hunting on the fertile ranchlands north of Harlingen; swimming at "the Beach," as we called South Padre. It was heaven.

My Dad's father (we called him "Papacito") settled there from his roots in San Antonio in 1941 to provide the concrete for an Air Force base that was built there during WWII. The company grew and provided many jobs in the Valley. It also provided my family with a nice lifestyle; in 1966, my Dad took it over and ran it for almost twenty years until we sold it in 1984. Once I turned 15, I spent almost every Summer until I graduated from college working in one or more of the various plants we operated, including driving a mixer truck delivering concrete to various job sites around town. We started batching trucks as early as 4:00 AM, so it was an early start, and I learned the value of hard work and discipline. I'm quite sure that was what Mom and Dad had in mind.

Papacito was an excellent amateur golfer – he shot his age at 74! - and gave me my first set of junior golf clubs when I was 9. Papacito was, for many years, a director of the annual Life Begins at 40 golf tournament held at the Harlingen Country Club. Very good amateur golfers from all over the country would come into town to play in the weeklong match play format, which was regarded by many as one of the best amateur tournaments in the U.S. Dad was also a really good golfer and carried a 6 handicap. We played many rounds of golf together, and I became a decent golfer of my own, doing well in local Junior golf tournaments and playing on my High School's golf team.

Growing up, Dad and I would watch all the major golf tournaments on TV. I learned an early appreciation for places like Pebble Beach, Augusta National, Pinehurst, Olympic & St. Andrews. He and I talked about one day going to Scotland and playing golf together, but it was a dream that was too large for me to comprehend at twelve years old. Me, play where the pros play? In Scotland? "No way," I thought. Little did I know that one day it would come true. I remember winning my first junior golf tournament in McAllen in a playoff. My trophy was beautiful, and it felt like it weighed a ton.

As soon as I got home, I jumped in our golf cart (I was way too young to drive a car) with my trophy in hand and headed to Papacito's house to show it to him. This man had won many golf trophies in his life, but this was my first. As I jumped out of the cart and ran into the house, he and my grandmother, Mamacita, appeared. I flashed the trophy in front of him, and he gave me a hearty hug. Mamacita smiled broadly and kissed me on the cheek; her chin whiskers gave me a bit of a chafe. Later, when I would be late to dinner at her house because my golf buddies and I were trying to finish 36 holes one day, she would reassure me that it was "ok, honey." She had a lot of experience with men in the family running late because of a golf match. A sweeter lady there never was.

Mom's parents also hailed from the "Valley"; her Mom was named Roberta, and we called her "Momma Bert." A tiny woman who barely stood five feet tall, she was as full of love as anyone I ever met. Momma Bert was born in the panhandle town of Roby, TX., one of twelve children. Her father, Robert Hudson Johnson, was a lawman. In the 1920s, he was deputized as a Texas Ranger, and they moved to South Texas so he could help protect the area from cattle rustlers coming over the Rio Grande from Mexico. His firstborn son, William Horace Johnson, became a Texas Ranger and fought alongside "Big Daddy," as everyone called my great grandfather. One night, patrolling the U.S. side of the river, they were ambushed by Mexican banditos, and William was killed in action. Many years later, Big Daddy became the first Chief of Police for the city of Harlingen. He and "Big Mamma" are buried in the F Street cemetery in Harlingen; his grave is adorned with a ceremonial cross that has the Ranger badge attached to it. In fact, when the Rangers first started wearing badges, they were stamped from the Mexican Cinco Peso silver coin because, back then, it was not illegal to deface foreign currency. Today, the Ranger badge is sometimes referred to still as the "Cinco Peso."

In 1821, Stephen F. Austin, known as the "Father of Texas," signed a contract to bring 300 families to the Spanish province, which is now Texas. By 1823, probably more than 600 to 700 people were in Texas, hardy colonists from the various portions of the United States at that time, who settled not far from the Gulf of Mexico. There was no regular army to protect them, so Austin called the citizens together and organized a group to provide the needed protection. Austin first referred to this group as the Rangers in 1823, for their duties compelled them to range over the entire country, thus giving rise to the service known as the Texas Rangers. Today, with women in their ranks, they are one of the country's most respected and successful groups of crime fighters. One of their more noteworthy successes came in May 1934 when a group of Rangers led by the legendary Capt. Frank Hammer took down nefarious bank robbers Bonnie Parker (born in Rowena, TX.) and Clyde Barrow (born in Ellis County, TX) on a rural road in Bienville Parish, Louisiana. For many years Dad had a beautiful, framed print on his office wall showing the weathered profile of a lawman wearing the Cinco Peso, which simply said: "One Riot, One Ranger."

Having lost State, it was me and my three sisters, Cindy, Gayle, and Shelley. Cindy was 13 years older than me, so she went off to college when I was just 5; I really didn't have a chance to get to know her that well. Gayle was 10 years older, and we did bond. As I grew older and started dating in high school, Gayle always took an interest in my social life and asked about any new girl at school I happened to mention. She gave me some very good advice about how to be a "good guy" and the dos and don'ts of relationships. As we both grew older, our relationship blossomed even further; I have always enjoyed our time together, and as time passed, we grew very close.

My third sister, Shelley, was almost exactly one year older than me, so we were "Irish twins." We were extremely close through our youth and remain so still. Shelley is unique: a wonderful combination of beauty and charm. She has this innate ability to put people at ease around her, much like Mom did. I was always "Shelley's little brother" on the first day of school, and she set the bar pretty high. Her wise counsel over the years has served me well.

Shelley got her driver's license on her 16th birthday (I was 15), and I tagged around with her and her friends as much as I could. She was a good sport about it but certainly didn't like having to share a vehicle with me during her Senior year in High School, especially since she knew, as the youngest sibling, I would have a car all to myself my Senior year. In fact, as a Junior, I had football practice at 7:15 every morning, which meant Shelley and I had to leave the house around 6:45 am to be there on time. Anyone who was late to morning practice had to run extra wind sprints (lots of them) after practice ended that afternoon. So, there was no way I was going to be late! Occasionally, it would be time to leave for school, and Shelley wouldn't be quite ready (girls take longer, you know?), so I would just drive off and leave her. I had to avoid her for the rest of the day at school because I knew she was hopping mad at me. Ahh, little brothers can be such a pain.

About once every six months, the local cinema would run a "midnight movie," which meant we could stretch our curfew to 2 am. Well, being high school kids, we decided to go to Reynosa, Mexico, to party instead. Back then, Mexico was safe, even for a bunch of 16-year-old high school kids out late at night. Reynosa is a bustling town of about 500,000 people across the border from McAllen. Our favorite spot was "Eddie's," which was an easy walk across the bridge; at least we had the good sense to park our parent's cars on the U.S. side!

All our friends and cousins would go to Eddie's on midnight movie night. We knew most football players from our rival schools in McAllen and Pharr and would see them there. The bragging and trash-talking would start after a few drinks, which would always lead to arm wrestling. No fights ever broke out, and we all made it home safely.

Cindy had married a man she met at U.T. and had her first child, a son, about a month after I turned 11. I became an uncle at a very early age, with two more nephews and two nieces born in succession after that. Since I didn't become a father until I turned 39, I had watched my sisters raise their children for 28 years before my daughter was born. The lessons I learned and the parenting styles they showed me helped immensely. I was a much more "chill" Dad than I probably would have been otherwise, watching my nieces and nephews grow up through their own bruises, cuts, and fevers. They all survived their accidents and hurts and turned out well, so I knew my children would, too. I remember thinking I wanted to talk "with" my kids and not "at" them. At least, I certainly tried.

Chapter 2: Leathernecks

Several years after WW II ended, in 1962, the Air Force base in Harlingen was closed. At that point, our family business ("Valley Ready Mix") had grown and was also manufacturing concrete pipe to help irrigate all the rich farmland in South Texas. But the base closing had a big negative impact on Harlingen, and many jobs related to it were lost. Several city political and business leaders in town met to discuss ways to use the massive facilities and buildings that were now vacant. One of the people present was a retired Marine Corps Captain who had seen many military bases in his time. He suggested turning the base into a military prep school for grades 7 – 12, emulating other schools around the country, like VMI in Virginia and the New Mexico Military Institute. Further, he suggested this new school be rooted in and based on Marine Corps training and principles. Thus, the Marine Military Academy was born.

Our family was deeply involved in "M.M.A." for many years. Papacito was a founding member of the Board of Directors and deeply loved the school and its mission. Other board members over the years included John Glenn, the first American astronaut to orbit the earth and later a U.S. Senator from Ohio; John Connally, who was Texas Governor from 1963 to 1969 and was in the car with President and Mrs. Kennedy that fateful day in Dallas in November 1963; Brig. General Walter McElhenny, whose family founded and owned for many years the famous "Tabasco" brand in New Iberia, LA. and Mary Moody Northern, the grande dame of the very wealthy Moody family from Galveston. When Papacito died in 1984, he gave his estate to the Academy; the beautiful headquarters building there bears his name and is located just down the street from the Iwo Jima Monument sculpted by Dimitri Vail. In fact, it is the original sculpture that Vail created: the one in Washington, D.C., near Arlington National Cemetery, is actually cast from the original, which now resides in Harlingen.

Mom served as "social directress" for many years coordinating the dances and parties for the cadets. We would often see them walking to and from the campus (most were from out of town and had no cars), so we would always try to stop and give them a ride. They were very nice young men and always appreciative of the lift. The highest-ranking cadet was a "Major" from Annapolis, MD. named Bill Foster; he and Gayle met at one of the social functions and fell hard for each other. They would eventually marry in 1972 at St. Alban's Episcopal in Harlingen and settle in Annapolis. My brother, State, was a student at M.M.A. and played football for the school. He talked the coach into letting me be a "water boy" during their games, and I loved it. It was so much fun being around State and his buddies, and we are still in touch with many of them through social media.

State was also a member of the precise "rifle team," which performed around Texas and was often featured in parades and military ceremonies. In 1971, they were invited to New York City to perform at the huge Marine Corp Ball held there at the Waldorf Astoria Hotel, which they did. While in New York, they were asked to perform on The Tonight Show hosted back then by Johnny Carson, which was broadcast live on network television. I remember anxiously staying up past my bedtime to watch State and his buddies throw rifles around and over each other with perfect precision. His Drill Sargent, Robert Lacourse, was a brusk man who barked orders and expected perfection. He had a distinctive speech impediment from having his tongue cut down the middle as a POW in the Korean War, which added to his tough guy aura. But I recall vividly how after the performance, he sat down with Johnny and the other two guests, Bob Hope and Ella Fitzgerald, and charmed their pants off! I think State and his buddies were shocked to see this softer side of Sgt. Lacourse because they talked about it for weeks.

Papacito did offer to pay my way at the "Academy," as we called it, but I had my heart set on going to Harlingen High School and playing football for the Cardinals. I've sometimes wondered how things might have been different if I had taken his offer. But, in hindsight, I'm glad I chose the path I took because I fully enjoyed the experience at H.H.S.

Chapter 3: All You Need is LUV

I took an early interest in business and watched Dad intently as our family business, later named "Varmicon Industries," grew and prospered. We all attended the annual stockholder's meetings, and I would always pepper Dad with questions about something I noticed on the Balance Sheet or Income Statement. Dad was a great mentor (he once told me that I had "a lot of business acumen for such a young boy only 13 years old"), and I took a great interest in business and the stock market. I learned how to read the stock pages in our local newspaper and would grab the Wall Street Journal off Dad's desk after he had read it.

In the early 1970s, two Texas entrepreneurs, Rollin King & Herb Kelleher from San Antonio, decided to start an airline linking the three largest cities in Texas: Houston, Dallas, and San Antonio. The Feds governed the airline industry in Washington D.C.; airfares were tightly regulated, and access to certain markets was strictly controlled by the Federal Trade Commission and the Federal Aviation Administration. But as a "regional" carrier, meaning they only served cities in one state, King & Kelleher knew they did not have to listen to Washington. Instead, they were regulated by the much less stringent Civil Aeronautics Board (C.A.B.). Thus, Southwest Airlines was born with that swashbuckling, wildcatter mentality that Texas was known for. S.W.A. could charge whatever fares they wanted and were determined to undercut the larger airlines serving these markets back then, namely Braniff, American, and Texas International. King & Kelleher knew they would have to control costs and make efficient use of their airplanes; most airlines at the time were stodgy and boring. Southwest wanted to make it fun to get on their flights and go somewhere, as long as it was Houston, Dallas, or San Antonio.

So, they decided they would only use 737 aircraft; that made it easier and cheaper for their maintenance people to service one type of plane rather than several types like the "major" airlines had in their hangars. And they decided they could fly more flights with fewer aircraft if they could "turn them around" in ten minutes. It was unheard of at that time for a plane full of passengers to unload upon arriving at their gate, then refill the plane with departing passengers and push back from the gate in ten minutes for the next flight. But Southwest figured out how. And it worked. I recall pretty well flying Southwest back then, and the flight attendants (all adorned in very attractive hot pants – it was the mid-1970s, after all) would come down the aisle after the plane levelled off to collect fare money from the passengers! Just like they still do on trains. This eliminated having to pay gate agents to do that job and saved Southwest a ton of money in their early formative years.

It was an instant success, and Southwest was turning a tidy profit very soon. Naturally, the major airlines hated them and filed many lawsuits to stop them, claiming that the majors couldn't charge the lower fares Southwest could because they didn't answer to the C.A.B. Ultimately, it led to the deregulation of the airlines which levelled the playing field and literally forced the major airlines to improve their performance and passenger experience. And lower their fares to compete with Southwest on common routes. It would save the flying public millions of dollars and vastly improve service and reliability in the airline industry for years to come. Southwest was a true corporate pioneer and the darling of the airline industry; people who lived in Houston, Dallas, and San Antonio LOVED flying them (their ticker symbol on the American Stock Exchange, when they went public, was LUV. They are now traded on the New York Stock Exchange and the symbol has never changed). Other cities were clamouring to get Southwest to provide service to their airport and its paying passengers.

In 1975, King and Kelleher decided they would expand Southwest and start serving a fourth Texas city: good ole' Harlingen. Harlingen was located at the geographic center of the Valley and had a nice, modern airport served by Texas International Airlines (it was actually the original Air Force Base that Papacito had helped build back in 1941.) So, it drew potential Southwest passengers from the entire Valley and Northern Mexico, a sizeable population area even back then. Well, I was no genius, but even for a 15-year-old, this sounded like a great investment! I had a passbook savings account (at Tropical Savings & Loan in downtown Harlingen) from working at Valley Ready Mix that summer (we changed the name in 1980) and some birthday money from my parents and grandparents. In fact, I had a whopping $750 to invest, and LUV was trading at $15 a share. Which meant I could buy fifty shares. Clearly, my world voice was speaking to me again.

The only problem was I was too young to open an investment account in my name. So, I had to get Dad to agree to be my "custodian" for this big plan to work. I pitched the idea to him, and he was cautiously receptive. "Are you sure you want to use ALL of your savings for this investment?" he asked me. "Yes, sir," I replied enthusiastically. I was sure this was going to be a home run and was already counting my profits. Dad consented and drove me down to Tropical Savings & Loan, where I withdrew all $750 of my money. We then drove over to his friend's office at Merrill Lynch, and I put in the buy order. The first thing the next morning, he called to say the trade went through, and I was the proud owner of 50 whopping shares of LUV. Man, I was stoked, and every morning I would run down to the end of the driveway to grab the newspaper, flip it open to the stock sheets and see where LUV had closed the prior day.

It went nowhere. In fact, it went DOWN to $14 a share. "Hey, wait a minute, I thought, this isn't supposed to happen!"

"What about that world voice? Should I not have listened this time?"

Lamar Muse was the President of Southwest, then hired by King and Kelleher to run and grow it for them. I had the mailing address for Southwest's home office on Regal Row (near Love Field) in Dallas, so I wrote Mr. Muse a letter explaining my mammoth investment in this company and my "bet it all on you" gamble. About a week later, I got a very nice letter from Mr. Muse personally thanking me for my confidence in him and Southwest and assuring me he had me and all shareholders of LUV in mind every day as he guided this (still upstart) airline through its early stages. I still have that letter in my files.

Eventually, LUV rebounded. I guess Mr. Muse is an ok guy after all, I thought. I knew if I sold it, I had to pay a commission, which I loosely calculated to be 25 cents per share. That meant LUV had to close at 15 ½ the day before for me to have an actual profit. Many trips to the end of the driveway followed over the coming weeks, and then it finally happened. I stood at the end of the driveway on a Saturday morning (it was not long after sunrise, so I had to squint) and found LUV on the stock sheets. And there it was: the closing price the day before was 15 ½.

I was overjoyed! I turned and ran back to the house, busted through the front door, and shouted, "Dad! Dad! Dad! Southwest Airlines closed at 15 ½ yesterday!" In my joy, I forgot it was before 7:00 AM on Saturday, and Mom and Dad were still asleep. I'm sure I scared the hell out of them as I bounded up the stairs to their bedroom and rushed in. "Look!" I said, "Dad, LUV closed at 15 ½!" and shoved the newspaper stock sheets under his nose. He broke into a big smile, and Mom gave me a warm look, too. As the owner of 50 shares, I now had a paper profit of $12.50. Could I pick 'em or what? I couldn't wait for the market to open on Monday and make me even richer! This was like shooting fish in a barrel.

I held that stock for two years and saw it split several times - I had to get Dad to explain what that meant. At that point, I had doubled my money, and in my naivete, I thought there was no way

I could improve on that. So, I sold my LUV (I think at this point I owned 100 shares) and put my $1,500 proceeds into Tropical Savings & Loan. It was time to find my next home run; I just hoped that same world voice would speak to me again.

Chapter 4: A Writer?

One of the coolest things about Mom and Dad was that they were always "tuned in." By that, I mean they were always looking beyond the borders of South Texas to see what else was "out there." And they found plenty of it.

One day, when I was about fifteen, Mom announced that she and Dad were taking Shelley and me to Houston to the "Johnson-O'Connor Research Institute" for some "testing." Now, at fifteen, I had no concept of what that meant. Today, I probably would have been very worried, but as Mom explained that it was a fun series of aptitude tests that lasted almost a full day and ended with a "consultation" to go over the results, I bought in.

And it was a fun series of aptitude tests that included number memory, word association, musical note and pitch recognition, hand-to-eye coordination, and a bunch of other cool "skills tests." The day flew by, with only a short lunch break. Then the four of us gathered to hear the results of the "skills tests" and their recommendations about what Shelley and I might do with our lives. (Sidebar: it was so cool and fun that several years later, Mom and Dad went back for their own tests.)

The staff at J.O.R.I. was an energetic and bright group; they were good at their jobs and very good at going over the data they had collected and their conclusions. They made it interesting and intriguing; I was pretty anxious to hear what they had to tell me. At first, it was pretty much raw data with bar graphs comparing me to all the other people they had tested in my age group and how I compared to them. This wasn't a competition; the data was used to measure your areas of strength (a good place for you to study and make a potential career) and weakness (a place to stay away from and leave to others). I was, at that time, completely immersed in high school football. I was very fit, knew every college and NFL football player in the country, and was rather convinced that I was as good as them and even better than some. So, I was expecting to be told that I should take my skills and strengths and either be a professional athlete or try out for the Olympics.

Through the consultation, I learned that I was left-eyed dominant (really?) and that I had a "magnet for numbers." When they said that, I quickly recalled a few hours before when I was taking the "numbers" test: I was shown a flashcard with a random set of six numbers and given three seconds to read it. Then, I was given ten seconds to repeat the six numbers back before I was shown the next flashcard; as I recall, I was shown about thirty such flashcards.

And I nailed it. I didn't miss a single number. And that was apparently a big deal because they said it was at the end of the day.

I must admit, at fifteen, I was proud that I scored in the 100th percentile of number memory, but I had no idea how that was going to help me in the real world or make me better at football. But Mom was hanging on every word and asking all sorts of questions, so I just decided to wait for the "good stuff." And then the big moment arrived. We had been there all day and worked pretty hard, actually. I could tell this consultation had set Mom and Dad back a fair nickel, so I was confident that these people had taken good stock of me and my strengths and were about to send me on a rocket ship to life's best reality and how to seize it!

"So, Cinco," the project leader said, "you have a cool set of unique strengths. And we had seen this before and counseled many young men like you". Man, my heart was pounding. I couldn't wait to hear what the future looked like for me! "And," he continued, "we are convinced that you should be a writer."

My heart sank. What? A writer? What the hell is that? This wasn't something I could take back to the locker room and brag to my teammates about! A writer?? No way, I thought. This place is a rip-off. Mom could sense my disgust and did her best to smooth my lost senses, but the bubble for me had burst, and there was no chance of refilling it. Now, I had actually read a few books: Call of the Wild by Jack London and Airport by Arthur Hailey, and I really enjoyed them. But me? A writer? Didn't those guys hang out in SoHo and smoke pipes or teach college courses in cardigan sweaters??

'Ha!' I thought, that will never be me! But here I am today, writing a book, writing real estate classes I teach all over the state, and thinking that the good people at J.O.R.I must have been on to something that day.

If I have learned anything from my world voice, it is to be open to where life might take me and to never make assumptions about myself or anyone else. Ever seen a picture of Stephen Hawking? (He wrote another great book, by the way: *A Brief History of Time.*) Would anyone think he was a brilliant M.I.T. physicist, given his physical limitations? How did a long-haired, dope-smoking Nair-do-well who used to live on a tiny sailboat on the dock of the Thames River in London become one of the richest and most innovative entrepreneurs on the planet? (Google Richard Branson for his fascinating story). If we were all the same, we would all DO THE SAME THINGS, which would be boring as hell. Like Hawking, Branson, Hailey, and London, I am glad that I learned to be open to ideas that sounded crazy at the time. And by the way, being open to crazy ideas can be a bad thing: do a Google search on Adolph Hitler and the Third Reich. As the poem, Desiderata says, "Go placidly amid the noise and haste and remember what peace there may be in silence." Be open to your world voice but be careful, too.

Chapter 5: It's Concrete, Not Cement!

Our company, now named "Varmicon," owned and operated four ready-mix concrete plants across the Valley. We also operated a concrete pipe and prestressed concrete products plant in Harlingen. The company was growing, with over 200 wonderful employees that all seemed to enjoy the company's success and share in it. Christmas bonuses were very attractive and tied to each plant's profit that calendar year. And they could be as much as 50% of your annual base salary. Often, they were.

Consequently, we bought a lot of cement for our various plants. We were a very good customer of Centex, Alamo, and Longhorn Cement companies, all of whom had cement mills and corporate offices in Texas.

We were good customers of several trucking companies, too, who would haul cement from the mills to our plants around the Valley. Dad was very good friends with the C.E.O.s of all these companies and was often invited on various hunting and fishing trips to their respective deer leases and bay houses scattered around Texas. Mom would sometimes go when the wives were included, and she loved it. In fact, she became so endeared by these corporate leaders that they started having a lot more "wives included" events just to see her and be with her.

Mom and Dad reciprocated the invitations, and I was getting to know these successful construction industry people myself. We would greet them at the airport as they flew in on their corporate jets, and I would help drive them to whatever hotel they happened to be staying in that weekend. I couldn't wait to tell them the story of my success with LUV (I was only 17, after all) and impress them with my solid investment know-how.

They were very gracious, and I was really surprised by how natural and approachable these men were; I mean, I read about some of them in the Wall Street Journal and saw their companies on the stock sheets every day. For me, it was pretty heady stuff.

Longhorn Cement was run by a very gregarious man named Gaines Voigt. Gaines was about ten years older than Dad, a diehard Texas Aggie, a WWII veteran, and a sharp guy. He loved his scotch, and after a few good belts, he liked to sing Italian opera (he sounded pretty good to me) and cussed like a sailor. Gaines was a great business mentor to Dad and gave him a lot of solid advice in those days about how to improve our company. The two of them became very close friends. Gaines and his wife, Lois, had a son, Eric, who was a year older than Shelley and two years older than me. We were often invited to Longhorn's beautiful hunting lodge near Junction, TX, called "Maynard Ranch." Our families enjoyed each other very much, and we created many wonderful memories with them and other San Antonio families at Maynard over the years.

During one of the Maynard trips, I learned that we were Longhorn's second biggest customer, so I asked "Mr. Voigt" (it wasn't until many years later I had the courage to call him "Gaines") "So who is your biggest customer?".

He told me it was Halliburton, the multi-national oil field services company headquartered in Dallas. Apparently, Halliburton bought a ton of cement from Longhorn to service the oil drilling operations of their own customers, companies like Mobil, Phillips 66, and Chevron.

Gaines was good friends with Eddie Paramore, Halliburton's C.E.O. Dad had met Eddie and some of the other Halliburton bigwigs a few times at Maynard Ranch. Halliburton had two very nice, side-by-side condos in Vail, and we were invited, with the Voigts, to use them for ski trips a couple of times. It was an awesome place, and we had a blast. Eddie and his wife, Jennie, flew down to

Harlingen a couple of times to hunt and socialize with us, and I was always sure to tell him how much we enjoyed the Vail trips and his generosity.

Well, my money in Tropical Savings & Loan wasn't growing to my satisfaction, so I told Dad I wanted to buy some shares in Halliburton.

Would he sign off for my custodial account? I asked. He consented, of course, and I bought some shares. I began watching Halliburton's stock in the newspaper and was doing ok with it. Since my communication with Lamar Muse at Southwest had gone so well, I decided to write Jack Harbin, the Chairman of the Board at Halliburton, and let him know of my investment in the company. Sure enough, a letter arrived a few days later with the distinctive Halliburton logo on the envelope's upper left corner. It was from an Executive VP of Halliburton, Tom Cruikshank, explaining that Mr. Harbin was "out of the country on an important matter" but that Mr. Harbin asked him to respond to my "kind letter" in his absence. I still have that letter in my files, too. Mr. Cruikshank said, "Mr. Harbin would be delighted to meet you at our next shareholder's meeting in Dallas on such-and-such a date if my schedule allowed."

'If my schedule allowed?' I thought. I was pretty sure I could free up my schedule for the Halliburton executives and ran it by Dad.

He was immediately receptive, so we made plane and hotel reservations and flew to Dallas for the shareholder's meeting.

Dad and I both wore dark suits and ties, very appropriate for the day's events at the home of a worldwide oil services conglomerate. As we walked into their posh offices in a swanky downtown Dallas high-rise, I was immediately awed. "Wow," I muttered to Dad, "this is really cool." Eddie Paramore's assistant greeted us and said, "Mr. Paramore will join you shortly."

We took a seat in the reception area, and in a few minutes, Mr. Paramore (Dad called him "Eddie") walked in and gave us a warm welcome. "Let me show you around. We still have a few minutes before the shareholder's meeting starts," he said and led us on a quick tour of the executive offices.

There were large photographs lining the walls of various drilling sites and ocean platforms all over the world; the offices were large, well-appointed, and comfortable. It was quite an eye-opener for me.

The shareholder's meeting was held in a very nice, small auditorium a few floors below the executive offices; I guessed it held about 200 people and was filling up quickly. Eddie guided us over to where Mr. Harbin and Mr. Cruikshank were standing and made a brief introduction. They welcomed us to the meeting and were very nice to this young man from deep South Texas. I was glad we accepted their invitation to the meeting and very glad I wore a suit and tie that day.

About that time, a very lovely, well-dressed lady walked up to our group. She was dark-complected, stately, and carried a serious air of confidence. She stuck her hand out to me and said, "Hi, I'm Anne Armstrong." I shook her hand as firmly as I could, and she then greeted Dad. Anne hailed from New Orleans originally and had married into the Armstrong family; they owned one of the biggest ranches between Corpus Christi and the Valley, and I was pretty sure they had oil under all of it. Anne served on Halliburton's Board of Directors and was obviously there in that role.

Additionally, she served on the Boards of General Motors and American Express. And as if that wasn't enough, she was the current United States Ambassador to Great Britain. In the political circles of the time, she was at the very top, having served Presidents Carter, Ford, and later, Ronald Reagan. She was charming and gracious, and after a short conversation, she moved to the front of the room and took her seat with the other Directors.

Dad and I enjoyed our trip very much, and I knew that this all happened just because some busy executive got a letter from some small-town kid he didn't know and was kind enough to respond. I vowed to remember how gracious all these important people had been to me and try to always treat people with gratitude and humility.

Just like they had.

Chapter 6: The Boys of Fall.

I was a decent athlete growing up and naturally wanted to play football. I played it through Junior High and High School and loved it. We had some pretty good teams and competed for the district championship in my Junior and Senior years at Harlingen H.S. The comradery with my teammates and the hard work we put in bonded us well. I'm still very good friends with some of those guys and enjoy catching up at reunions and various events when I see them. Fortunately, most of us escaped any serious injuries. However, I recall my left knee popping hard on one particular play – I had no idea at the time how bad it was, but I certainly wasn't going to say anything to my coaches or parents. It felt ok after a few days, so I concluded it wasn't a torn ligament. Arthritis from that injury is something I deal with daily.

All of us suffered the occasional ding to the head, with instant dizziness and confusion. I remember vividly the spring game of 1977; I was trying to make varsity as a junior that fall. Like all teams, at the end of spring training, we were divided into two squads, the red team and the white team. I was the starting center for the white team which meant I had to go up against our returning All-Valley nose guard, Eddie Casas. Eddie was a strong bulldog of a guy, and I'm sure he expected to push me around all night. He was stout, quick, and very talented. I wasn't going to let Eddie dash my hopes of making varsity that coming fall, so I gave him all I had. And I think he was a little surprised at how well I played him. Well into the game, with the two of us literally beating on each other every play, I drove him out of the "A gap," and the running back went right through it. I kept driving Eddie backward for several more steps (I wanted to see this on film the next morning!) when suddenly, I felt this huge blow at the crown of my helmet. Eddie gave me a "forearm shiver," and it knocked me seriously loopy. I struggled to get back to the huddle and tried to remember the snap count that was called for the next play. I was literally seeing stars but just hoped the series would end soon so I could go hide on the bench until my senses returned. Gratefully, the game ended soon after that, and once home, I downed a ton of aspirin to curb the bad headache I had.

The next morning, I felt ok and headed down to the gym, where the list of varsity players would be posted in our locker room. I pushed through the crowd of my teammates and found my name on the list. I was so happy and knew it was my play the night before against one of the Valley's best defensive linemen that sealed my place. Just then, I turned towards my locker and saw Eddie sitting on the bench in front of it, with his arm in a sling. He looked up as I walked toward him, and I asked, "Why is your arm in a sling, Eddie?". He took a long breath and said, "Well, you remember that hit I gave you on your helmet last night?" Boy, did I ever. "That hit on your head broke my arm," he said. He had a cast from his wrist up over his elbow! "Well," I said, "can be the first to sign it? After all, it was my head that you broke it on!" We had a good laugh, and I did sign his cast; in big, thick letters. Eventually, he recovered, and so did I.

The real threat to our health was the infections we all had on our knees and elbows from the constant cuts and scrapes from hitting the ground. It's a miracle we didn't have a staph outbreak in the locker room, and I remember wearing long pants and long-sleeved shirts to cover the infections so Mom wouldn't see them. I was afraid she would make me stop playing football. To us, it was just a part of the sacrifice we made to represent our school and our team on Friday nights in the Fall. We were all in great shape from weight room routines and wind sprints, and I liked the way I looked and felt.

I had some really good coaches playing football during those years. Most cared deeply about the game and about grooming us as young men. We worked hard in practice, and when we hit the field, we were prepared and ready to give it all we had. We didn't win every game, but I think we all knew that we gave everything we had every time. San Benito was a big rival since we literally shared a common city limit line with them, though our city was three times larger than theirs. We always knew they were going to play us hard, especially when we were the visiting team; our 9th-grade game with them was especially tough and a back-and-forth battle.

We ultimately won the game at the very end and headed to the bus as quickly as we could. Tension was high. As we were ready to drive back to our gym, a very loud bang hit the side of our bus. We knew it meant our bus was being "rocked" by San Benito fans. It was scary, and we all put our helmets back on and ducked our heads as low as we could. Several louder "thuds" hit the side as the rock throwers unloaded on us. As we pulled away, a rock hit the window, with shattered glass spraying into the bus. Everyone was yelling, "Stay down, stay down," as more rocks peppered the side of the bus. Fortunately, no one was hurt, and we were very relieved to be back in the safety of our own locker room. But that feeling stayed with us any time we played on the road for the next four years; passions ran high in South Texas high school football.

In my Junior and Senior years, our biggest rival was McAllen. There were several good teams back then in our district, but McAllen vs. Harlingen was special. They had a brand-new stadium that held well over 15,000 people, and in my junior year, we traveled to play them there in the last game of the season. We were confident that we had a solid chance of beating them (both teams had only lost one game so far that year), and we were ready. McAllen was a very good team with great coaches and really good players. You just knew they were going to execute well and give us one hell of a fight, which they did. It was a tough defensive game which we ultimately won 7-0. Our classmates and friends stormed the field at the end, and we were showered with hugs and congratulations. What a great feeling running off that field and celebrating in the locker room, where someone had Queen's song "We Are the Champions!" blasting through the speakers. The bus ride back to Harlingen was exuberant, and we were pretty sure it meant we had made the playoffs. Unfortunately, we ended up tied with PSJA, who also had one loss in District play. But our loss was to them earlier in the year, so they owned the tiebreaker; no playoffs for us in the fall of 1978.

Chapter 7: Service

I had become actively involved in Key Club at our high school, a boys-only service organization sponsored by Kiwanis all over the U.S.A. I really enjoyed taking a leadership role in certain activities. The Governor of the Texas-Oklahoma District was a classmate of mine, though he was a Senior, a year ahead of me. I decided to run for Lt. Governor for the T-O District, representing about twenty high schools all over the Valley on the T-O District Board of Directors my Senior year. The election was held in January at the Regional meeting at South Padre Island; my opponent was a young man from San Benito who was a year younger than me, John Scaief. I won the election and was thrilled to be accepted and elected by my contemporaries around the Valley. John was a really good guy, and we would become very good friends. I was going to be inducted as one of thirty Lt. Governors at the T-O District Convention in Dallas in May of that year as my junior year was wrapping up. I immersed myself in the activities and work of Key Club and began working with the local Kiwanis sponsors and T-O District staff.

The current District Treasurer was David Durr from Nacogdoches. David had announced he was going to run for T-O District Governor in May at the Dallas convention. One of the candidates to replace David as Treasurer the coming year was also a Nacogdoches guy named Jeff Warr. I soon became good friends with them, and on one particular weekend of Key Club meetings, David asked me to consider running for T-O District Secretary in May at the convention in Dallas. The Secretary was 2nd in command under the Governor, representing almost 200 Key Clubs in Texas and Oklahoma and over 5,000 members. I was very flattered but wasn't sure if I was really ready for the tremendous responsibility of serving as the number 2 man in the district. David and Jeff really encouraged me to do it, and I listened intently. After discussing it with Mom and Dad, I called David and said, "Ok. I'll run".

Running for a district office meant traveling every weekend (I became a frequent flyer on Southwest Airlines!) between March and May to visit Key Clubs all over Texas and Oklahoma. I had campaign posters and leaflets printed up and created a "platform" for my goals if elected district secretary for the 1978 – 1979 school year. While it was a lot of fun, it was also a lot of hard work. I shook many hands and answered lots of questions as a candidate; this was a serious political campaign, and I was only 17 years old! Mom and Dad were very supportive and encouraged me every step of the way. I did have an opponent from a small school in Oklahoma. Still, I guess my natural love of people and my passion for "Key Club magic" showed thru – I won the election that May together with David and Jeff. We were inducted as the top 3 officers for the T-O district on the last day of the convention in front of almost 3,000 people. I called Mon and Dad to deliver the good news, and they were happy and proud. I was very excited to start to work supporting the good members and the many, many service projects that Key Club organized all over the two-state district.

Chapter 8: Doolittle

The first order of business was to get all of the active files from the outgoing District Secretary, Mitchell George. Mitch lived in Hereford, which was way up in the Texas Panhandle, easily a ten-hour drive from Harlingen. Fortunately, Mitch offered to leave his files in Dallas with one of our Kiwanis advisors so I could just drive there and pick up his full file cabinet. This was 1978 and way before digital file storage! I took the Suburban and drove first to Nacogdoches to visit David and Jeff. One quick overnight there, and it was on to Dallas. As I drove south from Dallas, I knew I would be hitting San Antonio around dinner time. Being an 18-year-old, I had not made any plans for a place to stay that night. So, I stopped at a phone booth, called M.E. and Ski York (this was also way before cell phones), and asked if I could bunk in their guest room that night. They graciously said "Yes," and I arrived there just before dinner.

M.E. (short for "Mary Elizabeth") and Ski were very good friends of Mom and Dad's, and we had gotten to know them through Lois and Gaines Voigt. I would learn through the relationship that Ski was in the Army Air Corps in WW II (which was before a formal Air Force had been created) and had flown in the Doolittle Raid. His office was a small museum of his days in the A.A.C., and it was obvious he had served bravely and proudly. Like most WWII vets, he didn't talk about it much, but I did my best to draw out some of his stories and memories from the war.

When most people think about our country's entry into WWII, they immediately think of D-Day and the Normandy invasion of France. That's not surprising given the widespread popularity of the Steven Spielberg movie "Saving Private Ryan," which documented the Normandy invasion on June 6, 1944. But we had been fighting in the Pacific since Japan bombed Pearl Harbor on Dec 7, 1941, almost 2 ½ years before D-Day. The bombing of Honolulu that fateful Sunday morning caught the U.S. completely flatfooted, destroyed the bulk of our Pacific naval vessels, and killed thousands of men. Many people were convinced that, with our defenses so weakened, Japan would next sail towards California and bomb our military operations and key population centers there. It was a time of fear and even panic as we waited to see what the Japanese Emperor, Hirohito, would do next.

Our military knew we needed a quick and strong response and decided to strike back hard. Finally, the "Doolittle Raid" was created and planned. The idea was to modify 16 B-25 bombers (our lightest bombers available) and fly them off an aircraft carrier in range of Tokyo; each B-25 would carry a crew of five for a total of 80 men. This was going to be a huge task and required that the pilots be trained on carrier takeoffs and low-level flight lest Japanese radar spots them. President Roosevelt needed a bold and innovative pilot and leader for the mission, and he chose Jimmy Doolittle. Ski was one of two wing commanders for the mission.

The men of the Raid trained in bases around the country for a couple of months. Mastering a short-field takeoff was crucial, and while the "Raiders" were not told specifically they were launching off an aircraft carrier, they began to have their suspicions. Ski told me that they knew "this was something very big. After all, Jimmy Doolittle was one of the most Senior commanders in the Army Air Corps at the time. We knew that if he was in command, this must mean we were going to strike back at Japan. But we had no idea that we were actually bombing Tokyo!". After training at Wright-Patterson A.F.B. in Dayton, Ohio, and the Naval Air Station in Pensacola, Florida, the men gathered in San Francisco. The bombers were loaded onto the U.S.S. Hornet and left port in early April 1942. There is an iconic photo taken of the Hornet sailing under the Golden Gate Bridge on its way first to Hawaii and then on to Tokyo. It was later that day that Doolittle gathered the men and told them of their ultimate mission: all 16 crews were going to drop their bombs on Tokyo, and Doolittle would pilot the first plane off the Hornet and into the sky.

The bombers had been significantly refitted for the mission to lighten their overall weight so they could get airborne off the short runway on the Hornet. Non-essential gear was eliminated; the gas tanks were significantly reduced to eliminate weight, which meant their operating range was much shorter than usual for this aircraft. Consequently, the bombers would have to take off only about 300 miles from Tokyo. The entire fleet was ordered to "radio silent" not long after leaving Hawaii and had to communicate with each other via Morse code, lest the Japanese Navy pick up their transmissions and attack. The plan was for the crews to bomb Tokyo and then fly on to China (our ally in the war), land there and wait to be picked up and flown home by U.S. planes. China was very nervous about aiding the attack; they feared retribution by the Japanese, who had earned a well-deserved reputation for their combat zealotry and cruelty to prisoners.

The mission was going smoothly until our fleet spotted a Japanese fishing boat about 700 miles from Tokyo. Immediately, there was a conversation about scrapping the mission and turning for home; they were certain the fishing boat had spotted them and would alert the Japanese Navy. After considering all options and consulting the 16 Doolittle crews, it was decided to launch the bombers immediately and complete the bombing raid. But that meant the crews would likely not have enough fuel to reach a safe part of China and would have to bail out over areas controlled by Japan. The risk of being captured by the Japanese was high. Ski told me, "There wasn't any talk among us about aborting the mission. We were well-trained and ready, and we wanted to punch back at Japan decisively". So, the order was given to scramble to the crews and launch as quickly as possible.

There was still some doubt about whether the bombers, even though they had been stripped of a lot of weight, could even get airborne in such a short distance. Doolittle told the men that if the planes couldn't make it into the air and were going to ditch into the sea, he wanted to be the first one to test it. Fortunately, Doolittle climbed easily off the deck and into the air. Once all sixteen bombers had taken off, they regrouped and made a heading for Tokyo. Doolittle told the pilot of each plane it was up to him and his crew to decide where they wanted to go after they dropped their payload, so each crew made their plans and held a steady course. Soon, they saw the coast of Japan and the capital city coming up on the horizon.

The Doolittle Raiders had made it and unleashed a bombing hell storm on the Japanese. In a matter of minutes, the bomb bay doors were closed, and each crew was on its own to find a safe place to land or bail out. When news reached the U.S. homeland, there was jubilation that our "boys" had hit back at the Japs for the deaths they caused at Pearl Harbor only fifteen weeks before. We had taken the fight to the enemy in their homeland and proven that our military was up to the challenge. It was a huge morale booster for our citizens and our people in uniform. The United States of America had officially entered World War II.

Fifteen of the sixteen bombers were lost; some crash-landed in China, and some ran out of fuel, so the crew was forced to bail out into complete darkness. One crew was shot down, and all five were lost. Many of the Raiders were captured by the Japanese and were treated horribly. Three were summarily executed while in Japanese prison camps; two died from the sickening conditions. Of the eighty men who flew off the Hornet, seventy returned home. Ski and his crew made a safe landing in Vladivostok, Russia. The Soviet Union was not officially at war with Japan, so under international law, they were required to intern the crew and confiscate the bomber, which is exactly what they did.

Ski and his four men were "held" by the Russians for 18 months, often moved from one city to another without any advance notice. Bob Emmens, Ski's co-pilot, wrote a fascinating book called

"Guests of the Kremlin," which told of their ordeal and the bleak conditions they had to survive, including a Siberian winter. Eventually, the crew was placed on a train and moved close to the border of Persia (now Iran). Once there, they were allowed to escape and walk over the border to the closest U.S. consulate, who greeted them warmly and arranged for their transport home. They had not seen or talked to their wives and families for a year and a half, but at least they were alive.

Years later, the Doolittle Raiders would have an annual reunion where they gathered to recall their adventure and toast those that had died the year before. Ski took one of Emmens' books and had it signed by all the surviving Raiders for Mom and Dad. I recently found that book on Dad's bookshelf and plan on donating it to the Pacific War Museum in Fredericksburg, TX.

Chapter 9: A Change of Priorities

Through the summer of 1978, I worked at the family company and traveled almost every weekend to visit many of the local Key Clubs around the state and the clubs across the Valley. Many times, I was the featured speaker, and I became a very good public speaker as my confidence grew. John Scaief was elected Lt. Governor to fill the spot I vacated, and we worked closely together over the next twelve months. I quickly became very impressed with the passion that Key Clubbers had for the mission of the organization and got to know many of the adult Kiwanis advisors in Texas and Oklahoma. Our district board comprised David, Jeff, me, and our Convention Coordinator, another Nacogdoches guy named Vance Tiller, whom David appointed to the board. We were supported by roughly 30 Lt Governors – we all worked hard and clicked well. It was excellent training for me in executive management and group effort; I remember taking calls from district board members and working on reports in my bedroom well into the night many times that year. Sometimes I would totally lose track of time and would hear a knock on my bedroom door. "Cinco," Dad would say, "it's two in the morning. Go to bed". My fire was lit, and I had found a passion in my Key Club work.

When August 1978 rolled around, my senior year was weeks from starting. It was an exciting time, but as I thought about starting football two-a-day workouts in a few weeks, my heart just wasn't in it. Our head coach was all about football, but he really didn't inspire me much. (I recall during one particular tense game the prior season, one of our running backs was hurt and lying on the ground right in front of our bench. Our head coach walked over to him and said, "Get up, Son! You're just trying to get the sympathy of the crowd!" I was shocked.) Our head coach had his favorite players, and for whatever reason, I wasn't one of them.

I really liked our offensive coordinator, David Smith, and our defensive coordinator, Gil Ledbetter, but I just wasn't as motivated by football as I had been before. In fact, our head coach openly mocked my Key Club title and responsibilities at team functions, which really rubbed me the wrong way. He clearly thought we were only supposed to play football and anything else was a distraction. I saw the good service work Key Club did in our community and around the state and just couldn't understand his disregard for it. I was burned out by football and just wanted to focus on Key Club and the great people in it.

So, I asked our head coach for a meeting right before two-a-days started and also asked Coach Ledbetter to attend. Though I had played offensive center most of my career, they had switched me to outside linebacker during spring practice earlier that year, so it made sense that Coach L was there. I basically laid it all out for them and explained that I just didn't have a passion for football anymore. Our head coach didn't say much (I think quietly he was kind of glad I wasn't going to be around if I wasn't all-in for football), but Coach Ledbetter protested strongly. "Cinco, we need you this year as a senior leader on the team," he told me. "You are my starting weak-side LB and our backup center on offense," he continued. "We have a legitimate shot at the playoffs, and you don't want to miss that, do you?"

Against my true feelings and ignoring my trusty world voice, I agreed to stay on the team and reported for two-a-days a few weeks later. Coach L was a great coordinator, and our defense coalesced well. I was beginning to feel my mojo coming back as practice went well at outside LB, and we prepared for our first game, a match-up on the road at Alice. Alice was a really good team who made the state semi-finals the year before. They were well-coached and had lots of playmakers; we knew we had our hands full playing them in their home stadium. The week before the game, our starting center, Dean Anderson, twisted his knee in practice; immediately, I was switched back to offense and started working with our first team offense as the center, the position I had played the year before.

The game against Alice was the slugfest we expected. Our offense moved the ball but couldn't put any points on the board. I glanced around the huddle at my teammates, and we shared a look that said, "Dang, these guys are good." And they were. Alice's offense, on the other hand, clicked early, and we found ourselves down 14 – 0 at halftime. My replacement at LB was a talented junior named Shane Jones, and he was performing well; our coaches gave us some good halftime adjustments and got us fired up for the second half. We scored a quick touchdown, and our defense was really giving Alice hell. We held Alice scoreless in the second half, but we could only manage a touchdown and a field goal against their tough, talented defense and lost the game 14-10. I was never happy after a loss; it tore me up to practice so hard, play so well, and then lose. But on the two-hour bus ride back to Harlingen, I had a good feeling about our team, and I think all of us did. We knew we could hold our own against the best teams in South Texas – this was going to be a good year.

The morning after a game, we would routinely meet at the gymnasium for a film review and game planning for our next opponent. Any injuries from the night before got treatment, and we all gathered to pick each other up emotionally after the tough loss the night before. As the meetings and workout ended, Coach L called me into his office. "Cinco, our starting center's knee is much better, so he will get reps with the first team offense this week," he told me. "And." he said, "We're pretty set at LB, too, after the game we got from Shane last night." So, I was suddenly a backup at both center and LB. I didn't blame Coach L; he was right about Dean and Shane. But I was definitely dejected, and the old feeling of detachment came over me. Being a backup for the first time in my football career didn't excite me at all. I knew I wanted to spend time with Key Club; that gave me true purpose and satisfaction.

So, I saw limited playing time during my senior year, and I'm sure the coaches knew I was pretty much going through the motions. I couldn't wait for practice to end so I could get home, check my mail and voice messages, and get to work on my Key Club duties. Our team went 7-3 that year and lost a couple of games we shouldn't have; when we missed the playoffs for the 2nd year in a row, I was actually glad the season was over. I could focus on schoolwork, Key Club, and the SAT test. I had my heart set on attending the University of Texas next year and wanted to put my focus on that.

Chapter 10: Big "D"

As the Christmas holiday passed, the new year of 1979 meant I had only five more months of living at home. Shelley had graduated a year before and was attending an all-girls college in Fulton, MO. So, I had Mom and Dad all to myself (as well as Dad's hunting Suburban!) my senior year in high school. My grades were good, the company was prospering, I loved Key Club, and life was good. We hunted and fished when we could, and Mom and Dad traveled frequently, which left me home alone. I guess they trusted me and figured I could handle the responsibility of being home without adults around. While I did have a few people over (against their rules, of course), I never staged any big parties or did anything that would have gotten me in real trouble.

It was nice having football behind me, which meant my spring was free from off-season weight training and daily workouts. We were all excited about graduation and the exciting plans for college after that. I was ranked in the top 10% of my class academically, and I did well on the SAT; soon, I submitted my application to U.T. It was the only college I applied to, and while I felt confident that I would get in, I was overjoyed when the letter arrived telling me I was accepted! I yelled out to Mom and Dad and ran through the house to show them the letter. My plans for post-graduation from H.H.S. were set.

Key Club and schoolwork kept me busy that spring, and we worked hard preparing for our T-O District Convention that May at the brand-new Loews Anatole Hotel in Dallas. There were over 3,000 people registered for the convention, and while the Kiwanis advisors helped quite a bit, we, as the district staff, handled most of the planning and coordination. Quite a job for a bunch of 18-year-olds, but we were definitely up to the task. John Scaief was running to replace David as Governor, and he had our full support – he was ready for the job, had great people skills, and was the right man for the responsibility.

The opening night of the convention was held across IH 35 at the Apparel Mart, which had a very large open convention floor perfect for us. I was so happy looking down from the stage at Mom and Dad sitting in the front row, and I could see the pride on their faces as they watched me gavel the proceedings to order. There were a few speeches from Kiwanis dignitaries, introductions of local and state politicians in attendance, and brief recognition of the district staff and the lt. Governors. The Governor, by tradition, waited patiently in the back of the hall to be introduced by the District Secretary (me in this case) for his entrance down the main aisle and up the steps onto the stage.

As I stepped to the podium and looked across the hall of thousands of people, many of whom I had worked so closely with that year, I was filled with emotion. I had visited their schools, stayed in their homes, grown to know their parents, siblings, and girlfriends well, and genuinely loved my service to the Texas-Oklahoma District of Key Club International. I took a deep breath, unfolded my prepared remarks, and spoke straight into the microphone. "To the Key Clubbers from the great states of Texas and Oklahoma," I started, "welcome to Dallas and the world-famous Apparel Mart!" The place erupted in loud, energetic shouts of enthusiasm. The energy and anticipation were palpable. "As the District Secretary for the grand T-O District, it is my honor and privilege to officially call this annual convention to order!" More shouts and hoops from the many high schoolers in the crowd. They were feeling it, and so was I. "My friends," I continued, "we have some great speakers lined up for the next three days and some great educational opportunities to help you grow your membership and service to your schools and communities." The shouts and applause grew louder. They knew what was coming next. "But before we go any further, there is someone missing up here on this stage with us!

We have been represented by the most hard-working, dedicated, and devoted Key Clubber I have had the privilege to know and serve the past year! I have watched his tireless passion for service and his relentless drive for excellence in the T-O district, and we all owe him a big thank you and an enthusiastic greeting! Please welcome to the stage, from Nacogdoches, Texas, Governor David Wright Durr!!" The place absolutely exploded in noise and sound.

David is one of the most likeable people I have ever known. Both of his parents were college professors and devout Catholics. He is the third of five children and a devoted family person. David oozed confidence but also humility and a genuine love of people. Almost everyone in the crowd had met David over the last two years he served on the district staff, and he was loved by everyone there. As David appeared at the back of the room and began walking down the middle aisle, he could hardly make it thru the crush of supporters and hand-shakers. He was also slowed by the fact that, due to a swimming accident several days before, he had cut his foot badly and was on crutches.

It was the perfect start to a perfect weekend. We had awards ceremonies (naming the top 25 clubs in the state according to a points-ranking system) where the staff wore tuxedos; we introduced 10 Key Club sweethearts and had lunches with inspiring and humorous speakers. All of it was meant to inspire the Key Clubbers in Texas and Oklahoma to support their schools and communities with service projects and leadership. I was proud and pleased to have twenty members of my high school Key Club there – they were so supportive and enthusiastic for one of their own to be the second-ranking officer in the two-state district, and I was pleased to represent Harlingen H.S. that way.

The final event was lunch on Sunday, where David, after another short introduction by me, gave his farewell address. It was a wonderful talk about his year as Governor, and he made many thank-yous to everyone who had been a part of it. As I listened to

David and again glanced down at Mom and Dad, my mind drifted back over the last year as T-O Secretary. In the beginning, I had no idea what a wonderful experience it would be or how much I would grow from it; David, Vance, Jeff, and I are still friends to this day. I had traveled the far corners of both Texas and Oklahoma and participated in many service projects there with the wonderful Key Club members and our Kiwanis Club advisors.

As David ended his speech, which was interrupted several times with applause and ovations, I rose from my seat and embraced him. We held each other tightly as 3,000 people cheered and applauded our last official acts as Governor and Secretary of the wonderful T-O District of Key Club. We gave each other a warm "I love you, man," and then Jeff and Vance joined us. As we turned to face the crowd, we grabbed each other's hands, raised them high into the air together, and smiled broadly. When the crowd settled back in their seats and the noise abated, David introduced John Scaief as the newly elected Governor of T-O, and he joined us onstage. Accepting the gavel from David, John said some quick remarks and called the convention to a close. He was going to be a great Governor.

With that, I stepped down (literally) to the floor and found Mom and Dad for another big hug. I was bushed but running on adrenaline. They were flying back home that afternoon, so we said a quick goodbye, and I made my way out of the hall and up to our suite in the hotel with David, Jeff, and Vance. The 4 of us got out of our suits and put on some comfortable shorts and T-shirts. We sat talking and relaxing for a few hours and then ordered room service dinner. The next day we said our goodbyes, and I flew back to Harlingen for the last week of school before graduation. I had already enrolled for the summer semester at U.T. and would only have about four days between graduation from H.H.S. and moving to Austin to start classes.

The next weeks went by fast. I was still exhausted from the convention but also so excited about our upcoming graduation ceremonies. And I was very glad I didn't have to give any speeches or make any introductions! Mostly, I just wanted to spend as much time as I could with my friends and football teammates. We had had a great 4 years together and bonded well. My high school class was 85% Hispanic, but there were never any racial issues among us. No one gave race a second thought - we were all just good friends who shared a common school and some wonderful friendships. It was a great example of kids from all races and backgrounds coalescing together.

Graduation was over Saturday night, and Tuesday morning, I loaded up Dad's Chevy Suburban and made the five-hour drive north to Austin. I was going to live in a high-rise dorm right on campus and was excited to officially be a "college guy." Naturally, I was a little sad to be leaving home; Shelley was back from college and would work at Varmicon that summer. So, I was missing some time with her. But I was going through fraternity rush and was sure the parties and social scene at U.T. would be great.

Rafting the Animas River with the kids.
Durango, CO. Summer, 2008

#51   Fall 1977

Glacier National Park Montana September 2022

Alyeska Resort, Alaska. March, 2021

Annette & John Bender.   Spring, 2021.

Argentina soccer fans. Santa Clara, CA. 2016.

Arlington National Cemetery.

Arches National Park Utah Summer 2021.

Botswana with the Clowes 1985

Breckenridge, CO. Spring 2018

Charbel, me, Ron & Cynthia Evans. Fall, 2015.

Christmas 2020.

Chicago Art Instituite   July 2022

Colaney & Marshall. Chicago. Summer, 2022.

Colaney, Marshall, Savannah & Jordan. Fishing South Padre
Island. 2023.

Cotton Bowl. Dallas, TX. October, 2016.

Costa Rica. March, 2017.

Destin, FL. March, 2017

Eli Santos, Marshall & Joon Kang. Las Vegas, NV. March, 2022.

Fins Up with Jimmy Buffett fans. June, 2017.

Flyfishing. Crede, CO. 2005.

Gaudalupe Peak, TX. Fall 2020.

Harley Davidson Heritage Softtail. Austin, TX. 2014.

Harley riding in Lousianna. 2014.

High School friends Jerry Trevino, Annette Shepherd, Me, Chip Glispin, Wynn Searle & Shawn Swanson. Fall, 2022.

Hiking the Swiss Alps. September, 2018.

How very true.

Joy Cocke. Kerrville, TX. 2016

Marshall & me. 2004.

Laredo groundbreaking. Stacy Locke, Gayle Cocke, Bee Bee
Crooks & me. December, 2022.

Marshall. Turks & Caicos. 2018.

Me, Darrell Royal, Al McNamara & Robert Howden. 1996.

Mom & me. Kerville, TX. 2015.

Mt. Kilamanjaro, Tanzania.

My 38th Jimmy Buffett concert. Dallas, TX. 2015.

Portriat of Guy Staton Cocke

Provo River, Utah. September, 2021.

Savannah & Sydney. 2016.

Queretaro, Mexico. Industrial Buildings tour. July, 2022.

Savannah 2014

Savannah barefoot in the sand Port Aransas 2014.

Savannah O.U. graduation. May, 2021.

Washington D.C. Lincoln Memorial 2014.

Turks & Caicos 2018

With Tucker Graves, Lane Prickett & Nino Corbett.   San Miguel Allende, Mexico. January, 2022.

With Wynn Searle & Tucker Graves. June, 2017.

Wrigley Field, Chicago. Summer, 2022.

Robert Fowler and Rhonda Curry W/ Me,
Shelley, Mom, and Dad. Alaska Fishing 2003

Arc De Triomphe Paris 2007

W/ David and Martha Clowe Zimbabwe 1985

Victoria Falls Zimbabwe 1985

Augusta National Golf Club, GA. 2005

Dinner in Paris, 2007

Mom and Me London 1996

L to R: Robert McBee, Rodney Moore, Dad and
Me Narin, Scotland 1999

Marshall W/ Shelly Harrison Air Force VS Army
Colorado Springs, CO 2007

Savannah w/ Air Force Cheerleader, Air Force VS Army.
'West Point, N.Y. 2008

L to R   Jeff Warr David Durr Me Vance Tiller Spring 1980

Libby and Me Algodon Ball Summer 1980

Shelley Cocke Fall 1980

Part Two:
After High School and on to
U.T. Austin

Chapter 11: Anchors Away

May 1979 drew to a close, and with it, I left behind my high school experience, including Key Club, and any thoughts of ever calling Harlingen & South Texas "home" again. As I navigated Dad's Suburban up the highway through the vast expanse of mesquite-covered ranchland, I was excited about the next phase of life. I mean, I was going off to college! And not any college, either. In three days, I was going to be enrolled at THE University of Texas at Austin. This was a dream come true.

I had been to a couple of frat parties already and knew I would enjoy the rush experience. Dad & my Uncle Hill were members of Kappa Sigma at U.T. so naturally I wanted to give them a look. A couple of guys from Harlingen were current members of S.A.E. and Pi Kappa Alpha, so they were rushing me pretty hard. The outings and parties were a blast; these guys knew how to entertain Rushees, and there was always a bevy of pretty Texas sorority girls around.

Austin, TX, in 1979, was way bigger than Harlingen but still a bit of a small town. The state capitol was there, as well as U.T., but it was not yet the high-tech juggernaut it would become over the next 30 years. There were some tall downtown buildings but none much over twenty-five stories tall – you could see the capitol building from all angles. As I took the 19th street exit off IH 35 and turned left towards my dorm, I glanced at the "Special Events Center," where basketball games and concerts were held. On the marquee advertising the upcoming shows, it said in bold letters: "Tonight…Earth, Wind & Fire". "Tomorrow: The Bee Gees." I was in heaven. All thoughts of missing South Texas flew out the window, and I was ready to immerse myself in U.T., Austin, fraternity rush, and everything that came with it.

I was enrolled in two classes, Biology (which I hated but needed a science elective) and something else I don't remember. But walking the campus, attending class, and going to rush events 4 or 5 nights a week was great. I might have missed home a little, but I felt very comfortable in my new surroundings. I liked the SAEs and Pikes a lot; the Kappa Sigs were nice guys, but they just didn't seem to have the polish and swagger that the other two frats did. Even though I was only eighteen, I had had enough exposure from travel around the U.S. and abroad to appreciate a certain level of sophistication; I saw it in the Pikes & SAEs but not in the Kappa Sigs. Dad didn't push anything on me, but I think silently he assumed I would follow him and pledge Kappa Sig. When I left Austin after six weeks of classes to wrap up the summer at home, the SAEs were my first choice, followed closely by the Pikes.

Returning to Austin in August for the fall semester, there were more parties followed by "bid week," when frats and sororities invited Rushees to join. On the first day, I went over to the SAE house excited about the prospects of joining. They invited me back to a small conference room (standard procedure for bidding a guy) and asked me if I wanted to join. I immediately said, "hell yes!". That was followed by more parties and plenty of celebratory drinking.

School started several days later, and then so did the hazing. I was still in really good shape from football, so doing pushups was no big deal for me, even with actives yelling in your ear about what a "pond scum pledge" I was. The verbal abuse was hard to understand after being rushed so hard all summer, and I saw a side of certain guys that really surprised me. Most of my pledge brothers were not athletes and not in the kind of shape I was, so after a dozen or so pushups, they collapsed on the floor, exhausted. So, the actives would yell at me & the other strong guys that we had to "do his pushups for him!" The whole idea was to bond the group much like they do in basic military training. So, I would routinely do 200 – 300 pushups every day during the noon lunch hour. I'm pretty sure some of the actives were amazed at how I and a couple of my pledge brothers could just keep going while they yelled in our ears about being "worthless & weak." Looking back, it was pretty funny.

What wasn't funny was waking up the third or fourth morning with my biceps so swollen I couldn't raise my hands above my waist. I mean, I couldn't feed myself or even brush my own teeth. I looked in the mirror; my arms were so swollen I looked like the Hulk! I got dressed – my roommate had to button my shirt for me – and headed over to the house for more pledge "activities." When several actives saw my condition, they took a worried interest in me. "No more pushups for you," the chapter President said. I started feeling weak and a little sick, so I appreciated his help. But several of the other "gung-ho" actives thought I was being a weakling and took it upon themselves to administer a few swats with the paddle to make sure I wasn't "slacking." At one point, I nearly grabbed that paddle out of the guy's hands and was ready to beat his ass with it. Fortunately, my arms were so weak I don't think I could have managed to hold it or swing it.

That night we were supposed to gather back at the SAE house for our pledge class photo in a coat & tie. I couldn't button my shirt, much less tie a tie, so that would be a problem. My strength was diminished, and my spirit was pretty low. I stepped into the shower to try to get ready, and when the warm water hit me, I instantly needed to pee. I really didn't want to climb out of the shower and back in – every minor task was a big effort at this point – so I just decided to pee in the shower. Well, as I looked down, I saw that my urine was the color of iced tea: dark brown. "Uh oh," I thought, "that doesn't look good." Once I arrived at the SAE house, they helped me finish dressing, and the photo was taken – I found it hard to smile. My pledge trainer (I forget his name) was a good guy and genuinely concerned about me, as were the two actives from my hometown. When I mentioned that my urine was dark brown, they became even more concerned and drove me to a doctor; he was the father of one of the actives and an SAE alum, so there was no way he was going to rat to the U.T. officials or SAE national HQ. Hazing was against the rules, but in 1979 it wasn't yet against the law.

Dr. Arnold took one look at me and was clearly worried. I gave him a sample of my urine, and he went back to the lab to take a look under his microscope. When he came back, he said, "Ok, your biceps are so swollen that they have ruptured. So, protein is leaking into your bloodstream, which explains why you are so fatigued." He continued: "Your kidneys are filtering the protein out of your blood and passing it into your urine. Hence, the dark color". I looked at Rick & Michael, the Harlingen guys who drove me there, and all three of us had a look of shock. Dr. Arnold wrote me a note to take back to the SAE house saying, "No pushups for 2 weeks. No exceptions". After a day or two, the swelling in my arms was abating, and my strength gradually returned; I could actually feed myself now and brush my own teeth!

In no way could I have predicted the reaction from some of the active members when they learned I was "off limits" for two weeks. Most of the guys were concerned, but the chants & insults from the "gung-ho" gang returned. And so did the "licks" with the paddle. I guess every frat has its rogue members, but these guys wrote the book. I took it for as long as I could; I had not shared any of this with Mom & Dad (I was worried about causing a backlash for the chapter), but I decided it was time. After two weeks of being sick and now singled out as "weak" (let that set in for a moment), I called them and gave them the story.

Their reaction was very parental: Dad asked several questions, and Mom was pissed. This was not what they sent their boy off to college to endure. They felt strongly that I should not continue to expose myself to "this senseless abuse," as Dad called it, and after about 15 minutes on the phone, I agreed. "This is bullshit," I told myself and decided I could not be associated with these guys anymore. Now, let me say this: there were & are some great guys in that chapter. It's what happens when a bunch of 18 – 21-year-old boys, without adult supervision and too much alcohol, get together and try to "mold" a group of other boys into a bonded unit through a shared trauma. I remained friends with most of them and rekindled certain friendships later in life. But in that moment, sick & tired and knowing what every trip to the SAE house had in store for me, I decided to get out. My frat experience, it seemed, was going to be a short one.

Shortly after the news got around that I was out at SAE, I got a call from the Pike rush captain. "Come have a beer at the Pike house," he said. They were already well-along in their fall pledge class, but he told me if I wanted to pledge in the spring of 1980, they wanted me. I said "yes" and basically became a defacto Pike that day. It was the beginning of a wonderful association with the chapter that continues today. Did I do some pushups as a Pike pledge? Sure, I did. Were we made to stay up late working on party decoration "builds" and then clean up the mess the morning after on two hours of sleep? Yep, we did. But there were no insults, no "licks," and no rogue actives intent on inflicting pain. I had found my fraternity home and was very happy.

The end of pledgeship was going to take place in August so that we could be initiated right before the fall semester. During the Spring of 1980, I met a Theta (Kappa Alpha Theta sorority) named "Elizabeth Anne Vogelpohl"; everyone called her "Libby." She was born & raised in Galveston with some deep Greek roots and genes; her mother's maiden name was "Kanugrous." Libby was a beautiful girl, both inside & out. She had deep olive skin and a wonderful smile. She graduated #1 in her High School class and enrolled at U.T. the same year I did. We first met at a Pike mixer in the fall of 1979 – after the Christmas holidays, she asked me to a nice dinner at the "Theta" house, and we had a great time. We dated a little, and then about a month or so later, I had plans to drive down to Harlingen for the weekend to quail hunt with Mom & Dad, so I asked her if she would like to go with me. She said, "Yes, that sounds like fun", so off we went in my 1979 Ford Mustang.

The weekend went great; Mom & Dad really enjoyed her outgoing personality and true love of life. She even tried her hand at cleaning some of the quail we shot and laughed about it being good training for med school later. I saw a new side of Libby on that trip, and we fell hard in love then. She taught me so much about how to really love a girl, and she showed me true, genuine affection. Libby brought out the best in me, and I loved loving her. We dated through our graduation from U.T. and even after.

The spring semester wound up, and I headed home for the summer. Since I now had a year of college under my belt, I was sure that my job at Varmicon was going to be something a little more "dignified" and commensurate with my college-born intelligence. Imagine my surprise when Dad told me, "This summer, you're going to work on the tug boat." Gulp. Dad was a big man, easily 6 feet 3 or 4 inches, with broad shoulders, huge hands, and a voice he could inflect in a deep baritone when he thought he needed it. With me, he rarely needed it because there was no way I was going to cross this guy.

So, I packed my suitcase and headed to Port Harlingen to board the tugboat for the three-day trip to the Victoria Ship Channel, where we would tie up the barges and load them full of sand and gravel for the trip back to Port Harlingen or Port Isabel. The trip back took four or five days since we were so heavy and bucking the always present Gulf breeze blowing from south to north.

It wasn't particularly hard work, but the "maritime pay" was great; the day started at 6 am with breakfast for the crew of 5; there were two Captains, each paired with a Deckhand. I made the 5th crewman. I learned to cook and got a first-hand view of the beautiful wetlands along the Intercoastal waterway of Texas. This was way before cell phones, so the first thing I did when we made port was find a pay phone and call Libby. We would talk until I ran out of change, and then I would get back on the tugboat and not talk to her for several days until we made port again. Man, I was in love, and she was, too. We saw each other as often as we could during the summer, with either me going to Galveston or her coming to some family event in the Valley. There were Pike rush parties around the state, so we would always meet there and party with the chapter guys, their girlfriends, and a ton of high school guys going thru rush. It was a very happy time.

Chapter 12: Mom, R.N.

August meant it was back to Austin for the fall semester, and for me, it meant the end of pledgeship. There was one more week of it before initiation, and then I was going to be an Active. Again, we did some silly stuff "to earn the right to be a Pike," but nothing was too overboard or ridiculous. One thing we had to do was wear the same clothes all week: khaki pants, a white T-shirt, and high-top sneakers. It was just part of the process to show our "dedication to the frat" and our desire to pay our dues, if you will. My "pledge uniform" was getting pretty dirty after three or four days in the Texas summer heat, combined with some things we had thrown on us after meals, including raw eggs and buttermilk.

One afternoon a pledge brother of mine and I went down to the basement (it was a holy mess) to get some lumber to build some props for an upcoming party. Lumber and plywood were everywhere, and as we scavenged for the right pieces for our project, I accidentally stepped on a long nail coming out of one of the 2 x 4s. As I was about to learn, there was a bad bacteria growing in my very wet shoe that was delivered into my left foot, just between my big toe and the one next to it.

I dropped to the floor with the 2 x 4 still attached to the bottom of my shoe. My pledge brother pulled it off (the pain was pretty sharp), and I took my very damp sock & shoe off. I could see a small puncture on the bottom of my foot, so several actives drove me to the health clinic on campus so a doctor could look at it. He asked if I had had a recent tetanus shot ("Yes," I told him), so he prescribed some antibiotics for me. "Keep your foot elevated for several days and soak it in Epsom salt," he advised. And so, I went back to the Pike house to wrap up pledgeship. Elevating my foot and soaking it in a warm bath wasn't gonna happen there, and I knew it as I walked out of the clinic with a slight limp from the pain.

Over the next few days, the pain and swelling increased; I couldn't put a shoe on my left foot. Being eighteen years old, I figured that it would eventually heal and "go back to normal," so I ignored it. And no way was I going to call Mom & Dad about this, I thought. It will heal, and they will never know. Wrong again. Libby became concerned when she looked at my very swollen foot and saw the pain I was in; after ten days, she thought it was time to see a real doctor, and I agreed. Now, I had never had more than a common cold nor dealt with any serious health issues unless the swollen biceps experience counted. Libby got her Dad on the phone from Galveston; he was a successful cardiologist, and we hoped he could diagnose me over the phone. "Cinco," he said, "that sounds like a pretty bad infection. You need to see a doctor immediately". But who should I call? I didn't know any doctors in Austin other than Dr. Arnold, and I sure wasn't going to call him again!

Libby's Dad got me an appointment the next morning with a G.P. who took some x-rays of my foot. A few minutes later, he walked in with the x-rays in an envelope and sent me (with the envelope in hand) upstairs to an orthopedic surgeon named John Genung. Dr. Genung was a U.T. grad and even played back-up quarterback for the football team. He was a cool guy, and we hit it off immediately. He removed the x-rays from the envelope, snapped on the backlight of what looked like a classroom whiteboard, and quickly attached the x-rays of my left foot to the whiteboard to have a look. The light illuminated the "pictures," and I could see the skeletal structure of my foot. "Looks ok to me," I thought. Just then, Dr. Genung leaned closer to the x-ray and let out a long "hmmm." He pointed to a certain area of my foot, turned to me, and said, "see anything odd there?" On second thought, I did. "The main bone going into your big toe is gone," he said. My heart sank. "Oh wow," I said, "it really is!" It was pretty easy to see what he was referring to. I started to get very nervous.

"Clearly, your foot is very infected," he told me. "And the

infection is destroying the bones in your foot." He continued with more bad news: "I have no idea what bacteria it is (though I suspect he had a pretty good idea), but if we don't operate on it, you're gonna lose that foot." This was bad. "I'm scheduling surgery tomorrow morning at 7 am at Seton Hospital," he said and snapped off the backlight behind the whiteboard. My heart sank further. "Wait, Dr. Genung," I responded, "I can't have surgery tomorrow (a Friday). My sister's 21st birthday is Saturday, and there's a dinner party in San Antonio". (Mom & Dad were hosting a beautiful sit-down dinner at the Argyle Club in the posh area of Alamo Heights and had invited about 100 people to celebrate Shelley's birthday. Libby & I were planning on being there and staying over that night.)

"Cinco, you are losing your foot," he emphasized. Dr. Genung was a pretty cool dude, but I could sense he was very serious. And truly concerned. "Well," I said, "I better call Mom & Dad and let them know about this." He was shocked that after almost two weeks of pain & swelling, I had not notified my parents. Now, I had to break another story to them about an injury that occurred in the frat house, and this time, I was going to need surgery. And…. I was not going to be at Shelley's birthday party Saturday night. Once again, my spirits were sinking as I walked back into Dr. Genung's waiting room (using crutches he had given me during the exam) and gave Libby the news. Her eyes got big when she saw me and said, "Oh my God, Cinco, this is bad." She gave me a big, long hug (that girl gave me love and empathy in spades) and took my hand as we walked out to the car to go call my parents.

Ring. Ring. Ring. "Why won't they answer?" I thought as I sat in my apartment, calling Mom & Dad with the news. It was dinner time, so I thought maybe they were away from the phone. Finally, Dad answered. "Hello," I heard his deep baritone voice say. "Dad, it's me," I told him. "Can you & Mom talk?" I asked. "Sure," he said. "Let me put you on speaker phone". I heard Mom's wonderful, loving voice say, "Hi, Baby!" She called me "baby" until the day she died. "Hi, Mom," I managed to say. My voice was starting to crack a little, and my pulse quickened.

I laid the story out for them and apologized for waiting two weeks to let them know what had happened. To my surprise, they weren't angry (that helped relieve my angst a lot) but weren't sure about this quick surgery scheduled for first thing the next morning, either. "We want to talk to Dr. Genung before anything happens, Cinco," they told me. Fortunately, Dr. Genung had predicted this and gave me his home phone number in case Mom & Dad wanted to call him. Now, it was clear they did. I gave them his number: "he's expecting your call tonight," I told them. "Call me back after y'all talk." I hung up and silently prayed. I was raised in the Episcopal church but hadn't really been to church or thought much about faith since going off to college. Now seemed like a good time to talk to God.

Twenty minutes later (it seemed like two hours), my phone rang with Mom & Dad on speaker phone calling me back. They had talked to Dr. Genung and said he explained the dire circumstances and the need for quick action. "We can't be there that quickly," they said, "but Shelley will drive you to the hospital early in the morning." Shelley was living in Austin, having transferred to U.T. from William Woods College in Missouri. She & I were very close, and she had a very loving & caring demeanor. Mom & Dad had already called her and shared the plan with her. I felt better knowing she would be there. "Dr. Genung said he did not think you would be able to come to San Antonio for the party Saturday night," Mom said. I could hear the disappointment in her voice. "But," she continued, "I hope you will try," I assured Mom that I would be there, even if it meant being on crutches two days after foot surgery. I had even packed my suit & tie to take to the hospital with me so I could get dressed there Saturday afternoon for the dinner party that night. Clearly, none of us really understood the severity of my condition; we would very soon.

I had never even been to a hospital, much less been admitted to one. Surgery? That was for wounded soldiers and old people, not me. It was still dark as Libby, Shelley & I arrived at admissions and made our way to my assigned room. An I.V. was inserted on the top of my hand, and they told me to strip naked and "put this gown on." "Wait," I said. "Why do I have to be naked under this gown if they're operating on my foot?" The nurse explained they might need "access" to all my parts during surgery, in which case I couldn't be wearing anything else. It was all I could do to put on that damn gown; no way was I going to be naked underneath it. I didn't say anything to Libby or Shelley, but as I disrobed in the bathroom and donned that soft, cotton gown with the ties in the back, I left my boxer briefs on. "No way will the doctors & nurses in surgery ever know," I assured myself.

A few minutes later, the nurses arrived to roll me into O.R. Libby & Shelley both gave me a quick kiss on the cheek. "See you in a little while," I said, still confident that this was going to be a quick procedure and that I would be outta there in a few days. Afterall, it was September, and I was just starting my sophomore year in college. We had tickets to the Texas vs. Oklahoma football game in two weeks, and I was a newly initiated active of the PKA fraternity. This was a minor setback, I thought, as I was transferred from my portable bed on wheels onto the surgery table. It was cold in there; and very bright.

Dr. Genung walked in and gave me some quick words about what he planned on doing: "We're going to cut an incision on the bottom of your left foot, just over the puncture wound," he said. "It will be about three to four inches long, and then we will 'evacuate' whatever infection is there." He was all business; everyone was in scrubs, masks & gloves and scurrying to & fro in the O.R., prepping for surgery. "Sounds good to me, Doc," I replied and gave him a thumbs up. Did I mention it was cold? I mean, it was freezing in there. I'm glad I left my boxers on, I thought, and I had a wry smile knowing I was "breaking the rules" even in surgery. With that, I said another silent prayer, hoped for the best, and drifted off to a deep sleep induced by whatever drugs my anesthesiologist had just injected into my I.V.

I really don't remember waking up in recovery. The first thing I recall was being wheeled down the hall toward my hospital room with my elevated left foot wrapped in a huge bandage. Shelley was waiting for me in the hall, and even though I was still groggy from the anesthetics, I was so happy to see her. As she took my hand for the rest of the short trip down the hall, our eyes met. We teared up immediately because we both knew, in that moment, that there was no way I was going to be at her birthday party in thirty-six hours. I was crushed, and I was pretty sure she was, too. "Damn nail," I thought. "How could such a small object create so much trouble?" and drifted off to sleep again.

I was feeling better the next morning though the pain was pretty severe. I was on a 4-hour rotation of pain meds (administered by injections in my thighs – this was potent stuff!), and I started needing them after about 3 ½ hours. To my surprise, the IV had not been removed; some big bag of something was still hanging there, dripping into my arm, but I had no idea what it was or what it was for. Shelley & Libby had come to visit and were there by my bed when Dr. Genung arrived. By the way, I learned later that they thought Dr. G was pretty good-looking; being a guy, I hadn't noticed. But they loved seeing him and made it a point to be there every morning for my daily updates from him. He was a damn good surgeon and an even nicer man. The girls often talked about what a "hunk" they thought he was.

"The surgery went well," he told me. "We just got the lab results back, and the bacteria is called pseudomonas. Your foot was very infected, and there is a lot of bone damage, but I evacuated as much of the infection as I could". Evacuated, I thought, he uses that word a lot. "Well, when can I evacuate this hospital, Dr. Genung?" Libby

& Shelley were headed back to their apartments to pack for San Antonio and the birthday party that night, so he kept it short and to the point. "Cinco," he said, "you're gonna be here awhile. Maybe for a few weeks," he told me. "WHAT?" I said, "that's not funny, Dr. G."

He went on to explain that there was no oral antibiotic in the fall of 1980 for this type of bacteria and told me that's why I was still hooked up to an I.V. "The drugs dripping into your body right now are saving your foot, maybe even saving your life, but it will take a while to kill off all the infection that was there" he said. My spirits were falling. "And," he continued, "the damage to your bones doesn't show up on x-ray for several days, so we're chasing a moving target. We may have to operate again". Before I had a chance to react, he pulled his chair up next to my bed and said, "now we need to change the dressing from the surgery yesterday." I was due for a pain shot, and the nurse walked in with a needle ready. "Hold that for a few minutes," he told her. "I'm changing his bandages now, and he's going to need it after I'm done." Oh shit, I thought, this is going to hurt. He suggested Libby & Shelley get going, which they needed to do anyway. It was clear to me & them that he didn't want them in my room for what was going to happen next.

Because he wanted my foot to drain the infection out, he did not suture the 4-inch incision at the bottom of it. If he had, then he would have sealed off my foot with the infection still in it. So, he had to basically wrap my foot with layer after layer of gauze. I swear it was three inches thick and must have taken 20 or 30 feet of gauze strip. As I was about to learn, my incision had been bleeding and draining for about 24 hours, and every layer of gauze was now soaked with my blood & bodily fluids. And the outer layers had dried up, which meant he had to tug the gauze section on the bottom of my foot loose with a big jerking pull, layer after bloody layer, to get the gauze free. It was misery, and all I could do was try to hold still in my bed and wait for him to finish. He did his best to minimize my pain, taking a break every minute or so, but there wasn't much else he could do.

Finally, he took this big wad of blood-stained gauze in his hands, turned towards the bio-hazard trash bin in the corner, lifted the red plastic lid, and threw it away. My foot was a massive, swollen mess on the top; I could only imagine what the bottom looked like. The nurse stepped forward, jabbed the needle in my thigh, and pushed the painkiller in with her thumb. Whatever that stuff was it was strong, because immediately the pain receded, and my mood improved.

With the nurses' help, Dr. G rewrapped my foot with another 20 or 30 feet of gauze strip; "we'll have to go through this process every morning for a while, Cinco," he told me. "And," he continued, "I'm moving you to a room called 'isolation.'" "Isolation?" I asked. "What is that?" He explained that since I had an open incision on my foot, I was very susceptible to outside infection. So, everyone who came to see me, whether they were a doctor, nurse, or friend, would have to wear a mask, gown & gloves. An isolation room has a small "outer" room connected to it with a door between them; that door had a window in it that I could see through from my bed. Any outside visitors would step into the outer room first and, with the help of my nurse, gown up with a mask & gloves. It actually gave me a bit of gallows humor seeing everyone go through that process and walk into my room looking like the medical staff just for a visit.

On Sunday morning Mom & Dad arrived after the party the night before in San Antonio. I was feeling pretty good, and it was great to see them. It was their first chance to meet Dr. G, and they hit it off well. I think they felt confident in him and his plan for my care; I certainly did. We had a good visit, and they stayed in Austin that night. Mom wanted to stay in Austin with me for several days, but I told her there wasn't much to do. "Mom, what are you going to do? Sit there and watch these drugs drip into my body?" I asked. Against her maternal instincts, she agreed, and they drove back to

Harlingen together the next day. Shelley & Libby were there to take care of anything I needed, after all, and it was kind of fun watching them dress up like nurses when they came to see me.

I had tons of visitors. Guys from the Pike house made a constant stream through Seton to see me; Al McNamara, Paul Swope, Tucker Graves, Robert Howden & Tim Costello were all my poker buddies and good friends. David Durr had pledged PKA and were now fraternity brothers. The chapter president, Beau Frederick, and our V.P., Tom Webber, made frequent visits. They were both pre-med majors, so they took an especially vivid interest in what I was going through. Libby & her friends were there every day, it seemed. Shelley brought a lot of our Harlingen friends with her who were at U.T. then. I had a lot of company and was feeling pretty good. But when was I going home? I kept wondering as I looked up at the I.V. bag next to my bed, keeping me in constant company.

Towards the middle of the week, the pain in my foot returned. I mean big-time pain. Dr. G. was clearly alarmed. "With the meds you are on, you shouldn't be in this much pain," he said with a troubled look on his face. "I'm sending you downstairs for more x-rays."

The next morning, he arrived with that familiar envelope under his arm with the new x-rays inside. We didn't have a backlit whiteboard this time, so he had to hold the "pictures" of my foot up to the light fixture hanging from the middle of the ceiling in my isolation room. "See this?" he asked and pointed to the middle of my left foot. Sorta, I replied. "The infection is spreading," he said sort of nonchalantly. Is it spreading? I asked. "Yes, we haven't stopped it yet." He showed me where more bone damage had appeared. My heart sank; I knew this probably meant more surgery. I could barely listen to his words as he explained that he was going to operate on me in the morning; my mind was already thinking about the gauze wrap removal torture I was going to have to endure again and the fact that I had to call Mom & Dad and break the news to them. "Is there any other option?" I finally managed to utter. "I'm afraid not," he said. "I know this isn't the news you wanted to hear; see you in O.R. in the morning," and he made his way out of my room.

I have never been depressed. In fact, I am probably too positive for some people: how can this guy be so happy all of the time? I'm sure some people have wondered. But, in that moment, sitting alone in my bed in the isolation of this hospital, knowing that I was going to face another surgery and all that comes with it, I was "as low as whale shit," as we used to say at the Pike house. (Afterall, don't whales swim the deepest spaces of the sea? And if so, then doesn't their poop fall to the deepest crevasses on the ocean floor? What could be lower than that? we surmised.)

I decided to call Dad at his office; I knew Mom was going to be very upset with this news, and I wanted him to break it to her, not me. I was already dealing with all the emotions I could handle. When I told Dad that Dr. G wanted to operate again, he was very concerned. "what's going on here?" he asked out loud and to no one in particular. "I think it's time to get a second opinion," he declared with true paternal concern. Ok, I thought. Dad went on to say that he was going to call Dr. Bill Ferrante at Ochsners Clinic in New Orleans. Ochsners has a tremendous reputation, and for reasons I never knew, anytime anyone in our family needed serious health care, they went to Ochsners and Dr. Ferrante. Dad even called Shelley and told her to pack my suitcase and hers because he was booking us flights to New Orleans. "Your Mom & I will meet you there tonight," he told her. Now, I was in no kind of shape to be moved or go anywhere. The slightest movement in my foot caused shooting pain, notwithstanding the fact that I was pretty sure Southwest Airlines wasn't going to let me board their shiny 737 with an I.V. tube stuck in my right arm. But I was too tired and too sad to argue. "Let them figure it out," I thought.

Dad talked to Dr. Ferrante and asked him to call Dr. G, which he did. Apparently, Dr. Ferrante liked what he heard from Dr. G because he called Dad back and said, "Jimmy, the boy is in good hands. They are doing everything for him that we would do here. In my opinion, he is where he should be." That was music to my ears, and Mom & Dad quickly drove up to Austin for my surgery the next morning. It would be my second in seven days. This time as I donned the gown, with Mom's help tying the strings in the back, I stripped naked and left my boxers in my room. At this point, I really didn't care if someone, somehow, saw me naked during surgery. I had way bigger worries on my mind as I was wheeled down the hall and swung briskly into O.R. I immediately remembered how cold it was in there and wished I had my boxers on!

Dr. G was there all wrapped up in his surgical gear & scrubs and gave my arm a quick tap of reassurance. "I hope you get it all this time, Dr. G," I told him. He assured me he would do his best, gave the anesthesiologist a nod that meant "knock him out," and then stepped around to the bottom of the surgery bed I was laying on.

I woke up in my hospital room violently sick. As I had just learned, me and anesthetics don't get along well. The first surgery was a pretty quick one, lasting only about thirty minutes or so. This one went a good two hours because Dr. Genung opened two incisions on the top of my left foot and inserted a rubber catheter into each opening and out the bottom of my foot through the first incision he made there a week before. Obviously, I did not take the drugs well and was throwing up into the trash can Mom held for me. I guess the good news was I was so sick I didn't feel the pain in my left foot for a while. But when I did, it was a doozy. They basically kept me knocked out on morphine (I had asked them earlier what they were giving me) the rest of the day so I could sleep. Mom stayed with me in my room that night and was there the next morning when Dr. G. arrived.

That was the first time I heard about the two incisions and tubes thru my foot and his hope that this was the final solution to my infection. I had prayed for that in the O.R. the day before. Then it was time to remove the dressing. The nurse was ready with my pain injection, and I suggested Mom not stay in the room. She protested, as any Mom would, and vowed to hold my hand through the whole thing. She was a total trooper, and I was relieved knowing she was there. And I was going to do my best to "buck up" and not show the pain – if not for me, then for her. But this time, the gauze wrap was soaked on the bottom, AND the top, so instead of one big jerking pull with each layer, there were two. My big plan to endure it without showing any reaction flew out the proverbial window; poor Mom was near tears as I flinched with the removal of each layer of gauze. She asked if the gauze could be cut off, but it was just too thick and swollen from my drainage. Finally, it was over, and the nurse quickly jabbed me with another dose of pain-relieving solution as I let my body fall against the bed and tried to relax. My thighs were starting to look like pincushions from all the med injections they were giving me, but I didn't care.

A couple of hours later, a new doctor walked into my room and introduced himself. "Hi, Cinco. I'm Dr. Douglas," he said. (I honestly don't remember his name, and I don't want to because whatever misery I had endured in the post-surgical re-dressing of my foot bandages was about to seem like child's play.) He went on to say that I was starting physical therapy twice a day – the first session was scheduled in about 30 minutes, I was told. This was day nine of my stay at Seton, and it was clear that Dr. G knew what he was talking about when he said I wasn't going home anytime soon. This new doctor was younger than Dr. G and had a certain toughness to him; his bedside manner wasn't very warm. "I've ordered twice-daily P.T. for you, young man," he said. He sounded like a drill sergeant, so I thought maybe I should salute this guy or something. Turns out, he was a drill sergeant AND an M.D. in the army. In Vietnam, no less. And this was 1980, only five years after the end of that war.

"You have three open wounds on your foot," he told me. No kidding? I wanted to say. You're a brilliant physician! Instead, I just let Dr. Saigon keep talking. "We're gonna bathe your foot twice a day in a cleansing solution, ok? P.T. is ready for you; your nurse will take you down in a wheelchair. You'll have to roll the I.V. stand alongside of you – think you can handle that, Private?" Aye, Aye, sir. I thought he might order me to do some pushups, too. If only he knew THAT story!

Well, bathing my foot in a cleansing solution wasn't exactly what he had in mind. As I was wheeled into P.T. and met my "trainer" - I forget her name now, but she was awesome. We would become very good friends, and she would sometimes bring me a pizza and watch the baseball playoffs with me in my isolation room. Let's call her "Mary" - and she was sitting next to a small whirlpool bathtub. But it was empty. Next to it was a water pik machine. Full of Clorox bleach. Yep, Dr. Saigon explained that this was how they treated wounded soldiers in the jungles of "Nam" when they couldn't get them to medical care quickly enough: they shot Clorox bleach into their open wounds with a water pik gun! I looked at Mary, and she gave me a return glance that convinced me she had never done this before. "Uh, Doc," I said as I turned to protest. But it was too late. He was already gone, and it was just Mary & me there to sort this out.

"How long do you think this is going to take?" I asked Mary. She gave me a sheepish look and said, "I don't know. I was told to empty all of the Clorox out of the Water Pik machine. I guess 15 or 20 minutes." Hmmmmm. "So, you and I are the first people in this hospital to try this, huh?" I said. (Lord, I was pretty sure we were the first people not located in the jungles of Southeast Asia to try it!) "Yes, we are," she said and turned on the water pik.

All I can say is I gained an instant respect for the military men who served in Vietnam. At least for the ones who had their wounds treated this way; it was a living hell. Now, I know that most men are pain weenies; we don't like to hurt. We're just not wired for it the way women seem to be. But even poor Mary was hurting for me; as much as she tried not to wince and react when she would hit the trigger and start more Clorox shooting into my foot, she was a bad actress. We were about halfway through the tank of Clorox when Dr. Saigon reappeared. He had a sort of weird look of morbid satisfaction on his face, and I thought for a minute he might have a Nam "flashback" and do God knows what with his stethoscope. "Try to get the Clorox shooting all the way through his foot!" he told Mary. "We gotta make sure we wash all that infection out of there." She moved in closer, only about a half inch away from my open incisions, and gave it a shot. I grabbed the handles of my wheelchair and arched my back in pain. It felt like she was using a flame thrower on my foot, and I didn't try to hide my discomfort.

"You want me to order a pain shot?" Dr. Saigon asked me. "No," I said, "I want you to tell Mary to stop." I'll get the pain shot on my own, I thought. Gratefully, the Clorox was all but gone, so Mary wrapped it up and turned off the machine. "That worked well, men," he said as he took a close look at my foot. "We'll see you back here this afternoon," and turned and marched out.

I endured this "therapy" for the next 5 days until Dr. Saigon was convinced the treatment had worked. Dr. G was happy with my progress, and the latest x-rays showed no more bone damage. I was on the mend after 2 ½ weeks in the hospital. They even moved me out of isolation at this point into a "normal" room. As I felt better and was getting my strength back, I was ready to get out of there and return to school. The next morning when Dr. G made his rounds, I asked him: "when can I check out of here and go back to school?" The news I heard hit hard: "Cinco, my last pseudomonas patient, was here for six weeks." That meant I wasn't even halfway. (The Texas – Oklahoma football game was this coming weekend, so I gave our tickets to Libby, and she went without me.) SIX weeks? I thought. No way I was going to be here 3 ½ more weeks. Dr. G explained, again, that there were no oral antibiotics for this bacteria, which is why I was still on the I.V. and would remain on it until I left the hospital.

They had removed the I.V. needle and relocated it so many times I was pretty sure I could do it myself. At this point, I knew every nurse, supervisor, and doctor on the floor, and they knew me. Frequently, they would bring the nursing students from U.T. through my room to visit and check on me. One very young first-year girl with a white bow in her hair and a hopeful look in her eyes was tasked with starting a new drip bag for me. This meant pulling the clear plastic tube (coming from the empty bag) out of the needle inserted into my vein and then inserting a new tube (from a full bag of antibiotics) into the open slot. "Will it hurt him?" she asked Susan, the trainer who had brought her in to see me. "No," Susan answered, "he won't feel anything."

Well, I was bored to death, and the chance to prank this girl and create some humor in my life was a temptation I couldn't resist. Plus, I knew Susan pretty well, and we had become friends – I knew she would get a laugh, too. So as this newbie inserted the new tube into the I.V. needle over my left hand, and the solution began to flow into my body, I began to thrash in horrible pain. "Turn it off!" I screamed. "For god's sake, TURN IT OFF!!" I thrashed left & right for about five seconds, and this poor girl just froze. Then I burst out laughing and told her I was only joking. She was mortified and burst into tears. I felt horrible, and Susan & I both tried to console her. She finally collected herself, but I never saw her again. And I never pranked a nurse in the hospital again, either. Lesson learned.

I told Dr. G that I had to get out of there. Soon! He explained that the only way I could leave was if someone could give me twice daily injections of antibiotics for the next three weeks. I told him Mom would do it. "Is she a nurse?" he asked. "No," I said, "but she can do it and will do it if I ask her to." He consented to the plan, so now all I had to do was convince Mom. Fortunately, Mom & Dad had plans to be in Austin the next day, so when she arrived, I laid it all out for her. In the meantime, I had called my advisor at U.T. and asked about getting caught up on my schoolwork. His stern advice: take a medical withdrawal and come back in the Spring. Damnit, I thought, that's not what I was hoping to hear.

Mom was a little skeptical, at first anyway, at the thought of jamming a needle in my hips twice a day for the next three weeks. But it was my ticket to freedom, and it was clear now that I would have to withdraw from U.T. and move home. The nurse came in and gave Mom an orange to practice with. After a few tries, she got good enough at it that they let her try a real injection on me. I rolled onto my side, pulled my boxers off my hip, and waited for Mom to hit me with the needle. And waited. I heard the nurse say, "go ahead, Mrs. Cocke, pinch his skin a little and insert the needle right there." Nothing.

I looked at Mom and said, "Mom, I have endured so much pain and had so many shots the past nineteen days. There's no way you can hurt me more than that. I want to go home, so let's do this together". With that, she took a deep breath, plunged the needle into my thigh, and injected me with bacteria-killing goodness. The nurse gave her high praise, and I did, too. Maybe, I thought, this is the beginning of the end in this hospital. Dr. G ordered several blood tests so they could monitor the level of antibiotics in my bloodstream after each injection. They had to make sure the dosage was just right. After two more days, they were sure that it was, and Dr. G ordered my release.

Mom & Dad, with Shelley's help, had gone to my apartment and packed my clothes and essentials. The next morning, they drove up to the discharge driveway at Seton, parked Dad's Mercedes there, and came up to my room to bring me home. Mary leaned over (I was sitting in a wheelchair for the trip to the car) and gave me a kiss on the cheek. She and I had endured a lot together those five days, and I was going to miss her. Dr. G gave me a quick handshake, and I thanked him for his good care and for saving my foot. "Hook 'em Horns," he said with a big smile. "Hook 'em Horns," I said back with an even bigger smile.

Libby pushed my wheelchair with Mom, Dad & Shelley following closely behind. As we made our way down the hall, many of the nurses I had gotten to know so well were there with their goodbyes. There was Nancy, who helped me take my first true soaking bath two days ago when the I.V. had finally been removed. (Before that, it was just "bird baths" in my hospital bed.) All of them were there and happy to see me going home. I was ecstatic. It had been three weeks since the day that I was admitted for my first surgery. It was five weeks ago that I stepped on that nail. I had lost weight and was still pretty fatigued, but rolling out the back door of Seton and feeling the sun on my face for the first time in twenty-five days felt like magic.

We got to Dad's car, and I stood up to climb in. I was on crutches and would be for another two months, but the feeling of being upright at that moment was heaven. I gave Shelley a big hug and thanked her for everything she did to look after me while I was at Seton. (I found out later that she literally called Dr. Genung every day to get the latest updates and news on my progress, even though she was there every day anyway.) I turned to beautiful Libby, my wonderful girl who had been there every day and so lifted my spirits with her big, loving heart. I took her in my arms and held on for as long as I could; I didn't want to let her go, but I knew we had a five-hour drive waiting. We kissed quickly (my Mom was standing there, after all) and I turned and climbed into the passenger seat up front. Mom took my crutches and placed them on the back seat next to her.

The car was rather quiet as we drove away, and Dad took us down Lamar Blvd, along Shoal Creek, lined with mature, beautiful oak trees, and eventually to Interstate 35 South. We passed U.T and all the places I knew so well but had not seen in so long. There was the Special Events Center with its marquee advertising the next big show. There was the football stadium – I was going to miss a lot of U.T. football, but at that point, I didn't care. Finally, I let out a long sigh and felt Mom's gentle touch on my shoulder from behind me. Dad reached over and gave my knee a hearty pat, saying, "I'm glad you're going to be ok." I was going home. Home, I thought. Finally. With any luck, we would be there in time for dinner. Man, some home cooking sure sounded good.

Chapter 13: Gone too soon.

The rest of the fall was spent in a basic daily routine: Mom and I would meet in my room at 7 am for my daily injection of antibiotics; then, I would follow Dad to the office and do some light financial analysis for him or whatever business errands needed attention. At night we would gather around the small dining table in the family room (there was this beautiful stained-glass window behind the table that lit up at night) for dinner and conversation. I stayed in touch with everyone in Austin, and Libby came down a couple of times for the weekend. Life felt good, and I was happy. U.T. had granted my medical withdrawal and told me that I would be re-admitted for the Spring of 1981 without any further effort from me.

My good friend, John Scaief, had pledged SAE that fall even though we rushed him hard. He handled it well and came over to the Pike house to say "Hi" and "Thank you" to all the guys that had helped rush him at our house. I drove him back to the SAE house and decided I would walk him in. Needless to say, there were some nervous looks from the actives there when they saw us arrive; I'm sure they were thinking I had convinced John to flip his pledge to the Pikes and was there so he could deliver the news. The rush captain was a guy I knew well, and when he walked up to us, I congratulated him for getting John's pledge and asked him to take good care of John. The mood in the room quickly became very positive, and several guys came over to shake my hand and greet me. This was just a few days before I was to step on that damn nail in the basement of the Pike house.

My big brother at Pikes was a guy from Liberty, TX, named Greg Fourticq. Greg had a little sister named Dawn, who was my age and a member of the Pi Phi sorority. Greg was a good guy, full of life with a great sense of humor. John had started dating Dawn's little sister in the sorority and was truly finding his way around the SAE house and Greek life at U.T. Even though I was home, John and I talked often on the phone, and he kept me up to date on him and his life. He said pledgeship wasn't all that bad, so I was glad to hear that the "gung-ho" gang over there had been reined in. One morning as I was sitting at my desk down the hall from Dad's office, John called from his dorm room. "Cinco, can you talk?" He was clearly concerned. "Sure, I said, what's up, John?"

He then told me that Dawn Fourticq had been in a bad rollover car accident the night before and was clinging to life at Seton hospital. I was stunned. He gave me the details and said he and his girlfriend had held a vigil at Seton all night; he was going to bed now at 9 in the morning. This was way before cell phones, so I called Al McNamara in his room at the Pike house to see what he knew. Al confirmed the news and said Dawn was on life-support. I knew there was little chance of reaching Greg, so I asked Al to tell Greg I called & was saying prayers for Dawn and the family. This was three days before Thanksgiving, and everyone would be coming home for the holiday. I caught Libby on the phone in her apartment, and she was devastated. We all knew Dawn well and loved her greatly; I felt especially close to the situation since Greg was my big brother at the Pike house.

Dawn's condition did not improve, and she died on Thanksgiving Day. Her funeral was scheduled that Saturday in Liberty. Shelley & I drove to Galveston to stay with Libby's family so we could all attend the funeral, which was about an hour's drive away. John and his girlfriend were there, as well as many Pi Phis and Pikes. It was one of the saddest days of my life, losing such a beautiful and energetic girl. It reminded us of how precious life is and to be careful. Greg's parents were wonderful people, and we all gathered at their home after the service. I tried to find the right words for them, drawing on my own experience of losing State six years earlier, but I just seemed to stumble. Eventually, we drove back to

Libby's house, and the next day Shelley & I drove home to Harlingen. It was a Thanksgiving I wanted to forget.

I was done with the daily injections, and my foot was recovering well. We had plans to spend Christmas at home in Harlingen, and I knew finals at U.T. were wrapping up that second week in December. All of my high school friends would be home for the holiday from their various colleges, and I looked forward to seeing them. In about a month, I would return to U.T for the spring semester, and life would be "normal" again. What a fall it had been, and we were still recovering from Dawn's tragic death two weeks earlier.

Chapter 14: This time, I'm mad.

Mom, Dad & I were having our nightly cocktail before dinner. It was around 6 pm when the house phone rang. Dad answered, and I heard him say, "Yes, Val, Cinco is right here. Let me get him for you". Val Garcia was a Kiwanis advisor of ours from San Benito and a good friend; Val was short for "Valderama," and he owned a clothing store on Main Street there. I hadn't talked to Val in several months and was glad to catch up for a few minutes before we sat down for dinner.

"Cinco," he said in a somewhat hushed tone, "I have some very bad news." "What is it, Val?" not sure what he might be referring to. He cleared his throat and said, "John Scaief was killed in a car wreck this afternoon driving home from Austin for the holiday." I was beyond stunned; I couldn't process the words I had just heard. Dad turned to me, and Mom walked up, staring at me; clearly, they knew something was very wrong. "Val," I barely muttered, "I will call you back." I turned to Mom & Dad without even hanging up the phone and immediately broke down. "John Scaief died today" is all I could manage to say. They were as shocked as me; they had gotten to know John very well over those Key Club years, and he had been to our home many times. I'm sure the horrible pain of losing a son came flooding back to Mom as she thought about John's Mom and what she must be feeling.

I knew I had to go straight over to the Scaiefs' house, but I wanted a few details from Val, so I called him back, and he filled me in. Apparently, John was passing an 18-wheeler that didn't see him there; the 18-wheeler made a quick left turn, and John's car ran right under it. I then learned that Cathy Harris, a Harlingen girl and the daughter of some of Mom & Dad's best friends (Cathy's Dad was a doctor and gave me all my football physicals back in high school), was riding back with John. Cathy was hurt badly but was recovering from her injuries at the hospital in Harlingen. John died at the scene.

My mind was swimming, and Dad offered to drive me to the Scaiefs and be with me there. I accepted but knew that before we left, I had to call Libby. She knew John well and loved him like we all did; she and Cathy were sorority sisters at the Theta house. This was going to hit her hard. She answered the phone when I called, and I tried to keep my emotions in check. "Babe," I said, "I have bad news." There was no way I could prepare her for this, and no soft intros were going to help, so I continued without letting her say anything: "John Scaief died in a car accident today coming home from Austin." She was speechless. The next voice I heard was her mother's, who had taken the phone out of Libby's trembling hands. "Cinco, what is it?" she asked. "What has happened?"

I could hear Libby sobbing in the background as I explained to Kris Anne what I had just learned. Kris Anne was a warm lady and had been very supportive of us when we lost Dawn. Now, we were all going through it again. After a minute, Libby came on the phone and had obviously just remembered that Cathy was with John that day. "What about Cathy? How is she?" she asked in a very worried tone. Libby was trying to hold it together, as was I. I told her that Cathy was badly injured but recovering in the hospital in Harlingen. We talked for only another minute, and I told her: "Dad & I are headed to John's house now. I'll call you when I get home". With that, we hung up, and Dad and I headed out the door. I was beyond sad; this time, I was mad. Why John? Why all this pain? Why now? It doesn't make sense; it's just so unfair. When I see God in heaven, I am going to ask him. I hope he has some answers.

The next few days were a maddening rush of trips to the Scaiefs and making plans for John's funeral in San Benito. John had a younger brother, Michael, and I did my best to console him, again drawing from my own experience of losing my big brother. John's folks asked me to be a pallbearer, and I was honored to accept. The day before the service, I drove to the airport to pick up Libby and David Durr; they were staying with us, and we were all going to the service together. The Harlingen airport was a mass of U.T. students: SAEs were there for John. Thetas were there for Cathy. Pikes were there for John, Libby & me. Key Clubbers from all over Texas & Oklahoma had flown in, together with many Kiwanis advisors, too. Walking Libby & David to baggage claim to grab their gear off the turnstile, we could barely go two steps before someone we knew from Austin grabbed us for a consoling hug or words of sad disbelief. It seemed like people everywhere at that airport were walking zombies. I certainly was.

The service was held at the Scaiefs church in San Benito. I remember it was a bright, sunny December afternoon, and the church was packed. I arrived early so that I could gather with the other pallbearers and sit up front. David, Libby & Shelley sat together a few rows back. I was still too stunned and sad to really listen to the words spoken or the prayers that were read. We had all lost another wonderful friend way too early, was all I could think. Finally, we pallbearers were motioned to stand and follow John's casket down the aisle and out to the waiting Hearse. The rest of the congregation followed closely behind; it was going to take a few minutes to get everyone outside, I thought, so that we could load John's body inside that long black Cadillac with everyone gathered around. When we hit the door and started walking down the front steps, I saw a mass of people there, too. There were so many people that the church couldn't hold everyone, so a hundred or so stood outside and waited for us to bring John out to the car.

At the cemetery, we carried John's body to the mausoleum, where his casket would be placed. His middle name was on the entrance, and it said: "Deem." Funny, I thought, all these years, and I never knew his middle name was Deem. At that point, what difference did it make? I wondered to myself. Whatever his middle name was, I was never going to see him again or hear his wonderful, infectious laugh. I was mad again. One by one, we pallbearers removed our boutonnieres and placed them on John's coffin. Several of his closest friends walked up, touched the casket, said a few words, and sadly walked away. We all greeted his parents and Michael as we passed by their seats, but no one really had anything to say. It was just a situation we had to deal with and move on as best we could. We skipped the reception at Scaiefs' house after the service and headed to our house out on Bass Blvd. It was a beautiful, white stucco home set in 4 acres of thick brush and a welcome oasis from the day we had just had. We got into comfortable clothes and gathered for dinner. We said a special prayer for John, and I did my best to eat something. Frankly, I didn't have much of an appetite for several days.

Chapter 15: "I am not a Crook."

The spring semester started in January, and frankly, it was a nice return to a regular schedule after the fall of 1980. Libby and continued dating and life revolved around U.T. academics and Pike House social life. Spring Break was always a great time, and annually I would invite 4 or 5 guys to the Sunchase Condo on South Padre for the week. My best buddies to join were Al, Tucker, Kirk Williams, Mike Chitwood, and David Prigmore. There were always other Pikes down there staying at various places, and we would all gather at various parties and beach functions and have a great time. One night, very early in the morning, probably around 3 am, the phone rang at the condo. It woke me up out of a deep sleep; on the other end was a rather intoxicated fraternity brother named Gib Wood. Gib told me that they were way down the beach (you had to drive a good five miles or so before there was beach access for vehicles) and had gotten stuck in the soft sand; he needed us to come pull them out since I was in Dad's 4-wheel drive hunting Suburban. "Ok," I said, "which beach access do we use to find you?" He gave me the instructions as best he could in his beer-induced state. Right before we hung up, I had finally woken to my senses: "Gib," I asked, "how did you get this phone number?"

He proceeded to explain that he called "directory assistance" in Harlingen and got Mom & Dad's home phone numbers and called them. "Oh, shit," I thought. he woke them up in the middle of the night. After losing State, those late-night phone calls were always a source of immediate concern for them. "Yeah," he said, "your Dad sounded pretty pissed off because I forgot the number to the condo the first time and had to call him back a second time." I expected an ass-chewing from Dad for that one, but it never came up. Things like that happened often at the Pike house; after all, we were just a bunch of boys with time & freedom on our hands. I could tell a million stories about the chicanery we either found or created on our own. Fortunately, no one ever got hurt, and later on, we all laughed about the stupid things we did.

Each fall, we would all gather in Kerrville at my grandmother's house for Thanksgiving; it was an easy drive from Austin, and I always enjoyed it very much. Momma Bert was a tiny little thing but full of love. She really enjoyed having all of us there and put on a huge, traditional Thanksgiving spread. She was a wonderful lady, and we all cherished her.

One year Dad said that we had been invited to spend the night in Wimberly at the home of one of his fraternity brothers. Mom, Dad & I drove over on Friday after Thanksgiving in Kerrville. Bob Draper was from Houston, and he & Dad were very good friends at the Kappa Sig house back in the '50s. Bob married a girl named Claire Jaworski; they, too, had lost a son tragically and were kindred spirits with Mom & Dad. Claire's father was Leon Jaworski, the well-known partner in the Houston law firm of Fulbright Jaworski (the firm is now known as "Norton Rose Fulbright"); we were going to his home surrounded by beautiful hill country landscapes.

About ten years earlier, he was named special prosecutor for the Watergate trial that ultimately forced Richard Nixon to resign, the only U.S. President to ever resign from the position. Watergate was a hotel & office complex in Washington, D.C., where the Democratic National Party had its offices. Richard Nixon was up for re-election, and even though he was a favorite to win the race, he directed his staff to bug the offices of the D.N.C.; apparently, the goal was to get some tawdry news about the Dems candidate, George McGovern, or otherwise gain some campaign advantage. Unfortunately for Nixon, when his operatives broke into the D.N.C.'s offices (well after working hours), they were spotted by a security guard who summoned the police. The two were arrested and eventually spilled the story about why they were there and who they were working for. Once it was traced back to Nixon, all hell broke loose. All of Nixon's senior staff were implicated, although they all feigned ignorance for a while. There were congressional hearings about it with Nixon's chief of staff, John Dean, the focal point. His testimony was broadcast live and became must-watch T.V. for a week or so. Eventually, Congress appointed a special committee to investigate, and once charges had been brought, they needed a savvy attorney to prosecute the alleged. They chose Leon Jaworski.

Now, I had heard enough about Colonel Jaworski to know he was a big deal; and I was a little intimated as we drove up their driveway towards their nice home in the Texas hill country just west of San Marcos. We arrived and settled in, and soon it was time for dinner. Their formal dining room was very nice, though still modest and comfortable. I don't know whether it was planned or not, but I found myself sitting to Col. Jaworski's left during dinner. His grandson, Robert Draper, was to my left, and even though he was several years older than me, he was a welcoming dinner partner, and I was immediately more at ease. (Robert was a budding author & would go on to write many articles that were published in Texas Monthly, GQ, and New York Times). Col. Jaworski engaged me in conversation, and I quickly found him to be very nice and not at all intimidating. I don't really recall what we talked about, only that we both seemed to enjoy the evening very well. He put me at ease, and I was very grateful; again, it occurred to me how humble people like him could be. Not arrogant or entitled in any way.

The next day, as I was getting organized to drive back to Austin, Col. Jaworski came over and had something in his hand. "Cinco," he said, "I wrote a book about my life in law and the Watergate scandal. I have signed it for you and hope you enjoy reading it." The book was titled Crossroads, referring to the many times in his life he had a decision to make that could go down a variety of paths. I did read it and still cherish it. A few weeks later, I received an envelope in the mail from Dad; inside was a letter from Leon Jaworski responding to a thank you note Dad had written him for our time in

Wimberly. At the end of the letter, Col. Jaworski wrote, "please remember me to your son, Cinco, whom I enjoyed visiting with so much." That felt pretty cool.

Chapter 16: The Big Easy

During my years at U.T., I did ok academically, but honestly, I figured I had a job waiting at Varmicon, and as long as I made Bs & Cs, with an occasional A thrown in, Dad was cool with my progress. I did take some summer classes, too, to get caught up from the semester I missed after my foot surgery ordeal. As May 1983 approached, I was scheduled to graduate on time after four years of study.

One night at our weekly poker game with Al, Tucker, Kirk, David & Mike Chitwood, we started talking about how some of us had never been to New Orleans. Tucker had been there before helping his Dad (Jim Graves was Sr. V.P. for Dresser Industries, a huge oil field services company headquartered in Dallas) host a big group of people (Dresser customers, no doubt) at the Super Bowl. Tucker knew all about New Orleans and said he could organize a trip for us. The problem was none of us had the money to swing it. Tucker was always up for a good party and a bit of a rule-breaker, so he devised a plan: "Well," he said, "what if we get the Pike chapter to pay for it?" "How are we going to do that?" the rest of us said in disconnected unison. Al was the social chairman for the chapter that spring and was in charge of planning all the parties. Tucker suggested that Al have a "Mardi Gras" themed party in a few weeks and create a raffle for 4 plane tickets and 2 hotel rooms in New Orleans over one weekend. That part sounded good to us, but "How are we gonna win the tickets?" I asked. Well, Libby was President of the PKA Little Sisters, so Tucker suggested we get her to draw the tickets out of the fishbowl at the end of the party.; we all felt that would add a lot of legitimacy to the outcome.

Plans were going along well. Al booked the plane tickets and hotel rooms and planned the party for a week later. "Tucker," I asked a few days later, "how do we make sure that Libby pulls out raffle tickets with our names on them?" "That's the easy part," he said. "It doesn't matter whose name is on the tickets. She just reads our names and throws the ticket away before anyone sees who has really won!" It was devious and maybe even a little dishonest, but as a group, we had spent a fortune of our own money rushing new members over the past four years, so we concluded the chapter "owed us." The only thing I had to do was get Libby on board with the plan.

Over lunch, on campus one day at The Texas Union - a beautiful building right on the tree-lined West Mall leading up to the Main Building from Guadalupe St (more affectionately known by U.T Students as "The Drag") - I pitched the party idea to her. When I got to the part where she was going to read off my name & Kirk's name as the winners (normally, when we had done party raffles like this before the winner took his date that night), she got very excited. "We're going to New Orleans for the weekend??" she exclaimed. "Well," I said, "not exactly us." "I don't understand, she said, who are you taking then?" Her look was part confusion and part concern. I proceeded to tell her that I was taking Al & Willie (Kirk's last name was Williams) was taking Tucker. David & Michael were going to pay for their own plane tickets, and it would be 3-to-a-room once we got there, with one guy on the floor every night, literally.

Libby was disappointed at first but then gave me a big smile and said, "ok, I'll go along with this silly plan. You guys go have fun in New Orleans". What a great girl, I thought to myself. And I knew enough about women at this stage in life that I was sure I was going to have to make it up to her soon, somehow.

The party went off without a hitch, and a week later, the six of us found ourselves in New Orleans. It was early March and still cool at night as we walked the French Quarter going from bar to bar. I thought it was the coolest place I had ever seen. We spent hours at Pat O'Brien's drinking hurricanes, and God knows what else, staying out until sunrise both nights, followed by a staggering walk to Café Du Mond for hot beignets and chicory coffee. As we readied ourselves for the flight back to Austin Sunday, tired and hungover, someone suggested that we all take our girlfriends a "trip treat" from NOLA. We walked into the next t-shirt shop we passed and started looking around. Against the far wall was a display of women's undergarments, so that naturally grabbed our attention. We all agreed to buy our girlfriends a set of fishnet stockings and give it to them when we got back to U.T. I remember Libby was not very amused.

Graduation was going to be the last Saturday in May. All the family, my sisters & their husbands, were making plans to attend the ceremony at the Special Events Center. When the day arrived, we drove by it looking for a parking space, and the marquee read, "Today: Business School Graduation at 3 pm". Not exactly the Bee Gees, I thought to myself, but I'll take it! Mom wanted to celebrate my B.B.A., and I think she was really moved to make it a special occasion after all the crap I had endured to get there. So, a few weeks earlier, when she asked if I had any "special requests," I wasn't sure what she was thinking. But after a minute, it was clear that she & Dad had talked. "We'll have the Conquest available," she said. (They were flying up from Harlingen for the ceremony.) "Why don't we go somewhere in it?" she asked. Immediately, without hesitation, I blurted out, "Let's go to New Orleans!" She smiled that great "Mom" smile and said, "Let's do it!".

So, after the ceremony ended and with my B.B.A. in hand, we all drove to Browning Aviation at the Austin airport. I still have a picture of Libby and me, dressed in our burnt-orange caps & gowns, standing in front of the plane. With that, we boarded the Conquest and took off for N.O.L.A. Gayle & Rusty had a prior obligation in Dallas that day, so they flew to New Orleans on Southwest and met us at the hotel.

Mom had reserved a private dining room for dinner at Antoine's, just off Bourbon Street. All of us guys were dressed in coats & ties, and the girls had their prettiest cocktail dresses. Looking at my parents & sisters gathered around this beautiful table with white-jacketed waiters bringing every delicacy they had. Well, it was magic. Libby was as beautiful as ever and fit in so well with the family. She got her New Orleans trip after all, and this one was way better than the other one! Four years had gone by so incredibly fast, and this was one of the happiest days of my life: I had such a wonderful sense of accomplishment and relief. This was exactly what Mom had in mind when we started making plans to celebrate my graduation from the University of Texas at Austin.

Part Three:
Life after U.T. Austin

Chapter 17: They're all buying? Then Sell, Sell, Sell.

Libby took a job in Washington, D.C. working for Senator John Tower, and I had accepted a job in Houston as a "credit analyst" for a large commercial finance & leasing company based in New York City. I rented an apartment and started to work a week or so after the celebration in New Orleans. Dad suggested I get a job "outside of the family business at first to get some real-world experience" so I did. I enjoyed the work and the people in the company and was learning a lot; I think they appreciated my contribution and felt like I was making an impact. Six months after starting with them I got a 15% raise; I was "on my way". Libby and I saw each other when we could, with her coming to Houston or me going to Washington D.C. I had never been to that city, and she was a great tour guide; it was inspiring to see all the historical sites and share it with her. One weekend, she rented a house with some D.C. friends in Rehoboth Beach, Delaware, so I flew up and joined her.   It was my first exposure to the Atlantic seaboard (as an adult anyway) and I thought it was pretty cool. Very different from South Padre Island, Texas, I thought.

Shelley was getting married to her high school sweetheart, John, in August of 1983 and Libby was a bridesmaid. It was another chance for us to be together and share more fun times together, making special memories. The fall came & went, and I went to Austin for a U.T. football game when I could.

Libby & I spent Christmas together in Galveston and attended the grand opening of the Shearn Moody Plaza at the end of "The Strand" (Galveston's downtown historic street lined with buildings dating back to the late 1890s) on New Years' Eve. Her family knew the Moody family well and Ross Moody was a Pike with me at U.T., so it was natural that we would be invited.

The party was a lavish, black-tie affair worthy of Galveston's most blue-blooded family. The Moody's have been very generous to many causes and had spent a lot of money bringing this building back to its original, turn-of-the-century grandeur.   Several other Pikes were there with their dates, too and we took it upon ourselves to really enjoy the cocktails, food and dance music provided by Archie Bell & the Drells from Houston. Archie had played a couple of Pike parties back in our day and he would let Al & Don McCabe join him on stage when he & his band did the Blues Brothers' song "Soul Man". Al & Don would put on their vintage sunglasses, take the microphones and sing at the top of their lungs. Sometimes they would ad lib some of the lyrics into phrases that might offend certain people, but since we were college frat guys, we thought it was hilarious. Don wasn't there that night but as I recall, Al gave it his best shot. I could sense some of the stodgy people in the "blue hair section" of the party weren't amused. We clearly didn't care and danced until Archie quit playing at 2 in the morning.

Spring arrived and I was busy with work in Houston and my life there. But I kept thinking that I wanted more. Was it time to move back to Harlingen and go to work for Dad? My world voice was asking questions this time. Libby and I had loosely talked about a future together (marriage?) the past New Year's, but she was happy in Washington, and I wasn't sure she would be happy in South Texas. I didn't give it a whole lot of thought at that point. "It's not broken", I told myself, "Don't try to fix it".

April 1984.   Dad called me at my office in Houston and asked if I could come "home" for the weekend. We still had the Sunchase condo on South Padre Island, so I flew in and met him and Mom there. What great Spring Break memories flooded back to me when I arrived; I even chuckled thinking about the night Gib called Mom & Dad and woke them up! Geez, I thought, we did a lot of stupid crap those years – it's a wonder we all survived.

Over breakfast Mom & Dad said they were considering selling the Company. Dad had grown it successfully, with the help and dedication of some very good people including my sister #2, Gayle. She had since met a guy in East Texas and married him, which took her away from the family business. "Your Mom and I think it is the right time to sell" Dad told me. They were very young: he was 54 and she was 56 but twenty years of running a materials business with 225 employees had worn them out. I watched them, as a very cohesive team, raise my siblings & me and grow the company together. Dad gave Mom as much credit as anyone in their success and was always sure to share the limelight with her.

Mom was a stalwart. She grew up in Harlingen, the oldest of four children. Her Daddy was a good man but wasn't the most robust provider. Mom knew little of the "finer life" until she was older. She married a WW II vet at nineteen years old and soon gave birth to her first child, my sister Cindy. Gayle & State followed and so did her husband's PTSD from the war. She didn't talk much about his drinking and the bad conditions of their marriage – Mom was eternally positive and thankful for whatever she had.   When they split up in 1956, she worked three jobs to support her children after moving back in with my grandparents. One of her jobs was to greet the members of the private "Motor Club" in town. She and Dad saw each other there from time to time and started dating. Mom was a unique combination of style, class & beauty mixed with some country girl roots.   You could find her camping out one night and hosting a nice dinner party the next. She did both with equal enthusiasm and comfort and she made everyone around her comfortable, too.

During my High School & college years Mom & Dad would host construction industry folks from all over the state to hunt whitewing dove in South Texas & Northern Mexico. It was always fun to see these corporate bigwigs pull out their beautiful Barretta shotguns (or some handmade side-by-side from England) and head out to field for the afternoon hunt. Mom would grab her little Remington automatic, and the show was on! That girl was as good a wing shot as I ever saw and usually showed up the men. They loved it though and it became quite a match to see who could get a limit of 20 birds with the fewest shots. Most of the time…Mom won.

All of us had a vested emotional stake in the company. It was very good to our family, and we loved the people and the times we all had worked there. I watched as Dad & Mom, over the last 20 years had bought out minor shareholders to consolidate ownership in the family. When Dad was named President in 1966 it was part of a big falling out between my grandfather and Dad's older brother, Hill. Papacito could be a very tough boss; in fact, he could be downright mean to his sons at times. As a self-made man and a child of the Depression, his perspectives and ideas were somewhat out of date and in some cases even detrimental to the company. Dad kept his eye on the bigger prize and swallowed his tongue many times. Uncle Hill, for whatever reason, didn't. So, after a particular nasty argument back in 1966, my grandfather fired my uncle and promoted Dad. I don't think Papacito and Uncle Hill ever spoke another word to each other.

Dad made sure that the company bought my uncle's shares back from him, but he had to fight my grandfather to do it. Dad's sister, Donald, also owned shares as did some of the early employees of the company. Dad did some excellent financial engineering, with the help of some very savvy advisors, to buy them out, too. Everyone was better for it but often that took some convincing. It was grueling and exhausting – I saw Dad so tired so many nights after a long day. Eventually, Papacito gave more & more control of the company to Dad and became a quiet figurehead. He was still alive in 1984 so his thoughts on selling the company were important. Fortunately, he saw the wisdom in it and agreed.

But sitting at the breakfast table that morning at South Padre with Mom & Dad hearing them talk about selling the company I needed a little convincing. I felt confident in my own ability to learn and to help grow the company like Mom & Dad had. We talked through several options and different scenarios, but it always came back to an outright sale being the best strategy. Mom & Dad made it clear they would not sell the business if I truly thought it was my life's ambition. My sisters were all married at this point and only Shelley was living in Harlingen, and they hadn't shown any interest in being involved in the company beyond shareholders meetings and corporate events. After a couple of hours, I agreed that we should do it. I had a pretty good idea what a company like that was worth and did some quick math in my head. My sisters and I owned stock as did Cindy & Gayle's sons; I knew this would be a nice financial "win" for all of us and told Mom & Dad "you have always made good decisions for our family; if this is what y'all want to do then I won't stand in your way."

Dad asked me to move down to Harlingen from Houston to help him and the assembled team of attorneys and investment bankers put the deal together. Little did I know that the experience over the next sixty days would change my life. In all candor, I was pretty much an errand boy; but, in several conversations with the "team" about some critical issues I drew on my knowledge of the company's operations and was able to give some good advice and a little different perspective. My confidence grew and I was really impressed with the level of expertise of Jim Rowe, our investment banker Dad hired to find a buyer, and our attorney, Jim Abbott, in McAllen. Both men were bright, energetic and absolutely loved Mom & Dad. I was in awe watching them work and it motivated me to later go earn my M.B.A.

In late May of that year, we signed an Agreement in Principle with the Barrett Family in San Antonio; they were a larger and very successful concrete and materials company there and we felt like it would be a really good fit for the employees of our company and theirs. Now the hard work of documenting the deal started; Dad chartered a Lear Jet (our Cessna turboprop was getting some scheduled maintenance in Wichita, KS and was grounded for several weeks) and he, Mom, the two Jims and I began flying to and from San Antonio, McAllen & Harlingen to facilitate meetings, negotiate the terms and prepare the documents. After several weeks the Barretts notified us that their bank had agreed to finance the deal and the Purchase & Sale Document was all but final. The negotiations were intensive and detailed but never adversarial. The Barretts wanted to buy, and we wanted to sell. This was starting to get exciting.

At this point, we were the only people who knew anything about the deal. Mom, Dad & I agreed that it was time to tell my sisters & their husbands. (Later when the formal closing was only a week or so away Dad sought the approval of the Board of Directors of our company, which they gave enthusiastically.) Since Gayle was in East Texas and Cindy was in San Antonio, we decided to call the family together in San Antonio to share the news. I remember many nights over dinner - after a long day of spreadsheets, documents, phone calls and flights to & from San Antonio - Mom, Dad & I would discuss and try to predict how my sisters would react to the news we were selling the company. We were pretty sure they would be puzzled at first, much like I was, but would see the wisdom in it and agree to tender their shares.

Dad booked rooms for all of us at the Four Seasons in San Antonio near the famed Riverwalk - he & Mom took a nice suite so we would have plenty of room to spread out and talk – and we jumped into the Lear Jet with Jim Rowe for the 50-minute flight from Harlingen to San Antonio. Dad wanted Jim there to help explain the genesis of the deal and the how & why of selling to the Barretts. Jim was a Wharton M.B.A. and I honestly think he might be the smartest financial guy I ever met – he did a great job of explaining to my sisters and their husbands the details of the transaction. I remember being very excited to share the news with the 3 girls and held my breath as Jim walked us all through the structure, terms & timing of the sale. They had some very good questions and were a little surprised at first. But after an hour or so they felt like I did: if Mom & Dad were sure it was best for all of us then they would certainly go along.

The next three to four weeks were a blur as we moved towards closing in late June; it would take place at our attorney's offices in McAllen. More flights to & from San Antonio followed by more meetings in McAllen. There were nightly dinner conversations with Mom & Dad about the myriad issues we had addressed that day and how we resolved them. At times it was exhausting but mostly it was a blast and I felt so blessed and privileged to have helped them put it all together. I knew I had matured greatly during those three months, and I sensed that Mom & Dad saw it, too.

We scheduled a celebratory party at the Harlingen Country Club the night before closing; many of the senior executives of both companies were there as well as members of the Barrett family. Mark & Mary Barrett had just returned from a safari in Tanzania and brought many of their photos for us to admire. (I remember thinking: "where the hell is Tanzania?". Several years later, I would visit there myself.) The mood was festive and the anticipation of closing the next morning in McAllen was keen. Arriving there the next morning I began stacking all the documents around this massive conference table for all of us shareholders to sign. We were about to sign the deal and "walk into the sunset". Or so I thought. As I circled the far end of the conference table with what seemed like fifty pounds of paperwork, I looked up to see Jim Rowe and Jim Abbott walk in with concerned looks on their faces. "Uh oh", I thought; this doesn't look good. "Is something wrong?" Dad asked them. Jim & Jim proceeded to explain that the Barretts attorney (who had flown in from vacation in Martha's Vineyard just the night before) had raised a last-minute concern about our company's bonus system. Essentially, he was claiming it was an unfunded liability that should have been identified on our Balance Sheet. If it had been, from his perspective, our company would have been worth about $1,000,000 less than the contract price. Dad was pissed; Mom & I were very concerned. Was this closing not going to happen after all? I wondered. All this hard work and late nights for nothing??

We knew we had disclosed the bonus structure to the buyers and were sure they had factored that into their pricing model. Their bank had seen it, too. I personally remember flying to San Antonio on the Lear (alone this particular time) to deliver that spreadsheet to the Barretts and their advisors. I reminded everyone in the room of that. Dad bowed up and told Jim A & Jim R to go tell the Barretts they had 10 minutes to come sign the documents or he was going to "get in my car and drive back to Harlingen". As Jim A. walked by Dad on his way to deliver the message, he whispered to him "you do, and I'll kick your ass!". I had never heard anyone talk to my Dad like that and I burst out laughing; and then so did Mom & Dad. I knew then everything was going to be ok: Jim Abbott was a smooth, smart, stately man with a calm demeanor. Whatever he told the Barretts worked (I doubt he gave them Dad's veiled threat to tank the whole deal!) because five minutes later we were all seated around the conference table signing the documents I had so meticulously piled in front of each seat.

After months of planning and hard work the whole thing was over in about fifteen minutes. "Wow, it's done" I kept thinking. As we all filed out the front of Jim Abbott's offices, I looked back to see him beaming from ear to ear. It was late in the afternoon, and we were all headed back to Harlingen for a celebratory dinner at home. Mark Barrett and his Dad asked if I could give them a ride to the airport so they could fly back to San Antonio on their own Cessna Conquest turboprop. "Sure" I said and loaded them into my car for the short drive to McCreery Aviation at the McAllen airport, a place I had come to know well the last six weeks. I gave Mom a huge hug and Jim Rowe & I embraced each other warmly. "Nice job, young man" he told me. I watched my sisters walk out the door knowing our lives had been changed in a big way and silently, I wished for my brother. He would have been proud of me, too, I thought as I steered my car onto Nolana Loop with Mark & Thurman Barrett riding along.

I dropped them off, shook their hands and started the forty-minute drive to our home on Bass Blvd exhausted but invigorated, too. As I drove east past the citrus orchards and rows of palm trees with the sun starting to set behind me, a Jeffrey Osbourne song come over the radio; the chorus says "it's been a lifelong love song" and it was the perfect words at the perfect time as I reminisced about the 23 years (I would turn 24 in three months) I had grown up in South Texas. I thoroughly enjoyed every year being the youngest of five children and working for our company business. A lifelong love song, indeed. With the sale done and the company no longer "ours" I knew it was time to look forward and see where life would go next.

Chapter 18: Is it really better to have loved & lost?

I wasn't sure what I wanted to do next or where I wanted to do it, at least not in the short term. I <u>was</u> sure I wanted to go back to school and get my M.B.A. So, in August I bought a small house in Harlingen and settled in there. I didn't have much furniture – I had been living with Mom & Dad since May – but I set up my house and made it a home. Dad & I leased a small office on the 7th floor of the former InterFirst Bank building; he was a director of that bank, and we knew all of the people there. Several people approached us about a variety of real estate deals, but I really didn't know how to evaluate them. And I was pretty sure I wasn't going to be in Harlingen that long, anyway. Gayle was married and lived near Longview with her husband, Rusty. They had a cool house right on the lake & I really enjoyed visiting them there. The tall pines trees were so nice and reminded me of my fun trips to Nacogdoches during Key Club. East Texas held some appeal for me. Jeff Warr was living in Tyler, as was another good friend from McAllen, Robert Fowler. Jeff & his Dad had grown a successful mobile home business for several years and Robert was in the oil business with his father-in-law.

Libby & I were still a couple, but I could sense that something was changing in her; and maybe in me, too. The long-distance relationship (she was still in Washington D.C.) over the last sixteen months had taken a bit of a toll. She had plans to attend a fund raiser for Phil Graham (John Tower had announced he would not be seeking re-election to the U.S. Senate after twenty-four years of service and Graham was the odds-on favorite to replace Tower in the Senate) at her parent's home in Galveston. Kris Anne was Chairwoman of the Republican Party in Galveston County and politically connected at some very high levels. So, I met Libby at Houston Hobby airport, rented a car and we drove to Galveston for the weekend. She was all business as she and her Mom worked the crowd, shaking hands and accepting donations. Her official role was to represent John Tower there and she handled it beautifully. But my intuition that her feelings might have waned was confirmed: we didn't really interact much at the party. The next day, she and I drove over to the beach for a nice walk along the gulf coast. As the waves crashed and seagulls chirped above us, she confessed that she did not see us getting engaged or married. "I think our lives are going in different directions" she told me "And I think our relationship has gone as far as it can go". While I knew we still loved each other very much, and was sure we always would, I also knew in my own heart she was right. So, we gave each other a long hug and drove back to her house to break the news to her parents. They were surprised but supportive; while Libby & I had plans to drive back to Houston the next day and fly home (me to Harlingen and Libby back to Washington) I had a different idea.

Mom & Dad had flown to Longview that weekend in the Conquest to visit Gayle & Rusty and were headed home to Harlingen the next day, as well. I called Dad, told him the news about Libby & me, and asked him if they could stop in Galveston and pick me up. "Sure" he said. "Are you ok?" he asked me. "Yeah, Dad, I'm ok" I replied, not really sure that I was. We settled on a time for them to arrive at the Galveston airport in the morning and ended the call.

That night Libby & I joined her folks for a pre-planned dinner at Gaido's - the local place to get good seafood in a nice, semi-formal setting - with Wendy & Phil Graham. I don't remember much of what we ate or talked about, and Libby & I were still affectionate with each other, though much-less than before our conversation on the beach. When we got back to her parent's house, I packed my bag and settled into the guest bedroom to go to sleep.

The next morning, we drove to the Galveston airport and arrived just as the Conquest taxied up to the tarmac. Our pilot,

Chuck Ritter, shut the engines down and Mom & Dad climbed out. After some quick hugs and a few tears, they boarded the plane and Chuck fired up the engines. I turned to Libby for one more kiss, gave her a huge hug and walked onto the plane. A few minutes later we were climbing out over the Gulf of Mexico with memories of her & our many times together rushing through my mind. While I was certainly sad, I also felt very blessed to have had her in my life at such a formative time. And I was pretty sure she felt the same way about me.

Chapter 19: Dr. Livingstone, I presume?

About six months later, Rusty invited me to come up to Longview and play in his Member-Guest golf tournament at Pinecrest C.C. So, I made plans for another of what had already been many visits to the area. About a week before the golf tournament Gayle called and told me she had met a really cute Longview girl and was setting me up with her that weekend. I was a little dubious about a blind date, so I told Gayle "Don't obligate past Friday night". I wanted to meet this girl first before spending both nights of the weekend with her. Her name was Neina Kennedy, and she was from an East Texas family with deep roots in the region. Her Dad grew up in Nacogdoches (I knew plenty about that town) and his family owned a jewelry store in Longview. Her Mom grew up in Longview and her family was very successful in the oil business. Neina was two years younger than me and was a Senior at T.C.U. in Ft Worth. She was a very pretty blonde and clearly intelligent and outgoing. Gayle brought her to the golf course and the four of us had a cocktail after Rusty & I finished our round. We went to the party that night at Pinecrest and had a great time; she was very easy to be around. We were both smitten and clearly, we both wanted to make the effort and see where this relationship might go, understanding that the distance between her life in Ft. Worth/Longview and mine the South Texas would be tricky to manage.

Besides, Mom, Dad & I had made plans for me to join them on their second hunting trip to Africa several months later. It was now one year since we sold the company. They had been to Africa once before, joining Dial & Weezie Duncan from Harlingen for a hunt in Zambia, and loved it. Some of Mom & Dad's good friends, Tom & Martha Clowe from San Antonio, were making plans to go on a hunt in Botswana and wanted to take their son, David.

Mom was wrapping up a trip in Europe with my sister, Cindy, and Mama Bert. Her trip ended in London, so Dad and I flew over on American Airlines to meet her there. We spent two nights at the Four Seasons Inn on the Park, and I really enjoyed having this special time with them. We did a little bit of touring the city but mostly stayed close to the hotel and listened to Mom's stories from her previous month touring Europe. We had a nice dinner the 2nd night there, when I inadvertently ordered steak tartar thinking it was beef wellington (what a rookie!).   When I realized my mistake, I was too embarrassed to change my order, so I toughed it out thinking about eating raw meat instead of a beautiful steak. Ahh well, travel is all about learning, right?

The next evening, we boarded South African Airways for the overnight, twelve-hour flight to Johannesburg, arriving in time to celebrate Dad's birthday on August 1st. I had no idea what Jo'burg was going to look like; my image was formed from pictures and articles in Time magazine which showed shanty towns and native South Africans in mass protests against apartheid. While that certainly existed, I was amazed at how attractive downtown Jo'burg was and how upscale the business & social communities appeared to be. I was learning that, even though there were serious racial problems and inequities, South Africa was an economic powerhouse with rich entrepreneurial traditions and vast natural resources. The issue was that only the whites were enjoying the fruits of it and the oppressed blacks wanted change.

We spent several days at the Carlton Court Hotel in downtown Jo'burg touring the city and having dinner with some South Africans that Mom & Dad met on their trip the year before. Then we boarded South African Air and flew up to Victoria Falls, Zimbabwe. This was towards the "dry season" in southern Africa so the landscape, in certain places, was pretty barren. But as we approached the Zambezi River (it supplied the water that flowed to & over the falls) it became lush & green. We checked into the Vic Falls Hotel and made our way out to the vast patio along the river. We could see the mist rising up from the falls and watched birds and baboons playing in the large trees that provided much shade for us. Wow, I thought, this is awesome! And it was. My horizons of the world, as a 24-year-old, were expanding rapidly.

After a couple of nights at Vic Falls, we were driven over the border into Botswana and met by our professional hunters, or "P.H." for short. They drove us to the small airport there where we boarded two single-engine airplanes, with all our gear, for the one-hour flight to our camp in the Okavango River Delta in northern Botswana. The camp was very nice with green tents and thatch roofs over the dining room. The weather was delightful: cool, dry nights followed by warm, sunny days. David and I shared a tent and settled in for 5 days of bird and big game hunting. Neina had clandestinely dropped a picture of herself into my carry-on bag back at the D/FW airport where she met us before boarding our flight to Africa. I found it later and kept it close the entire time I was there; I'm sure that was her intent, ha.

Our tents were nice with two cots and a wash basin just outside for morning routines. We were told many times NOT to leave our tents unzipped lest the baboons run in there and grab our things. They were "cheeky little buggers" as our P.H. said. The "shower" was about 50 yards (or should I say 46 meters since we were using the metric system in Africa) from our tent – it was a thatch enclosure with a bucket hanging from a long rope suspended in the middle. Warm water was supplied from a 55-gallon (208 liters) metal drum that had a small fire constantly burning next to it. When you wanted a shower, you simply called one of the camp orderlies and they would grab the bucket off the rope, run it over to the 208-liter drum of warm water, fill it and then reattach it to the rope in the shower. They then hoisted it up, tied it off to the frame and in you went. After a long day of bumpy, dusty rides in the Toyota hunting vehicles crisscrossing the African plains, a nice hot shower felt very good.   We would dress for dinner, meet around the wonderful campfire, pour ourselves a cocktail or glass of very nice South African wine and socialize about the day we had just experienced and make plans for the next day.

Most of the time we were bird hunting but the P.H. had an extra license for zebra, warthog & impala so they handed me their 7mm rifle and let me take target practice with it. I was pretty sure they wanted to see this young man handle their gun to make sure I knew how. All those days of hunting in South Texas had made me a pretty good shot and very comfortable with any long gun, be it rifle or shotgun. After a few shots found the target about 100 yards (92 meters) away I sensed that the P.H. was comfortable taking me out to hunt "big" game. Mom, Dad & I jumped into one of the Toyota hunting vehicles and the Clowes jumped in the other. They were wonderful friends, and we were all enjoying each other's company. I didn't know David that well before the trip, but he & I had many one-on-one conversations over those ten days. David was two years older than me and a delightful guy; we grew to be good friends on that trip and though we haven't stayed in touch (our lives just went in different directions) I will always remember him fondly as my first "tent mate" in Africa.

After several days there we all boarded more single-engine airplanes for a flight to a part of the Delta where we could fish for bream (kin to our white bass) and tigerfish. The camp was similar in every way to the hunting camp just left but it sat immediately along the Okavango River. If was an African oasis and beautifully scenic, with lush green palm and banana trees surrounding us. Each morning they would put the six of us, along with one or two P.H.s, into a power boat and off we would go looking for good places to fish. Now, we were told that every piece of water in the area was full of crocodiles and hippos and that we should never, ever go into the water. As we made our way over the crystal-clear water of the Delta, sometimes slowing down to navigate the think papyrus outcroppings that narrowed in our path, we would frequently spook crocs into the water from their sunbathing perch on the bank. They were huge and lightning fast, and I knew there was no way I was getting into the water with them! That was their turf, and I was determined to stay on mine.

We fished for several days and had a great time. I was just as hooked on Africa as Mom & Dad were and fully understood their fascination with the continent and their loving desire to return. The six of us were boarded onto a much larger airplane this time for a short flight over to the city of Maun. There we would board Botswana Air for the flight back to Jo'burg. The Clowes had plans to continue on to Cape Town, so we said our goodbyes there and Mom, Dad & I caught a cab over to the Carlton Court. I still had Neina's picture in my flight bag.

After a couple more days in Jo'burg we boarded S.A.A. for a flight to New York City and then home. We made a refueling stop halfway there at Isle de Sol, part of the Tenerife Islands off the western coast of Morocco. I wanted to get off the plane and have a look around even though it was about 2 am but alas we did not have visas; in fact, no one was allowed to deplane so I drifted back to sleep – it would be another ten hours before we landed at J.F.K. airport in New York. When we arrived in Harlingen, I was exhausted but invigorated by the wonderful trip and experience we had just enjoyed. Neina and I had a long conversation catching up – I had so much to tell her and share with her about Africa!

Chapter 20: "It's Five O'clock in Scotland!"

Towards the end of the conversation, she mentioned a trip she was taking with her parents in about three weeks. Her Dad had ancestral roots in Scotland and her folks were going there with some of their best Longview friends to visit - this would be their second or third trip but this time they were taking Neina. "Would you like to join us on the trip?" she asked. I didn't have to think about it for very long: "Absolutely" I said. I was making plans for graduate school and had no work commitments, so my time was mine. Spending a week touring Scotland with Neina & her family concluding with 3 days in London sounded like "jolly fun" to me!

I had gotten to know Neina's folks, George & Dorothy, pretty well already. But being with them on that trip solidified a wonderful relationship, especially between Dorothy and me. Dorothy Kennedy was a fun, gracious, thoughtful lady. I grew to love her very much over the next seven years that Neina and I shared, and I know she loved me. We saw some very cool places in Scotland and made a visit to the Turnberry & St. Andrews golf courses. Even though time didn't allow me to play there, I was in awe having watched the British Open (or simply "The Open" as the Brits call it) so many times on T.V. Even though we had many chances, given we were traveling internationally with our own hotel rooms, Neina & I never shared a bed on that trip. I wanted her to know that my feelings were real and show her complete respect. And her parents, too, who were hosting me in Scotland & London.

After a wonderful ten days of constant companionship, it was clear that we fancied each other. She was returning to T.C.U. in a few weeks for her final semester of college and I was applying to graduate school. Without giving it a lot of thought, I put my house on the market and rented a house in Tyler. I figured I could do some real estate deals with Jeff or go to M.B.A. school, as well. Either way I would be in East Texas and closer to Neina; she was glad to have me closer, too. Robert Fowler and I were good friends, too, so Tyler seemed like a good fit.   Once I settled in Tyler, Neina and I spent every weekend together and had fallen deeply in love. I really liked Ft. Worth and was putting a lot of miles on my car driving back & forth.   I rented a small office in Tyler and set about with applications to graduate school.

Chapter 21: Damn it feels good to be a gangster.

My grades at U.T. were ok but not the kind of work that was going to impress the admissions committee of a prestigious M.B.A. school. So, I knew my score on the GMAT (the Graduate Management Aptitude Test) had to be good. So, I bought the very thick GMAT study guide at the bookstore, sequestered myself at Mom & Dad's Sunchase condo at South Padre Island, and did nothing but study and prep for the exam for two solid weeks. It was my 8 hour-a-day, full time job and I took it very seriously. A few times I would go out to dinner but usually I would cook at home and enjoy a glass or two of red wine. I had no visitors and frankly, I didn't want any. I knew I had to do well on the test to have a shot at graduate business school.

After two weeks of solid study, I was ready. So, I grabbed a flight on Southwest Airlines to Austin to sit for the exam. I recall that it took about four hours to work through all the sections which covered math, finance & statistics. Once I was finished, I felt confident that I had done well and returned to Tyler to wait for the results. Finally, after three agonizing weeks, the test results arrived in the mail. I tore open the envelope and scanned the numbers on it looking for my grade. I honestly don't remember the raw score, all I knew was that it was in the top 25 percentile of anyone who had ever taken the test, meaning 75% of all the people who had ever taken the GMAT scored lower than me. I was thrilled and pretty sure I could make a case for graduate school admission. I called Neina with the news – she was happy and excited for me. Life was really good and getting even better, I thought as we wrapped up the call.

It was the spring of 1986 then; S.M.U.in Dallas had a one-year

M.B.A. program that started in August 1986, and I wanted in. So, I called the M.B.A. applications office and made an appointment. I knew I couldn't rely simply on my GMAT score to get me a place in the class and that I needed to meet, face-to-face, with the admissions officials and convince them of my sincere desire to excel in graduate business school. So, I put on a dark suit, drove to Dallas and sat down in front of the head of admissions. We had a nice conversation, and I did my best to explain why my U.T. G.P.A. of 2.5 didn't reflect my ability or commitment to academics. "It has been two and a half years since I graduated from U.T." I told the woman sitting across the desk, "and I am a more mature & disciplined person". I shared with her the story of selling Varmicon and the growth and wisdom I had gained from that experience. I told her of my life's goals and the entrepreneurial drive that was rooted inside me. "I know", I said "that given the chance to be an M.B.A. graduate of this school, you will be glad you accepted me". She, of course, did not make any commitments to me but my sense was she was impressed.

Back in the small house I had rented in Tyler, I was anxious and nervous. "What if they don't accept me at S.M.U.?" I thought. I was too young and too impetuous to even consider a "Plan B' if this didn't work out. I was just sure it would and kept thinking positive thoughts.

Neina & I had been dating for about six months at this point and I loved every minute we spent together. As the end of her time at T.C.U. approached, followed closely by the Christmas holiday, we were together constantly. Her Aunt & Uncle, Janna & John Robbins, had a very nice home in Longview and invited us to a small dinner party they were co-hosting with Neina's parents. Mom & Dad were invited, as were Gayle & Rusty, and were flying up to Longview for the weekend and the dinner party. Neina's Aunt Betty Davis and her husband, Charlie, would be there, as well. Naturally, her brother George and his wife, Marilyn, would be joining us.

John and Janna had been very warm to me those last months and John and I enjoyed each other's company discussing business, the oil market and political issues. John was smart and a cunning oilman but also easy to be around. Janna was delightful; she was an Oklahoma girl and had two younger children from a previous marriage to David Boren, the former Governor of Oklahoma who would later serve the state in the United States Senate. Later, he would become the President of the University of Oklahoma in Norman.

Neina drove in for the weekend and we stayed at her parents' house. After breakfast that morning she & I decided to take a drive down to Lake Cherokee where her family had a house. We had spent a good bit of time at the lake house and always enjoyed the quiet solitude set amongst the tall, green piney woods of East Texas. We were deep in conversation about nothing in particular when I was moved to turn to her and say "Neina, would you marry me?" We were sitting outside so I was wearing sunglasses. She turned to me, caught her breath and said "take off your sunglasses. I want to see the look in your eyes". I took my sunglasses off, laid them on the table and looked squarely at her. "Neina", I said, "I love you very much. Please marry me". Her beautiful face broke into a wide smile, and she said "Cinco Cocke, this may be crazy, but yes, I will marry you".

Now what? I thought. I didn't have a ring and I hadn't asked her Dad for permission to marry her. This was blue-blood East Texas with traditional values: some young buck from South Texas doesn't just waltz in off the prairie, woo one of Longview's most-treasured debutantes and then whisk her to the altar without asking her Dad first! We had to make a plan. And we only had about six hours before the dinner party at John & Janna's.

"Ok" she said, "we gotta figure out a way for you & Dad to be one-on-one this afternoon when we get back to the house. Then you can ask him for permission". She devised some way to get her Mom out of the house so that George and I could talk man-to-man. I agreed and added more strategy: "I want to tell my folks and your Mom about this before dinner. So, I'll call Mom & Dad and ask them to come over to your folk's house for a cocktail before dinner across town". She liked the plan and we drove back to Longview with our heads spinning about what we had just done. Now, I have always been a pretty conservative guy; a true planner who thinks several moves ahead at all times. Yes, and a little O.C.D. To be this spontaneous and carefree was strange to me, but it felt great. We were both excited about how the next few hours would play out.

Everything went according to plan: Neina and her Mom left for whatever errand Neina had contrived and I sat down with George. I told him about the conversation she & I had had that afternoon at the lake and asked his permission to marry his daughter. George was a jovial, gregarious guy who liked his cocktails and cigarettes; I found him easy to talk to and enjoyed our time together. He was very happy that Neina and I had made such big plans and immediately consented to our nuptials. We hugged boldly and he said some very nice things. I swore him to secrecy and said, "Neina & I want to tell Dorothy and my parents when we are all here together in about two hours". It was important to me that Mom & Dad learn this happy news at the same time Dorothy did. I was sure all three of them would be a bit surprised but very happy, too. "I won't say a thing" he promised me, and we parted to start getting ready for the night's events.

Mom and Dad arrived, and George greeted them at the door. They walked in exchanging pleasantries and George took everyone's drink orders. I helped him tend bar and once or twice he & I traded a look of knowing secrecy. Earlier, and without Dorothy around, he had given Neina a big hug and huge kiss on the cheek. I could tell Dorothy had no idea about what was going to unfold and was glad we had pulled this off. As we gathered in the Kennedy's den the setting was perfect. After a few minutes of small talk there was a long enough pause for me to jump in. I looked at Neina, who was beautiful and smiling boldly, and cleared my throat: "Um" I started, "I am so glad that we all were able to gather tonight before going to dinner". Dorothy chimed in and in her enthusiastic way said "I love this! It's so special for the six of us to be together". "It is, Dorothy", I said, "especially because Neina and I have some wonderful news we want to share". Mom, Dad & Dorothy were immediately curious and attentive. Without any pause I said, "I asked Neina to marry me today at Lake Cherokee and she said 'yes'".

Dorothy nearly jumped out of her chair and Mom & Dad were shocked, in a good way. We all hugged and kissed and laughed. Dorothy dabbed a few tears and then George made it clear that he & I had talked already, and he consented. "You mean you already knew about this, George??" Dorothy exclaimed. Mom & Dad were very pleased for me and felt certain that Neina and I had a bright, solid future in front of us. We gathered ourselves together, the girls re-touched their makeup after some joyful tears and we made our way over to the Robbins house for dinner to break the news, once again, to everyone there.

The rest of the night was a blur and the next day I drove back to Tyler and Neina drove back to Ft. Worth for the remaining few weeks of school.   Before she left, we looked at the calendar, and with Dorothy's support and input, decided the wedding would be May 3, 1986, in Longview.   When I later shared the date with Dad he jokingly said, "Good plan, there's no hunting season open then that we have to plan around!"   We had a good laugh at that one.

Chapter 22: A caddy joins the tour.

The months leading up to the wedding were a whirlwind of cocktail parties and planning. With all the very good friends our parents had, it seemed everyone from Longview to Brownsville wanted to host a party for us. It was flattering but exhausting, too, as we crisscrossed between Longview and the Valley as the honored guests. But it was mostly a lot of fun, and we enjoyed it immensely. Sweet Dorothy listened to all our wishes (as a guy, I didn't have many) and was determined to give us a beautiful ceremony. Dad pulled me aside one evening after a few cocktails at a particular party (the mood was festive, and Mom & Dad were really getting into this weeding planning stuff) and lots of wedding talk.

"Son", he said "you need to understand something about these wedding plans". (I had watched my three sisters all get married and thought to myself: this can't be all that hard, can it? Boy, was I naïve.)

Little did I know we would eventually have a cocktail buffet for five hundred people with the Dallas Brass Orchestra playing dance tunes. "Son", Dad repeated, as he threw his arm around my shoulders, "your job here is like a caddy on the professional golf tour". Mom & Dorothy were standing near and could tell Dad & I were having a serious word, so they leaned closer to hear this sage advice a father was about to give his groom-to-be only son. "A golf caddy, Dad?" I asked. "That's right" he continued. "Like a caddy carrying the bag for a professional golfer you have three jobs as it relates to this wedding: show up, keep up and shut up!". We all burst out laughing and it lightened the evening a lot.

But I knew he was right; as much as Dorothy always included me in wedding planning, I knew it was her and Neina's show and I was determined to say "yes" often.

By this point I had taken a very nice unset diamond that Mom & Dad gave me (they bought one for me and the three girls on their first trip to South Africa) to Paul Penaloza, a jeweler in San Antonio, to have it set in a ring for Neina. It was an oval shaped, two carat stone that shimmered brightly. Paul recommended surrounding it with two triangular-shaped stones, commonly known as "trillions". He showed me a setting that he would use, and I gave him the ok to do it. When I picked it up several weeks later (he shipped it to the Shreveport, LA. airport to save me Texas state sales tax) I thought it was beautiful. I honestly don't remember how or when I gave it to Neina, but I do remember she loved it instantly. She was pleased and I was, too.

As the months rolled by, we decided to go to Antigua for our honeymoon, so I began making all those plans. Mom & Dad were hosting the rehearsal dinner at a private club on the top floor of a downtown bank building. Wedding gifts were rolling in and it seemed like Neina, and I could barely keep up with the unwrapping and thank you notes. There were portrait sessions with Giddings; there were small, intimate dinners followed the next morning by enormous brunches and then cocktail dinner parties that night. The R.S.V.P.s were rolling in and Dorothy was repeatedly pleased that "so and so" from "such and such place" were going to be there; it pleased her that so many people accepted the invitation. It was beginning to sound like everyone invited was going to be there. Oh boy, I thought, I gotta practice my lines!

I had decided to ask Wynn Searle, a very good friend from Harlingen, to be my best man. It was a tough choice between him and David Durr; I literally flipped a coin to decide! All my good buddies from high school and the Pike house were involved, too, and we all arranged to rent tuxedos in Longview for the wedding. Neina & Dorothy had decided this was going to be a black-tie affair, with Wynn and me wearing white tie & tails. Dorothy had secured the Texas Boys Choir from Dallas to sing at the ceremony (when she asked me what I thought I remembered Dad's advice and said "yes"). Yep, this was going to be something. Our wedding photo even appeared in the Wedding pages of Vanity Fair. I caught a ton of grief from the Pike house guys for that one!

There was only one other teeny, tiny thing to figure out. I had proposed very quickly after meeting Neina, and we had been living apart the whole time, so we hadn't yet consummated the relationship. And frankly, with the jet-set schedule and burning the miles between Tyler and Longview that spring, we never really had the chance. One night as we had a quiet Moment, I asked her "You know, here we are getting married in a few months and we haven't even made love yet". She looked at me and said, "I was wondering when you were going to finally put the big move on me". We both laughed and it was the right icebreaker to a very important topic. As we talked about when and where we wanted to be together for the first time, we realized that almost every weekend, if not weekday, between then and the wedding was booked with some event or another. We certainly didn't want to rush anything, and we both knew how special we wanted that night to be. At almost the same time, we both said, "what if we wait until our wedding night?" So, that's what we agreed to do. And we did, at the Mansion on Turtle Creek Hotel in Dallas, about six hours after the wedding in a beautiful suite festooned with three dozen red roses I had delivered before we arrived. It was the perfect way to celebrate our wedding and all the wonderful times that led us to it.

Chapter 23: Master Cinco.

Neina moved into my modest rent house in Tyler right before the May wedding and we settled there after the honeymoon. We knew we wouldn't be there long: I had been accepted into the M.B.A. program at S.M.U. starting that August. We were moving to Dallas soon!

We found a small apartment a block off of Hillcrest Ave. across the street from campus. Together, we didn't have much furniture, but we did our best to make it homey. I started school and loved it from the first day. Since it was a one-year program, we took 18 hours over three semesters in twelve months. The pace was fast, and the workload was full, but I knew I was up for the challenge. My classmates were from colleges spread all over the country and their backgrounds and undergraduate degrees varied widely. One thing they all had in common was, they were smart as hell. I mean, wow, I was impressed. But that just made me even more determined to find my place within the curriculum and classes and make a visible impact.

Very soon, I knew this was going to be a full-time job. With Neina's support and encouragement, I was on campus by 7:30am and didn't leave there until after 5:30pm or so. Even on Fridays & Saturdays when we didn't have class. Almost all my classes were case studies of various companies and or business situations from many different industries. I drew on my B.B.A. and my experience with selling Varmicon to bring my perspective and comments when called on during class discussions; I was always prepared and knew the material well. This was way better than undergraduate studies, when half the time the prof just walked out, gave a 50-minute lecture and there was only a mid-term exam and a final to determine your grade. I was never a good test-taker, so that didn't fit my learning style at all. But case studies with notes and lively class debates and discussion with all these bright people?? Man, I was having a ball!

Neina and I would make Saturday night our date night and usually we would walk across the street to University Methodist Church Sunday morning for services. After a Sunday lunch and a few quiet Moments, I would hit the books or my Compaq laptop for work on a class assignment or case study. There were lots of group-study events with classmates, usually on Sunday afternoon for several hours before the start of another grueling week.

I was getting to know most of my classmates and became good friends with several. One guy in particular hailed from San Antonio and we discovered that our families knew many of the same people. Stacy Locke was married to a very bright girl named Joanie Neuhaus (remember the Wall Street investment banking firm Underwood, Neuhaus? Well, Joanie hailed from them.) She was working on her M.B.A. at Rice while we were at S.M.U. so we didn't see her very often, and since Stacy was there as a solo married guy, we tried to have him over when the schedule allowed for some social time. We would eventually become great friends with Stacy & Joanie and joined them in Paris for a week about a month after we graduated from M.B.A. school. Stacy and I are wonderful friends still.

As graduation neared, we knew we wanted to plan a worthy celebration of my graduate degree. Neina booked a very nice, private dining room at The Mansion on Turtle Creek and the family flew in. I got them rooms at the Mansion and the plans were set. Graduation day was warm, it was August, but I was so glad to be earning my M.B.A. and had proven to myself that I could perform well in a tough academic environment. All of the graduates gathered in front of Moody Coliseum (yes, the Moody's from Galveston) in our cap & gown; it was warm under that gown with a shirt & tie on! Because we were actually being "draped" with a bright scarf (recognizing that we were all college graduates already) we were told to wear our tassels on the left side. It didn't matter to me, I would have worn it between my eyes, all I knew was shortly I would have my M.B.A.

The keynote speaker was Trammell Crow, the very successful Dallas real estate developer. He was one of the largest developers of office & industrial space across the U.S. at the time and a big icon in Dallas business circles. His home was adjacent to the Dallas Country Club along Mockingbird Ln in Highland Park, just down the street from S.M.U. Unfortunately, I thought the speech was pretty sub-par; I'm sure he did his best, but I don't think public speaking was one of his strongest skills. I do recall a funny story he told, though: He reminded everyone that Dallas Country Club was completely surrounded by very expensive homes; they had no room to grow but had some expansion plans. Trammell said that one day he got a call from the Club President and after exchanging some pleasantries, the man told Trammell that the club needed to expand their facilities. "Would you consider selling your place to us?" he asked. "That's funny" Trammell replied, "I was about to ask you the same thing." It got a good laugh and shortly after that the ceremonies concluded with hugs & high-fives from all the family there.

Chapter 24: California is the place you ought to be!

Neina's and my first year of marriage was pretty much consumed by graduate school - although we did join Mom & Dad in Chub Cay, Bahamas for a week of bill fishing in April. I wanted to isolate myself from work and have some fun with her, besides we had income coming in and weren't worried about paying our bills. So, we just chilled for the fall. We saw her family in East Texas a couple of times and her Dad had a deer lease just outside Harper, TX so we hunted there once or twice. And the aforementioned week in Paris with Joanie & Stacy.

Dorothy was turning fifty in December and Mom & Dad had just bought a home in Breckenridge, CO. Dorothy's party was planned in Napa, CA. on Dec 18th, obviously one week before Christmas. Mom & Dad had invited us to Breckenridge for the holiday and we had accepted, so this great idea hit me: "Neina, why don't we drive out to your Mom's birthday party in Napa and then on to Breckenridge from there?" She thought it sounded fun, so we started putting the plans together. We decided, ultimately, to see the Grand Canyon & Las Vegas on the drive to California. I had never been to either place and was stoked about it. Stacy Locke gave us some places to see in So Cal and told me La Joya is "a must". Again, I had never seen the Pacific Coast and was very impressed with the scenery.

We spent one night in Los Angeles just to say we did, and I booked us into the Beverly Hilton Hotel. Neina went downstairs to get her hair done so I decided to head out to the pool. Even though it was early December, it was nice and warm in L.A. I threw on my trunks, pulled a t shirt over my head, slipped my feet into a pair of Topsiders, grabbed my magazine and headed to the elevator. I was standing there waiting for the elevator to arrive, when two men walked up to me. Like most people in that situation, we were trying not to make eye contact or otherwise act like we were acknowledging each other. But one guy had a voice I had heard before. So, out of complete reflex, I turned and looked at him. His eyes met mine as his very unique voice kept talking; it was Michael Douglas.

Michael Douglas was the hottest man in Hollywood at this time. Fresh off mega-hits like *Romancing the Stone* & *Fatal Attraction*, he had just released *Wall Street*. (Neina and I were going to be in Santa Barbara Friday night and had already decided to see it then.)

The 1980's saw an explosion of corporate mergers and acquisitions, and investment bankers and law firms were making obscene money in fees representing the buyer or the seller. "Corporate Raiders" like Boone Pickens & Carl Icahn would gobble up a company's stock, announce that they were buying more, and then sit back and watch the market run the share price up on that company, expecting tidy profits as it continued to rise. Pickens & Icahn would then announce they were replacing half the Board of Directors and possibly some of the Senior Management, and the fight was on. Ultimately, they would end up selling their shares back to that company (and pocket a mammoth profit quickly dubbed "Greenmail") so that the once-threatened Board members and Senior Management could keep their jobs.

It was crazy how every month or so, another announcement about another "hostile tender offer" had been made by a "buyer" against a company who didn't know they were going to be a "seller"! And every time, it seemed to set a new record for the size of the deal in dollar terms. The wizard who financed all these deals was a mastermind with Wall Street firm Drexel Burnham Lambert named Michael Milliken. Milliken officed in Beverly Hills (he apparently did not like New York City) and invented the "junk bond". When one company wants to buy another, they need financing to pull it off. No company has enough cash to pay the full price, so they have to borrow the rest. Usually, a bank will loan part of the money with the seller's assets pledged as collateral; it's called a "leveraged buyout" (aka l.b.o.) because of the debt involved. Often, the combination of cash and bank financing was still not enough, so the acquiring company would sell bonds (issued by Drexel) to raise the rest of the money they needed. Now, these bonds were rated by Moody's (no relation to the Galveston family) and Standard & Poor's, whose opinion on bond ratings was essential to creating a market for them. Well, they took one look at the bonds Milliken & Drexel were selling and rated them so low they were considered "junk".

But that didn't stop Milliken from selling them. The feeding frenzy of leveraged buyouts going on then meant everyone involved had "m & a" fever. Milliken would call a Drexel client who needed "l.b.o." financing to buy some "target" company and promise to sell enough junk bonds for them to close the deal. In exchange, they would agree to buy junk bonds from him on his next deal for his next client. Where would the purchase money come from to buy those bonds? Well, Milliken would just sell more junk bonds for them, and they could use that cash to buy Milliken's bonds they had promised to buy! It was brilliant. But also, illegal. Eventually, after about ten years of absolute barbarism on Wall Street, people started asking questions about this and the m & a era came to a close. Milliken would eventually go to jail, Drexel Burnham collapsed, and the reputations of many Wall Street bankers & brokers were ruined. But, for the ten years leading up to that it was a high-flying, corporate-raiding free for all. And the perfect time to make a movie about it.

I turned to Michael Douglas and said "hello". He very graciously nodded and said, "how are you?". Now, usually I would have given him a nice "fine, thank you" and left it at that. But we were standing toe-to-toe and the elevator hadn't opened yet. So, I decided to give him a real response, and said "you have an amazing body of work. You were great in *Fatal Attraction,* and I can't wait to see you in *Wall Street*." As we stepped into the elevator for the short ride down to the lobby, he thanked me and said he would love to hear what I thought about Wall Street after seeing it. We shook hands as the elevator doors opened; he slipped on his Wayfarer sunglasses and strolled out of the lobby to a red, convertible Porsche 911 waiting on the curb. It reeked of Hollywood, but I was stoked more than ever to see *Wall Street* now! Wait 'til I tell Neina I met and talked to Michael freaking Douglas.

We drove on up the Pacific Coast Highway and toured Hearst Castle along the way. Its owner, William Randolph Heart, had built the largest media business in the world, including newspapers, newsreels and movies. The Hearst family wielded massive political influence and were staunch anti-communists before WW II. As we walked through this massive, ornate home set in the California hills, I felt odd and a little creepy thinking about the founder's granddaughter, Patricia Hearst, who thirteen years before in February 1974, was kidnapped in her apartment near Cal Berkley by the Symbionese Liberation Army. The "S.L.A." was based in San Francisco and was a small, urban guerilla left-wing group. When they announced the kidnapping, they demanded that two of their members, recently arrested for the murder of the Superintendent of the Oakland, CA. public schools, be released. This was a huge media story; the full resources of California law-enforcement, led by the F.B.I., was called on to find and free Patricia Hearst. The updates from the search for her led the news every night and was the headline story on every newspaper the next morning.

Imagine everyone's shock, when two months later, in April 1974 Patricia walked into the Hibernia Bank in San Francisco brandishing an M1 military rifle and robbed it with her S.L.A. "captors". The entire event was captured on bank surveillance video and clearly showed her shouting at bank customers to "get up against the wall you mother f---ers!" and announcing her name was now "Tania". Two bank customers, who walked into the bank during the robbery, were shot & wounded.

The next month, "Tania" and her S.L.A. accomplices robbed a sporting goods store in Inglewood, CA. When the store manager ran out and tried to defend himself a gunfight broke out with Tania emptying the magazine of her rifle shooting up the storefront. Fortunately, no one was injured, and she drove away with the two other S.L.A. guerillas in tow. The manhunt to find Patricia Hearst had quickly taken on a very different tenor: she was now a wanted criminal and no longer considered an unwilling kidnap victim and prisoner.

Sixteen months later, in September 1975, Patricia Heart was arrested by the F.B.I. and a team of police officers in an apartment in San Francisco. Dollar bills that had been "marked" were found there and linked her to the armed robbery of the Crocker National Bank in Carmichael, CA. earlier that year. Very quickly, using their massive resources, her family hired famed defense attorney, F. Lee Bailey. His strategy was clearly to paint Patricia as the victim who had been drugged and brainwashed by the S.L.A. Many professional phycologists and experts in mental health were called to testify in her trial, some in her defense and others for the prosecution. She even testified in her own defense, a risky strategy that Bailey supported; according to interviews with several jury members after the trial, she came off as aloof and disaffected. Ultimately, in March 1976, Patricia Hearst was sentenced to seven years in federal prison. But just twenty-two months later, then President Jimmy Carter commuted her sentence, and she was released under strict probation. On January 20, 2001, President Bill Clinton, on his last day in office, gave her a full pardon. Wealth can certainly buy influence, but it sure can't guarantee happiness.

All of this was bouncing through my mind as we continued our tour of the "Castle". This was no Disneyland for sure, and in my humble opinion, the place was just way over the top.   I just didn't think it was all that pretty.   Sort of like parts of "Graceland" in Memphis or the guy who has a very loud tailpipe on his big pickup truck, for me it was just too much. Maybe I need to go have a second look because everyone else seems to love it. And I wonder if Patricia Hearst has ever been back.

Later that day Neina and I drove on to Carmel, CA. I wanted to go out to the Pebble Beach golf course (why we didn't stay there I'm not sure; someone recommended Quail Lodge, instead) and so we did. It was a grey, windy winter day with a brisk breeze blowing in off the Pacific. But walking out to the golf course and seeing the 18th hole there, it was pretty special. About thirty years before I stood there, Mom & Dad did.   Mom had flown out to San Jose to visit her sister and was considering moving there. Dad didn't want that to happen, so he flew out several days later, and together they went to the P.G.A. golf tournament being held at Pebble Beach that weekend. As the day wound up, Dad guided Mom over to the 18th green and proposed to her. She said yes and well, you know the rest.

Neina and I spent that night in Carmel and then drove on to San Francisco. I had a new Suburban, so we had plenty of passenger and luggage space and had offered to meet her parents and the Robbins at the airport. They were flying in for the birthday weekend in Napa and we were going to provide the transportation after two nights in San Francisco. Lots of Dorothy's friends were there, too, and as we arrived at the Auberge du Soleil hotel high up on Rutherford Hill above Napa Valley, it was pretty special.

The birthday dinner was hosted that night by Margaret & Robert Mondavi at their beautiful, very private dining room at the winery down the road. "Mondavi" was a wine label name everyone knew because of his vast distribution network. You could buy a bottle of Mondavi wine in all fifty states. Dorothy and her sister, Betty, took an annual "girl's trip" to Europe with about five or six of their best friends; they claimed it was a tour of "cooking schools" but we all knew better: it was just an excuse for a bunch of well-healed ladies from Texas to go to Europe and shop. But…. on one particular trip they actually took a "food & wine class" (I would guess it was at Hotel Creon in Paris, but I'm not sure) and low & behold, Margaret & "Bob" Mondavi were there, too. And they had become good friends with them over the years.

Walking into their vast dining hall, it was probably the longest dining table I had ever seen. It was set perfectly for dinner and as our group of thirty people (fifteen on each side of the table) took our seats I noticed at least seven or eight wine glasses at each place. "Whoa" I thought, "this is going to be cool". And it was. I don't recall a lot about the food they served, but every course was paired with another different Mondavi wine. And "Bob" served his red wines slightly chilled and his white wines just below room temperature. He said "Cinco, most reds are served too warm, and most whites are served too cold". And after that night, I agreed. But as the evening unfolded, with special toasts and hugs & tears, it was an awesome way to honor Dorothy on her birthday. And she looked beautiful. Neina & I had pre-arranged for a letter to be written from the Mayor of San Francisco, the Hon. Diane Feinstein, to Dorothy honoring her on her 50th and welcoming her to the area. I stood, and after saying a few words, read the letter to Dorothy from the Mayor. (Feinstein would later serve California in the U.S. Senate). She was very moved and clearly, she felt like the special guest and person she was. I miss her still.

Our time in Napa ended and Neina and I headed to Breckenridge, CO. to join my family for Christmas. We stopped along the way in Elko, NV. and I played a little blackjack in the casino that night. The next day we made the drive to Breck and arrived at Mom & Dad's home there. It was beautiful and Mom had appointed it with all her pretties. They had also hung all their (now many) game mounts from hunts in Africa; they had impala, wart hog, cape buffalo, sable, and kudu, and leopard. Mom even had a lion skin rug on the floor with the lion's head and gaping teeth staring at you as you walked up the steps leading from the entry into the living room. They had a panoramic view of the mountain range and ski slopes, and we were thrilled to be there. Several days of skiing, snowmobiling and general relaxation were going to be nice. Shelley & her husband were there with their first-born daughter, Sarah. We would have a very white and merry Christmas.

Chapter 25: They're all selling? Then Buy, Buy, Buy!

Neina & I made it back to Dallas and soon I took a job with a small consulting firm owned & run by Charles Lemmon. Charlie had recently taken a nice severance from MCorp, the former Mercantile National Bank in Dallas (he had run their leasing subsidiary for many years) and was setting up his own firm to help owner-managed businesses refinance their liabilities. The late 1980's had seen a meltdown in the financial markets; many Savings & Loans had made tons of commercial real estate loans and much like Drexel Burnham, they had loaned more than the assets were actually worth. The U.S. Government took over hundreds of failed S & Ls and the repossessed real estate that came with them. It was billions of dollars of failed loans, and the Feds became the largest owners, through the "Resolution Trust Corporation", of commercial real estate in the country. The economy was suffering and so were many of the owner-managed companies Charles Lemmon & Co assisted. Charlie would buy their assets from them and then lease them back; it helped these businesses raise cash (something many of them sorely needed) and the lease obligation didn't have to be shown on the Balance Sheet, in accordance with GAAP, so it was a slick vehicle. Often, there was real estate involved, so I took real estate classes at night and eventually got my license. It would be the beginning of a wonderful career in commercial real estate.

Chapter 26: Seretsi Khama

Neina & I traveled quite a bit during those years, visiting Paraguay & Brazil with her parents and a wonderful weekend in San Miguel de Allende with Mom & Dad, to name a few. In 1990 she & I joined Mom & Dad for another hunting trip in Botswana. Neina & I flew British Air thru London and then on to Gaborone, the capital of Botswana. There we were met by a representative of Vira Safaris, owned by a gentleman named Mark Kyriakou. Mom & Dad had hunted with Mark before, and we had gotten to know him well before the trip at the Safari Club International convention in Las Vegas (and a few weeks later in Dallas) earlier that year. While we were in Dallas, Mark & his mates from Botswana wanted to visit Billy Bob's in Fort Worth to see what a real Texas honky-tonk was about. So about eight of us loaded into my Suburban and made the drive. The place was packed that night with Restless Heart as the headliner. Mark and I muscled our way to the bar to get everyone a beer with Restless Heart belting out "The bluest eyes in Texas" right behind us; he was clearly impressed with the size of the place and asked the bartender "how many people are here tonight?" The bartender said "well, it's sold out so that means there are at least 6,000 people in the house". Mark shook his head in disbelief and then turned to me. "Cinco" he said, "that's more white people than live in the entire country of Botswana!" We were both struck by the scope and irony of the different cultures and people across the world.

Mark was a really good Professional Hunter and a very likeable fellow. Neina and I boarded a twin-engine plane in Gaborone, loaded with foodstuffs and kitchen supplies for the hunting camp, and flew into the Okavango Delta. After a short flight we landed on a dirt airstrip adjacent to the camp where we could see many of the green hunting vehicles, mostly open-air Toyotas, waiting for us to taxi over. We were pretty bushed from two consecutive overnight flights and anxious to stow our gear and grab a Castle beer (Botswana's national brew) around the ever-present campfire.

As we stepped out of the plane, Mom & Dad greeted us warmly with hugs & smiles. Standing next to them were some very handsome people who were clearly getting on the plane we had just flown in on to head to another camp. "Cinco" Mom said, I want to introduce you to Paetra Barretta." Standing there was a very nice-looking young man (with his very beautiful wife standing next to him) whom I reckoned to be about 10 years older than me. Fit, dark complected and well-dressed, Paetra stuck out his hand and with a heavy Italian accent said "it is nice to meet you. My family and I have enjoyed sharing this camp with Jimmy & Joy for several days." It was only after they had flown away and we were decamped around the campfire that Mom told me that Paetra was one of the members of the Barretta family, the owners of the iconic Italian gun company by the same name. His Dad was also in the group but had flown out of the camp earlier in the day; Paetra and his wife were boarding our plane and rejoining their family. Dad later told me that the Barettas always had two planes to transport them from camp to camp: one for the people and the other for their luggage and wine. He wasn't kidding. The older man, whose name was also Paetra, and Dad became quite good friends during the trip and exchanged contact info. About a month or so after we returned home a package arrived from Italy addressed to Dad; inside were two beautiful Barretta handguns sent warmly from Paetra himself.

We spent about ten days hunting in both the Okavango Delta and Kalahari Desert, taking a host of African plains game. The mornings were very cold in our tents, but the days warmed up quickly, so we soon learned to dress in layers. In the Okavango, one of our camps was literally on an island, so we had to be transported over to it on "mokoros", the Swahili word for canoe. They were literally dugout of large trees with a bow that was whittled to a point so that it could slip through the water. One of our guides would use a long pole to propel us and we were told to sit very still: these mokoros sat very low in the water and were not particularly stable. Any sudden shift in weight could tip us over into the clear delta water we knew was populated with crocodiles. We did as we were told and made it safely from one bank to another.

Another one of our tent camps sat right along the banks of a river nestled within some lush, beautiful palm trees. As we settled in and made our way over to the campfire to watch the sun set that evening, I noticed a thick, braided rope running the full length of the riverbank. It was probably about four or five inches in diameter and separated our tents from the river. "What's that rope for?" I asked Mark. "Well,", he said in his strong Zimbabwean drawl, "that rope is there to keep the hippos out of the camp". That was not the answer any of us expected to hear and I honestly thought he was kidding. "Come on" I said, "why is that rope really there?" Mark explained that it was, indeed, there as a hippo barrier. "Their gate is so low when they walk" he said "that they can't step over it. So, it keeps them from walking into the camp". I wondered if the Barettas had the same question when they were at this camp earlier in the week – no doubt they kept some high caliber rifles at the ready in case the rope failed to deter the hippos. I know we did.

We had a wonderful time taking some big game coupled with some nice bird hunts for guinea fowl, francolin and sand grouse. The entire trip was everything we had hoped for, and we really enjoyed Mom & Dad's company. At the end of the hunt, Mom & Dad flew back to Texas, and we continued on to Jo'burg and eventually Cape Town. We spent a day in the wine country and the next day we drove out to the Cape of Good Hope; it was beautifully scenic, and we could see where the warm Indian Ocean met the cold Atlantic: there was a cauldron of twisting & turning water there. We took a cable car to the top of Table Mountain and could see Robin Island where Nelson Mandela was still imprisoned. I didn't know much about South African history but was impressed with the can-do spirit we seemed to find everywhere we went. They pointed out that the first heart transplant ever done was performed in Cape Town by Dr. Christian Bernard. Pretty cool stuff I thought, and we became very fond of the country & its people.

Back in Jo'burg Neina & I boarded British Air for the flight to London with a short stop in Nairobi, Kenya; the pilot announced that our route of flight upon departure out of Nairobi would take us almost due north towards Tel Aviv, Israel (along the western border of Saudi Arabia) where we would bank left and make our way up the coast of Italy, over France and into London. This being September 1990, U.S. troops were fighting in Iraq attempting to liberate Kuwait from Saddam Hussein's invasion earlier that year. In fact, in our hunting camps back in Botswana we tuned in to BBC radio each night via short-wave radio for updates on the war. Under the command of General Norman Schwarzkopf, we were kicking ass, but the war was still fully on. After hearing the pilot tell us our route of flight I turned to Neina and said, "did you just hear him say we were flying to Israel and along the western side of Saudi Arabia?" "Yeah" she said, "so what?" "Well, I told her, "Let's look at a map because I think we're going to be pretty darn close to Iraq!" In fact, it is only about 330 miles (500 kilometers) from Tel Aviv to the Iraqi border town of Trebil. That was a little too close for comfort for me; but I assumed British Air knew what they were doing and if there was anyone who could maintain safe airspace over their country it was certainly Israel! We dozed off to sleep and woke up to the flight attendants announcing that we would soon be starting our descent into the London area. Thank you, Gen Schwarzkopf, and the Israeli air defenses, for a safe flight.

Chapter 27: The light comes on.

Growing up, my folks always had their cocktails at the end of each day; they liked scotch (preferably "J & B") with club soda. And Dad knew a lot about wine, so there was always a good bottle of red burgundy or Napa Cabernet available. I never gave it much thought and as I became an adult, I adopted the same pattern & routines each evening after work; it was just "what we always did". But Neina was a little bothered by it and I wasn't sure why. Until she opened up about her *adult child of an alcoholic* issues. George, as I mentioned, was an outgoing man who always greeted me warmly and who always seemed ready to "celebrate" when Neina and I were there. I sort of shrugged it off, but to her, his drinking was a problem. She told me some stories of past special occasions where her Dad would drink too much and then end up embarrassing her. Honestly, I had never seen that behavior in anyone, least of all her Dad. But as she shared with me the pain she carried from it, I decided to be more aware and try to look for these same patterns of behavior that she shared.

And I soon saw what she was talking about. His favorite quote was "it's 5 o'clock in Scotland!" so that he could give himself permission to drink at lunch. His gifts for Christmas and for my birthday were usually pretty extravagant and she would explain how he was "buying my silence". This was very new to me, and I must admit, I was still somewhat skeptical. I mean if the guy did something nice why should we immediately question his motives? It became a regular event that she would be in a crappy mood after a weekend in Longview watching & listening to her Dad drink too much. And sweet Dorothy wanted everything to be so happy that she looked the other way, too. At least when we were there. It would take Neina a few days to wash the hurt & frustration out of her head & heart once we got back from a Longview visit.

While I never saw my parents "abuse" alcohol I certainly understood Neina's discomfort with its constant presence in our lives. As she would say, "it's always there". What I did notice in my family was a growing distance between my parents and my oldest sister, Cindy. And I also noticed that both Cindy & Gayle drank alcohol frequently. Eventually, Cindy stopped coming to family events (like my graduation from S.M.U.) and I could tell she was having marital problems. I still wasn't clear about the "why" of it, and we had not been particularly close (either geographically or emotionally) for several years, but I would always tell her to please reach out to me if there was "anything I could do to help". Neina and I talked about it, and she was supportive; she understood the alcohol issue much better than I did.

One day, while I was at the office with Charles Lemmon, Cindy called. She told me that she was leaving in a few days and "enrolling" herself into a treatment facility in Wickenburg, AZ called the Meadows. She didn't offer a lot of details about "why", so I didn't ask. Again, this was all new to me and I had no reference about "treatment" or "recovery". I wished her well, thanked her for calling, and again told her to please let me know if there was anything I could do to help. I had no idea where that would eventually lead.

About a week later, Cindy called again; this time she said she wanted Neina & me to come out to Wickenburg for her "family week". I was non-committal, and honestly, I was a little perturbed. "A week?" I asked her. She told me this was an important part of her treatment and that it was important to her that the family all be there. She gave me the dates and we hung up, but I was pretty sure there was no way I was taking a week out of my life to fly to Wickenburg, AZ (wherever the hell that was!) for a week. Especially in August.

Neina was all in when I told her about the call that evening when I got home. She had way better instincts about these kinds of things than I did and I'm sure she knew it would be good for me, us & my family to go through some intensive counseling. I called Cindy the next day and told her we would be there. I reminded myself that I told her to let me know if I could "do anything to help" and for the first time ever, she did. Whatever is eating at her, I thought, if us being there helps her live better then I want to be a part of it. The world voice was speaking through my sister this time.

We rented two apartments in Wickenburg and arrived at the Phoenix airport to be greeted by Mom, Dad & Shelley. Gayle said she had no interest in "rehashing a bunch of old problems" and clearly felt no compulsion to support Cindy. None of us pushed her; I still thought it was all overkill but went with an open mind and open heart. If Gayle wanted to pass, that was completely her call, I thought.

The first morning we all got dressed and ready to be at the Meadows for breakfast at 8 and our first family session at 9. Except for Dad. He walked into the living room and quickly explained that he had "no interest" in a mud-slinging fight fest and was not going. I never crossed the man or tried to get him to change his mind and I wasn't about to start now. Mom pleaded for a few minutes, but he was resolute. So, Mom, Shelley & I got in the car (it was already about 95 degrees) and drove over to the Meadows for breakfast. I could tell that Cindy and her assigned counselor were disappointed that Dad wasn't with us, but they didn't make a big deal about it. I was still in a state of ignorance about the whole thing; I was there because I wanted to keep a promise to my sister.

Session 1 started and there were other families in the group with us, which sort of surprised me. I didn't know these people and very soon they were discussing their inner-most secrets about their "family of origin" and any issues that stemmed from it. I was a little uncomfortable with how open they were but just sat and listened as the counselors, one male & one female, asked questions and offered emotional support. At times, it got pretty tough listening to the "dysfunction" they described, and I thought to myself: man, I'm glad we didn't go through anything like that. And then it was Cindy's turn; and she opened up about the source of her personal struggle.

And finally, a lot of the dysfunction in my own family started to unfold. And it did make sense. The drinking. The distance between Cindy & the rest of us, especially Mom & Dad. And Gayle's refusal to attend these sessions; she had dealt with it in her own way and didn't want to reopen old wounds. And as I listened to the other families work through their issues, several of whom were there for alcohol addiction, my understanding of how & why people turn to their "drug of choice" to medicate bad feelings (be it alcohol, cocaine, sex, shopping or gambling) grew exponentially. I saw Neina's world through Neina's eyes, and it was both enlightening and very sad. Coming to grips with the deep issues in both our families was very hard.

The day wrapped up and on our way home Mom, Shelley & I agreed that we needed to call Gayle and "get her out here" as soon as we could. Our reasoning was that if we were going to rip this band aid off and go through whatever pain that brought us, then we all needed to be there. It was clear that we were going to leave there very different people and that anyone who wasn't part of this week was going to be confused about the new perspectives we had gained while there.

When we walked into the apartment at the end of day one, Dad was gone. There was a heart-felt letter he left behind, in his own handwriting, saying he couldn't be a part of it and was flying back to Texas. I was almost too tired and emotionally spent to care. Almost. And it pissed me off that he abandoned us.

Fortunately, Gayle agreed to fly out and once she arrived, she immersed herself in her pain and guilt. Her story and Cindy's were eerily similar to the addiction and dysfunction in the other families in our group, whom we had gotten to know well after five days. It was very eye-opening for me and some of the stories I had heard about Papacito started to have clarity. I always suspected there were issues between him and my aunt: she attempted suicide as a young girl in high school after a bitter fight with my grandfather at dinner. Dad found her on the bathroom floor, bandaged her wrists and got her medical attention, thus saving her life. He was probably 15 at the time. Many years later, about ten days after my grandfather died, my aunt committed suicide at home. This time, there was no one there to bandage her or call for help.

At the closing ceremonies in Wickenburg, as we all took turns sharing how the weekend had "changed us" we were all given a medallion with the Serenity Prayer on it. I understood the power of the words and I actually did feel some peace with it all. I just wanted to fly back to Dallas and take a few days to absorb everything I had been hit with that week. As Neina and I sat on that airplane climbing out through the Arizona sky, it was clear we had a unified vision: "the dysfunction stops with us" we both boldly claimed. And we agreed to start seeing a counselor in Dallas to help us manage this new reality with our families. We knew that wouldn't be easy: we had come out of the darkness of enablement; some of them were still in it.

After three or four sessions with Jan, our counselor (sometimes Neina & I would go together and sometimes at Jan's suggestion, we went alone) she and I talked about how I felt about Dad leaving the Meadows. "I think he chickened out" I told her. "After all, he could have given our family a lot of recovery, but he chose to run away". Jan asked me if I thought there was any way Dad would consent to meeting with the girls in counseling. I told her that I thought he would "if I tell him & Mom, they have to do it". So, I called Mom & Dad and asked them to meet Neina & me in Dallas for a "serious conversation". They were making plans for a visit anyway and booked a room at a hotel in Las Colinas.

Neina and I arrived, and the pleasant "hellos" and hugs were shorter than before; they could tell we were there for business only and quickly I got down to the point of the visit. I told them about Jan and the work that Neina and I were doing to "stop the dysfunction" that the generations before us had perpetrated. I told Dad about how much I had learned about addiction and the toll it takes on families. And then I said "Dad, you are a coward for leaving the Meadows". My tone grew firmer, and my will became more resolved; I drew on strength I never knew I had. I was fueled by my love for my family; they knew I was confronting Mom & Dad and wished me well. Finally, I told Mom & Dad that they, as a couple, had an obligation to Cindy & Gayle to go meet with them, in whatever setting and environment the girls wanted, to get everything "out in the open" and allow the girls to vent whatever feelings they still had boxed inside.

Dad protested saying vague things like "I don't know how to help them" but I cut him off. "Dad, ask the girls what they need. They will tell you". I knew from my conversations with them during the weeks leading up to this meeting the girls were very clear about what they needed. And then I made it very clear that I was walking out the door of their hotel room and would not communicate with them again until the girls told me they were "as ok as they could be" with this situation. Again, Dad tried to talk me out of it and then, as Neina and I rose to leave, he downright pleaded with me not to go. "Dad, I think I have been clear about my goal here and what you & Mom need to do. Your next move is to call the girls and get the ball rolling. Until then, I'm out" I said. And we walked out.

I guess the gamble worked because a few weeks later the girls shared with me that they had met with Mom & Dad and "worked through some things" with them. Gayle was able to turn loose of it pretty quickly; it took Cindy longer and she & my parents would meet for counseling sessions for several months. Eventually, though, she found a comfortable place & was able to reengage with us for holidays and special family events. There was a certain sense of peace with it all, though no one pretended we were this "perfect" family. Let's be honest, they don't exist. But, as I reread the Serenity Prayer from the Meadows the words really did connect: *"God, grant me the peace to accept the things I cannot change. The courage to change the things I can and the wisdom to know the difference"*. With God's help, I was able to muster the courage to confront my folks and consequently, my sisters were able to regain some sense of wholeness in their lives. Both have been alcohol free for over twenty-five years and are strong, successful women.

Chapter 28: Going off script. WAY off.

After a couple of years in Dallas Neina and I were getting the itch to move back to Tyler and the pine trees and smaller crowds. I had met some real estate people in Tyler and had bought a small twelve-unit apartment building from the R.T.C. with Jeff Warr. We fixed it up, stabilized the rents and sold it a year later at a nice profit. I thought there was more profit to be made from other deals there, so we bought a house near Hollytree C.C. and made the move. We had settled in, and I was working feverishly looking to make commission income and find other real estate opportunities. I came across an office/retail center in town called "Commerce Square" that the RTC owned. It was roughly 76,000 sf and had some decent tenants, but not a lot of excess cash flow. Dad had a fraternity brother from Tyler, Jimmy Wynn, who was successful in oil & real estate, so I showed him the deal. He eventually bought it for $760,000; $10 per square foot!   Several years later I kicked myself that I didn't buy that property, but those were the kinds of deals going around in the early 1990s.

Neina and I made a drive down to South Texas in March 1992 - Mom & Dad had bought a 2,000-acre ranch northwest of Raymondville and we wanted to see it. Neina's 30th birthday was in April and May 3rd would be our sixth anniversary. On the drive back to Tyler, I asked her what she thought about starting a family later that year. Her reaction surprised me: Neina loved children and really enjoyed spending time with her niece & nephew, so I expected her to be very positive about the idea. But she really wasn't. She said the thought of delivery and labor was not appealing to her. I just figured I caught her at an odd time and let it go. Later, I would understand her response, but at that Moment, it didn't seem like any big deal.

I had a fun birthday party for Neina at the Country Tavern in

Kilgore.   The Country Tavern is known for its ribs and dance floor with jukebox music playing and it was a nice setting for a very casual party celebrating her 30th birthday. Many of her good friends from over the years came, as well as George & Dorothy and Janna & John Robbins. After several beers and the fun, casual atmosphere set it up, Dorothy came over to me and in her wonderful, sweet way she said "Cinco, you & Neina have been married six years now and she is turning 30 today". This big smile came over her and she went on: "I think it's time you two had a baby, so I want you to flush the birth control pills down the toilet tonight and get going! I want some grandchildren". We had a good laugh, and I knew she was somewhat serious, but she also knew I would not be offended, either. I told her I would "do my best" and we had a nice hug.

The following Friday afternoon I wanted to play golf, so I left the office early and swung by the house to grab my golf clubs. Neina's car was not in the garage (which wasn't unusual) but as I walked into the house, I immediately sensed something was different. Our dog, a sweet little wire-hair fox terrier she named "Prissy" was gone. And so were some of Neina's clothes. As I walked into the kitchen, I saw a brown manila envelope sitting there addressed to me. The return address was *The Law Office of Samuel George* with a Tyler address. "What's this?" I wondered as I tore it open. Inside was a Petition for Divorce filed by Neina. My eyes literally darted all over the pages and my mind was reeling. "Can this be true?" I asked myself. What the hell is going on??

Neina and I didn't have a perfect marriage but had never had any major issues, either; like all married couples we had our tough Moments, but nothing too serious. I put a lot of pressure on myself to be successful and to keep good track of our household expenses and budget. I'm sure at times I didn't handle that very well. But as far as I could tell, we were very much in love and had a bright future together. Obviously, Dorothy thought so, too, given her comments to me at the birthday party six days earlier. As I stood there in the kitchen looking at the legal document in my hand, I just couldn't believe what it said. Needless to say, I did not head to the golf course. Instead, I picked up the phone and dialed the number for George & Dorothy's house in Longview.

Dorothy answered the call and when she heard my voice, she immediately became reserved and measured. Gone was the fun, outgoing tone I was so used to hearing from her. "Dorothy, is Neina there?" I asked. After a brief wait, Neina came on the phone; she was all business. "Neina, what is going on? I asked. "I'm standing here looking at divorce papers from you?". I was absolutely floored by her response: "Cinco" she said, "I don't love you. In fact, I have been waiting for six years for the love to come and it hasn't. It's time for me to get out of this marriage". I tried to get some clarity on it from her, but it was clear she made up her mind. Nothing I could say was going to make any difference, so we ended the call and I tried to make sense out of something that just didn't make sense to me.

So, I did the only two things I could do: I hired an attorney to represent me, and I found a good counselor. Since I didn't know any divorce attorneys in town, I had to make a few calls. One good friend, when I told him Sam George was representing Neina, told me "then you have to hire Coye Conner". "Why is that?" I asked. He proceeded to tell me that Sam had a reputation as a ball-busting cowboy attorney who would run over a meeker one. "The only guy in town who can go toe-to-toe with Sam is Coye" he said.

Now, I didn't want a fight, so the thought of getting into one of those "nasty divorces" went against everything I felt in my heart & mind. In fact, I thought there was still a chance to save the marriage, so I was determined to be as cool and calm as possible. My counselor, Tom, was a huge help in keeping my emotions in check and my focus squarely on NOT being a hot head. "If this marriage can be saved", he said "you have got to be the nice guy every chance you have". I promised him I would, and I did. I did not lock her out of the house or change the alarm code. I made it clear that I would, in fact, move out so she could move back in (she was staying with her parents at the time) if she wanted to.

But her tone wasn't changing; in fact, more & more she hid behind her attorney and our phone calls became fewer & fewer. She did consent to a one-hour session with Tom; he suggested it and said that hearing her side of the story would help him help me. So, I asked her if she would do it (at my expense, of course) and she did. I was scheduled with Tom for the hour immediately following hers and I was very hopeful that she would still be there when I arrived; my rationale was Tom was going to "reach her" and this would be the start of our reconciliation. To my disappointment, his office was empty as I walked in. I took my seat across from Tom and he could sense my sadness. "Cinco" he said "we had a very good session. She shared some good background with me, and we discussed her interest in trying to work things out." And? I thought. Then Tom said as clearly and succinctly as he could "in my professional opinion this marriage is not going to be saved. You need to prepare yourself to be divorced from Neina".

I was crushed. I had gotten over the initial shock of all of this and had sort of settled into a pattern of working, going to see Tom and trying to keep my emotions in check so Neina would see me for who I knew I was. But it didn't help. It was over. And it was time to call Mom & Dad and let them know.

Over the next couple of months, there were letters back & forth between Sam & Coye with Sam making some baseless accusations about me "hiding funds" and being "emotionally abusive". Coye explained it was typical tactics by opposing counsel: "he wants to paint you as negatively as possible in case this goes to trial" Coye told me. "Trial?" I asked. "Geez, Coye, that sounds awful. Why would we have to do that?" He told me he didn't think it would, but my head was spinning. Two months ago, we were having a wonderful birthday party (with Dorothy planning our family for us!)

and now this? I was still very young and had never been in any kind of legal fight, much less with a girl who I loved very, very much. I started smoking and lost 15 pounds in about six weeks. Without Tom's help, it might have been worse.

Sam set a hearing at the courthouse to see if he could get a judge to make me pay Neina "temporary support" while the divorce was pending. "Temporary support?" I asked. "Coye, this girl has plenty of oil income every month and close to $100,000 in savings. And she lives with her parents. How in the world could she need 'temporary support'?" Coye explained that it was, once again, legal gamesmanship where Sam felt obligated to throw s--t against the wall and see if something would stick. Otherwise, he could be considered "negligent" in the way he represented Neina and after all, given her family's social status in East Texas, this was now a high-profile divorce.   That's exactly what I was hoping wouldn't happen. "So", Coye told me, "put on a coat & tie and act like a gentleman". I reminded him that I had already promised Tom I would; "you're doing fine" he said, "just keep a smile on your face and don't let anything Sam says rattle you".

It was now August and the Texas summer had set in. It was a bright, sunny & hot day in Tyler, TX when we all arrived at the courthouse for the hearing. Dorothy came with Neina (as moral support, I suppose) and as we walked into the courtroom, I had a very empty feeling. I had only seen Neina once since the day I saw the divorce papers in the kitchen and looking over at her in this dingy courtroom made me sad. "So" I thought, "this is where you have brought us?   After all the beautiful places we have visited and all the wonderful times we have shared, this is where we are now?" It was very sad.

Coye and I had talked about a "settlement" offer "just in case we can negotiate something" before the hearing he said. Neina & I had kept separate personal finances and I made 100% of the down payment on the house. So, Coye surmised, if she would relinquish any claim on the house what was I willing to offer her? She had already gotten everything out of the house she wanted since I had not locked her out and told her to come & go as she pleased. While that might have been risky, it was a risk I was willing to take to show her how much I still cared. So, Coye & I came up with some sort of "kicker" that Neina could have if we could settle the divorce that day. Before the judge entered the room, Coye & Sam stood at the back talking. A minute or two later, Coye came over and said, "they are willing to drop the motion for temporary support and agree to a divorce".

Whatever we offered must have worked, I thought. "So, you mean we will walk out of here TODAY divorced?" I asked. Coye said "yes, that's what I am saying". I was equal parts relieved and equal parts depressed. Never in a million years, I thought, would our marriage end this way. "Ok" I said "then let's do it. But I want to have one minute alone with Neina to say 'goodbye". "Lemme see what I can do" Coye said and walked over to Sam to pitch the idea. Just then, the judge entered, and we heard the words "all rise!". My heart started racing and Coye could sense how nervous I was. As we took our seats I listened for a few minutes as both Sam & Coye said a bunch of legal mumbo-jumbo to the judge that I could barely understand. I was still trying to absorb the finality of it; I was still trying to make any sense of why we were there. And I was determined to keep my promise to Tom and be a gentleman through it all.

Sam asked Neina to stand and be sworn in. He read the final terms we had agreed to and asked her if she was ok with it. She said she was. Coye then had me sworn in and asked me the same question. I said" yes". The judge then asked which of the two attorneys would draw up the final order for him to sign? Well, these two tigers, who had been at each other's throats during this divorce with hot letters and veiled threats flying back & forth, suddenly became pussycats. "Oh, Coye can draft it your honor" Sam said, "he has always sent my office really good work". "That ok with you, Mr. Connor?" the judge asked. "Yes sir" Coye replied, "Mr. George is very easy to work with". It became clear to me that these guys were probably decent friends and had been through this little charade before: make their clients think they <u>hate</u> the other attorney and that they can't wait to carve them up into little pieces. But when the ship finds the dock (and they had milked as many legal fees as they could from both emotional parties) they will both make sure the landing is a soft one. I was a little disgusted with the whole thing, to be honest, and I just wanted to get it wrapped up and get out of there.

The judge said some more legal mumbo-jumbo and then I heard the words "as of this Moment, the two of you are divorced". Meaning Neina & me. We were no longer married. That was it. Four months after her birthday and a month before I was going to turn 32, I was single again. As we gathered up our things and turned for the rear exit, I walked over to Neina and wished her well. And I thanked Dorothy for all the very good times and warm chats she & I had had over the years. They were both a little quiet, but I knew Tom would be proud of me. But there was no sense of accomplishment here for me. No thoughts of "winning". It had failed. I had failed. And I wondered if I would ever love another girl that much.

Four years later I was at a U.T. football game in Austin walking out of the Alumni Center across from Memorial Stadium. I had moved to Austin after the divorce and had put my life back together. Thoughts of Neina were fleeting and few. I looked over to my left and saw a young couple from Austin whom I knew well. "Mary" was originally from Longview and was a senior manager with the Texas Exes Alumni Association of U.T. A year or so earlier she had asked me to be involved in a big fund-raiser for U.T. Student-Athletes honoring our former legendary football coach, Darrell Royal. I was tapped as "table sales chairman" for a gala event the night before the Notre Dame game in Austin at the Four Seasons Hotel (it was fall 1996) with Willie Nelson as the headliner. It was a sell-out and a huge success; Mary and I had become good friends working together on that event.

Mary and her husband came over and we exchanged warm greetings. After a Moment, Mary asked "have you heard the news about Neina?". "No", I replied "what news?" My mind immediately thought that she had been diagnosed with some sort of cancer or was involved in a bad car accident or something. Mary then explained that recently, both of Neina's grandmothers had died. (Her grandfathers were gone before I met her.) "So" I asked, "what does that mean?" Mary then told me that once Neina's grandmothers were gone (again this is conservative, blue-blood East Texas and Neina was a social princess) she finally felt ok telling everyone she was gay. I'm sure the look on my face was total shock. But it finally made sense. Neina had two girlfriends, one from high school and one from college, who were clearly different in their manner than her other girlfriends. I was always aware of it but didn't give it much thought. Until that Moment just outside the front door of the Alumni Center. Well, I thought, Dorothy won't be getting those grandchildren after all. It made me sad for her.

Chapter 29: Off we go into the wide blue yonder. Well, almost.

During the preceding four months I asked myself often if I would stay in East Texas when the divorce was final. It was certainly a little isolated from my family and I wasn't sure there would be sufficient social life as a newly minted single guy. With the divorce final I decided I wanted to be closer to South Texas. Austin was the perfect place to go so I listed my house in Tyler and started making plans. After a quick trip to Breckenridge, I arrived home and had a full price offer on my house. Things were happening fast. While I knew I was going to Austin I had not found a place to live or even look for a job. Mom & Dad suggested that I put my things in storage and live with them at the ranch in Raymondville to buy some time. That sounded like a good place to convalesce after the last 5 months I had endured so I accepted their invite.

Before Neina & I split up I had started taking flying lessons in Tyler. It was something I had wanted to do since I started spending time in the cockpit of our Conquest with the pilot, Chuck Ritter. Chuck was a very seasoned pilot and patiently walked me through the various avionics, gadgets & gizmos that controlled the plane. I really enjoyed flying along with him, listening to the radio transmissions between all the planes in our area and A.T.C., and gaining a strong knowledge of what it took to be pilot-in-command. So, I called Tyler School of Flying at Pounds Field and drove out there for my first flying lesson. My flight instructor was a young guy from Belgium with a slight dialect named Yuri Von Leeuw. Yuri & I hit it off immediately and over the next weeks and months I was getting pretty perficient as the pilot of a small, single-engine Cessna 172. After one particular lesson, Yuri turned to me after signing my logbook and said "Cinco, I think you are ready to solo".

We had discussed it before, and I wasn't surprised when he said that – by this point I was doing 90% of the flying when we would "go up". I had mastered all of the maneuvers needed to fly a small plane in a controlled manner; both Yuri & I were confident I could handle the plane on my own.

Now, flying solo and earning my "Solo Certificate" means doing three consecutive "touch & go's" coming to a full stop after the third landing and taxiing over to the hangar where Yuri would be waiting. The only real trick to a touch and go is keeping the plane pointed straight down the runway once you touch down and immediately bring the flaps up and push in with full throttle. Very quickly you are at takeoff speed since you've already created a ton of speed on the landing. Yuri had shown me the technique and stressed how crucial it was: because the prop spins counterclockwise (as viewed from inside the cockpit) the left-hand side of the prop is moving downward, and the right-hand side is moving upward. The disproportionate torque of the two effects gives the plane a "left turning tendency", meaning the plane wants to veer left at full throttle and take off speed – a pilot has to know this and be ready to counteract this tendency by applying right rudder pressure. After practicing it a few times it becomes second nature – the muscle memory takes over and the process is almost mindless.

After several solo flights, all inside the "pattern" of the airport, it was time for me to fly "cross country", so I filed a flight plan and climbed into the cockpit. Alone. I would take off from Tyler and, after climbing to about 3,000 feet above sea level, I would make a heading for Sulphur Springs. That airport was kind of cool to land at because the runway extended out into the lake. From there I would climb back to altitude, make a turn to the Southwest and do a quick touch-and-go in the town of Corsicana. Then it was back into the air and a return flight to Tyler. The whole thing probably took about two hours. Because I was operating under Visual Flight Rules (a.k.a. "VFR") it had to be a clear, sunny day since I was navigating by referencing things on the ground, like highways, lakes and other large, notable items on the ground. So, I had to be able to see them. I was not yet proficient in navigating using only my instruments (known as "I.F.R." or instrument flight rules) even though Yuri and I had practiced it some by placing a hood over my head so all I could see was the instrument panel. You never know when a clear day can suddenly get foggy or cloudy, so every pilot trains for those conditions. Yuri and I had flown this route before so it was really a matter of repeating the process. As I climbed into the air and found my first ground reference the air was clear, and the ride was smooth. My first solo cross country, and fortunately everyone after that, went off without a hitch.

I sat for the F.A.A. ground exam, which I passed on the first try, and continued to fly my solo cross-country flights to cities like Rockwall and Kaufman. Sulphur Springs was really my favorite due to the aforementioned runway out into the lake. Soon, I would do my check-out flight with an F.A.A. flight instructor riding along and giving me various maneuvers to show him, like figure eights, stalls & "turns-around-a-point" on the ground.   But before I could do that, Neina filed for divorce. So, my flying time was limited as I focused on "keeping my head together". Honestly, I was not in a good place mentally to be flying an airplane and exercising the kind of concentration that is needed to satisfy the F.A.A. license people. But after I sold the house in Tyler and settled at the ranch the desire to fly returned. So, I called the F.B.O. at the Harlingen airport and arranged for an instructor to fly with me. It had been about six months since I was last pilot in command, and I felt like I needed an instructor along to help knock off any rust that might have accumulated. I don't recall his name (let's call him 'Rick'), but I felt comfortable with him and after a few flights together I felt confident enough to get back to some solo cross-country flights. I did notice, though, that the Piper we were training in had a "hard" right rudder pedal. From time-to-time it was difficult to depress it on touch and go's, which is not great given this airplane's "left turning tendency". After it happened a couple of times (it did seem to depress after I applied a little extra pressure with my right foot) I mentioned it to Rick. "Hey" I told him, "I am feeling some stiffness on the right rudder foot pedal from time to time right after landing. You should have the mechanic in the hangar check it out". He told me he would, so I didn't give it any more thought, at least until the next time I tried a touch and go on the Harlingen runway.

As I banked the airplane into a left turn from the base leg and lined up for my final approach, I could see the very long runway off my left wingtip. I dropped the flaps to 20 degrees (the landing gear was fixed so no need to lower them) and steered the airplane into a straight descent, neatly lined up on the runway for landing. Smoothly the airplane descended onto the runway with the bump of the wheels hitting the asphalt and the squeal of the tires making contact with the ground. Instinctively, I flipped the flaps lever up to bring the flaps to zero degrees of slope and pushed the throttle all the way forward for full power. Because I was already in-flight mode, with plenty of speed behind me, I was at takeoff speed very quickly; in this case, probably 75 or 80 mph within a few seconds.

As I always had before, I began to push in the right foot pedal to offset the left-turning pull of the nose. Except it didn't depress. Quickly I was reminded of the times this had happened before and went through the same process: ease the pressure of my right foot back just slightly and then depress the rudder pedal again quickly; it had always worked before. No response. Now the airplane was at top take off speed and quickly headed off the runway to the left! Soon I was careening through the grass, then up over the taxiway and back into a grassy area with the apron full of parked airplanes coming at me very fast. Holy shit, I thought, I'm not sure I'm gonna get this airplane stopped. I had pulled the throttle back to reduce speed; the brake pedals are located at the top of the rudder pedals (but operate independently of each other) so I was breaking as hard as I possibly could with both feet. In fact, I was breaking so hard that I literally lifted myself off the seat and was suspended about 3 inches above it! Everything happened so quickly, and the thought flashed across my mind: if I don't get this airplane stopped, I'm gonna run into those parked planes straight ahead and it will probably kill me!

Fortunately, that didn't happen, and I got the plane under control after what seemed like fifteen minutes. It was probably more like thirty seconds. As I eased my feet back from the brakes, and my butt settled back onto the seat, I steered the plane to the left and found a parking place right in front of the F.B.O. hangar door. My palms were a sweaty mess, and my heart was racing fast. I took several quick, deep breaths and regained my composure. "Jesus, that was close" was all I could think. I unfastened the seat belt and harness that ran across my chest, removed the headphones from my ears and killed the power. As the prop slowed to a stop, I could see Rick walking towards me with a puzzled look on his face; he expected me to be gone a lot longer than I had been. "Why are you back so quickly?" he asked. As I climbed out of the left side of the airplane and stood on the ground, my legs were still shaking. "Did you have the mechanic check the right rudder pedal?" I asked. "Yes, I did" he replied, but it didn't sound very convincing. "Why?" he asked me.

I turned and pointed to the tire indentions I had just left across the grass between the taxi apron and the parking area where we were standing and said, "you see those tire marks through the grass right there?" His eyes grew wide and bulged. He gulped and said "uh, yeah". He knew what was coming next. "Well, the right rudder pedal completely locked up on me on the first touch & go just now. I had no control of the airplane and came flying off the runway, over the taxiway, into the grass there and up onto this apron!" He was shocked. "So", I continued, "if you did actually have the mechanic check that pedal then it needs to be checked again". I was pissed now, and he knew it. He knew he didn't have it checked and could have been responsible for a serious incident if I had crashed that plane. He promised to have it checked again as I brushed past him, climbed into my car and made the 40-minute drive to the ranch.

The drive up there gave me time to settle my nerves and to consider whether or not I was going to tell Mom & Dad. As I made my way through the front gate and up the winding, gravel road back to the house sitting in a nice mot of mature mesquite and palm trees, I could see Mom & Dad sitting outside on the upstairs deck. It was after 5pm and they gave a warm wave; as I walked towards the front door Mom called to me: "make yourself a cocktail and come out and join us". If ever I needed a cocktail to calm my nerves, it was then! So, I made a stiff scotch & soda and dropped myself into a nice lounge chair overlooking a freshly mown field of grass adjacent to the house; some white tail deer were eating the corn on the ground that was just thrown by the automatic feeder there and the constant south Texas breeze was flapping the U.S. flag hoisted to the top of Dad's flagpole. I had decided during the drive from the airport I wasn't going to tell them about what had happened during my last flight; the whole thing ended well and there was no reason to concern them at this point. What they didn't know couldn't hurt them, I concluded. Mom had lost one son, I thought; no need to tell her she had almost lost another one. Then the phone rang.

I wanted to run and grab it (I had a sneaking hunch it was a call from Rick asking how I was doing) but Dad was nearest the door and got to the phone almost before I had a chance to rise out of my lounge chair. I could hear his deep voice grow into a concerned, serious tone. It was a sound I knew well, and it usually only came out when he was deep in worried thought & conversation. Mom could sense something was up and stopped talking so she could pick up what Dad was saying. He wrote something on a piece of paper next to the phone, said "yes sir, I will certainly tell him to call you" and hung up. He then walked back outside to where Mom & I were sitting and handed me the piece of paper: on it was a long-distance phone number from an area code that was definitely not in Texas. "Cinco" he said sternly, "you want to tell us why the F.A.A. just called from Washington, D.C.?" Uh-oh, I thought. My well-conceived plan to keep the news from them just went down in flames.

Chapter 30: Austin City Limits.

I knew a bunch of guys who worked at CBRE (then it was called "CB Richard Ellis") in Austin and a good friend of mine, Mike Chitwood, worked for the Weitzman Group in Dallas. Michael got me an interview with Weitzman in Austin, and I also met with the manager of the CBRE Austin office, Jerry Lumsden. While my first choice was CB, Jerry was moving kind of slowly and Weitzman offered me a job literally on the spot. After a few days of thinking about the options, I accepted the job with Weitzman. I had just closed on a nice 3 BR, 2 BA townhouse near downtown but it needed a lot of work. So, I pushed my start date with Weitzman into the Spring of 1993 so I could focus on getting my new home finished.

Almost from day one I felt like Weitzman was not a good fit. I was hearing some bad rumors about the founder and owner, Herb Weitzman, and how he had shafted the government on some of his own real estate loans. The guy who ran the Austin office ("Tom") even made jokes about it; I began to wonder if these guys shared my value system. I would soon find out my suspicions were accurate. The RTC would conduct major auctions of commercial real estate all over the country. It was easy enough to get on their mailing list and we all got mailers announcing the time & place of the next big auction, which in this case was Dallas on a Sunday. I flew up to Dallas to review the property "files" that the RTC had compiled in large conference rooms; there were a couple of properties that I thought were particularly interesting, and one was a free-standing Pier One Imports store near Fort Worth. As I dug through the lease and the property data, I was convinced this was a good prospect. I took tons of notes (you weren't allowed to remove the files or even make copies of them) and then came back to Austin to write up my findings and conclusion.

We were told often that Weitzman was an active and qualified buyer of property (how they got around Herb's prior issues with the government I have no idea) so I called Herb and mentioned this deal to him. This was before e mail days, so he asked me to fax my notes (duly organized and typed as they were) to him. A day or so before the auction I called Herb to see if Weitzman was going to buy it; he told me no. But I had already bought a plane ticket and there was one other property in the auction that interested me, so I flew up to Dallas, grabbed a cab and headed to the Marriott hotel on the north LBJ Freeway. As I walked in there was Herb checking in with a man he introduced as "Issac"; Issac was Herb's cousin. Herb looked surprised to see me, but we all walked into the auditorium and the three of us took a seat.

The auction moved quickly, and the Pier One property was the seventh property to be sold (out of about seventy). Very soon it became clear that Herb's cousin was interested in buying it because he started peppering Herb with questions. Herb didn't know any of the answers, so in an attempt to be helpful, I pulled my notes out and handed them to Issac. He looked at my work and then said "Herb, this is what you sent me, right?". Herb became very nervous (he knew I was now aware he was going to shaft me out of a commission) and replied "yes, it is". I was pissed for being treated so poorly and it was a clear violation of the ethics we, as real estate licensees, are sworn to uphold. Issac bought the property and Herb leaned over to me and said I would get "one third" of the gross commission; he was going to keep two-thirds of it! And, I then had to split my one third on a 50/50 basis with his company! It was a total screw job, and I was livid; I hadn't been with the company six months, and this was happening. Wow, I thought, this guy is a real piece of s—t.

Monday morning, back in Austin, I walked into Tom's office and shared the story with him in hopes he would call Herb and renegotiate the commission split. I was expecting him to go to bat for me; instead, he just laughed it off and said, "well you got your first 'Herbectomy'". Herb had done it to so many people they actually coined a term for it! I was getting out of there for sure; the smell of cheating and low business morals stunk the place up. I decided to go out on my own and started doing well right away; I was learning the Austin market and making a name for myself.

While I did have a good social life, I was pretty guarded about who I dated. I knew I needed some time to get my mojo back after the divorce. While I had some nice relationships, none of them went much farther than a few fun dates and some travel together. For Christmas 1996, Mom & Dad rented two nice apartments in London and invited all of us to join them. Shelley was recently divorced and didn't want to be away from her daughters, so she did not join us. But Cindy & Gayle did and brought their sons. Gayle's husband, Pete, joined us, as well.

The apartments were very nice and a short walk to Hyde Park. We saw a great play starring Gene Wilder and enjoyed some beautiful dinners. On Christmas Eve we all dressed up in coats & ties and cocktail dresses and went to the Tea Dance at the Dorchester Hotel, complete with a live symphony. Mom was a great dancer, and we had a wonderful time; even her grandsons all danced with her and there were smiles on everyone's faces. After the dance, we all walked down to Trafalgar Square and sang Christmas carols with many local Londoners. Christmas morning, we went to church at Westminster Abbey followed by a late lunch at the Four Seasons hotel. It was truly a magical holiday.

It rarely snows in London, but the morning of Dec 27th as we sat on a Continental Airlines DC-10 we were in the que for deicing. It delayed our flight about an hour, so I started chatting up the flight attendant sitting opposite from us. When I told her I lived in Austin, she mentioned that the flight attendant working first class had recently moved to Austin. Her name was Peggy Susan, and everyone called her "Peggy Sue". She made her way back to our seats about an hour after we left London, and we had a nice chat; she had responsibilities in First Class but made her way back to us several times during the 10-hour flight to Houston. Most times, she brought a bottle of wine or a treat of some sort. I found her attractive and very easy to talk to.

Peggy & I started dating soon after that and enjoyed each other's company. She flew frequently but we spent most of our time together when she was home in Austin. Eventually, I would go with her on her trips and layovers if there was room on the flight. We visited some cool places and traveled to & from the hotel in the crew van. Since I had some cockpit time of my own, it was interesting to me to talk to the pilots about the avionics and such in these big jets. Peggy had given me a nice knit shirt with the Continental logo on it and occasionally I would get a seat in first class. Peggy & the other flight attendants would really fawn all over me with service & attention without giving up the fact that we were all friends. I'm sure my fellow passengers must have thought I was some airline big shot. It was a lot of fun.

One day we were about to take off from Houston on our way to San Francisco on an MD-80. The first officer, Ben, was from Austin, too, and his wife was one of the flight attendants on the trip with Peggy. Ben came to my seat before we pushed from the gate and said "after we level off knock on the cockpit door and we'll let you in. But don't have any alcohol to drink before that". Wow, I thought, this is going to be cool. Now, this was 1997 and way before 9/11 and the terrorist attacks on the World Trade Center, so things were much more loose then. So, I did what he said and walked into the cockpit about 30 minutes after we took off. I expected to sit in the jump seat behind the pilot but when I stepped into the cockpit Ben slipped out of the co-pilot's seat and motioned me to sit there. So, I did.

It was a beautiful day and a cloudless sky as we cruised along at 33,000 feet above sea level on autopilot. Ben & the pilot began showing me some of the cool features of the plane and I listened to the transmissions between us and air traffic control on the headset. I was loving it. I sat there in the "right hand seat" for about 20 minutes and then they said my time was up. Ben took his place back in the co-pilot's seat and I went back to my seat in first class. The looks I got from the other passengers was awesome – they clearly thought I was another pilot or airline exec! Needless to say, it was a very fun trip.

In December of 1997 Peggy & I had been dating for a year and talked about getting married. She had a trip to fly one upcoming weekend (again to San Francisco), so I bought a ring and flew out there to surprise her and propose on her layover. Now, she normally didn't take nice clothes on her trips since most of the layovers were short and mostly about resting up for the next day. So, I tried to figure out a clever way of getting her to pack a dress for dinner, but she wasn't getting the hint. Finally, I just blurted out that I was meeting her in San Fran to get engaged. She was very touched and a little surprised and quickly threw a nice outfit in her crew luggage. We arrived in San Francisco, changed into our nice clothes and went to dinner at a place near the airport that I had reserved. I popped the question and she said "yes", and we celebrated over a nice bottle of champagne. It was December and we decided to get married in Austin in March 1998. The next day she went on with her trip and I flew back to Austin to start making wedding plans.

Chapter 31: Into Africa. Again.

Peggy and I decided on a small ceremony at the Episcopal Seminary just north of the U.T. campus in March 1998. Her parents and siblings all flew in from California and we had a nice, intimate service followed by dinner & dancing at Barton Creek Country Club. I wanted her to see Africa and felt like it was important that we have that shared experience, so we booked a ten-day honeymoon trip to tour Kenya & Tanzania with Abercrombie & Kent. She suggested that we fly non-rev on Continental to & from London which sounded good to me. But I knew we had to arrive in Nairobi on a specific date, so we bought full-fare tickets from London to Kenya and back.

The morning after the wedding we flew over to Houston from Austin and quickly learned that the Continental flight we wanted to take was booked. British Airways had a flight leaving in an hour, so we rushed over to their ticket counter and Peggy gave them her Continental credentials. B.A. had two seats available and when we told them it was our honeymoon, they booked us into business class. We had a very nice flight to London and then flew on to Nairobi the next day, again on British Air. As our tour group gathered at the hotel, we were excited about being in this very foreign place. We checked into the Norfolk Hotel, a classic Nairobi place with beautifully landscaped grounds and gardens. That night we had dinner on the Delamere Terrace of the hotel; Lord Delamere governed Kenya (then called British East Africa) which was a colony of Great Britain until 1963. Fans of the movie "Out of Africa" will recall the scene where Meryl Streep's character, Karen Blixen, kneels to Lord Delamere asking for him to not relocate the Kikuyu tribe from her lands once she returned to England. It was all very cool to be part of the history of the country; several of our tour group members toured Karen Blixen's former home the next day before we departed for our first lodge, Amboseli Serena.

The Amboseli Serena was located in Kenya, very near Mt. Kilimanjaro, which is just over the border in Tanzania (originally German East Africa). I had seen pictures of it from a trip that Mom & Dad had taken several years before and was very excited about seeing this striking mountain for ourselves. As we crossed the border into Tanzania and drove ever closer, we began to see zebra, impala & other African wildlife. It had been a particular rainy spring there so the grass was tall & green; the countryside was lush and full. But, as we got nearer, most of Kilimanjaro was shrouded in a dense afternoon fog. I was really disappointed to have come this far and now we might not get to see it. Our guide was a wonderful Kenyan fellow named "Cosmas" and we would grow to be very good friends over the next 10 days. "Cosmas" I said, "is the mountain always covered like this? I really hoped to see all of it" I told him. "Not to worry, Cinco" he replied, "in the morning the fog will lift, and you will see all of its beauty". I hoped he was right.

The next morning, we all met for breakfast and Cosmas told us we were going to hike out of the camp, which was nestled in a wooded area, and into a clearing where we would see Kilimanjaro. An armed guard went with us just in case we walked up on a lion or elephant. When we walked out of the woods and looked up, the morning was bright & clear. And Kilimanjaro loomed hugely in front of us. Now, I have seen many beautiful sights, including the Grand Canyon and Alaska. But this was different: because Kilimanjaro is a volcano it stands alone. It is not part of a larger range of mountains like the Rockies or Andes. The flat east African plain fed right up to the mountain, the tallest peak in Africa, and then Kilimanjaro sloped up & up to its snow-capped flat peak. It was not only beautiful but surreal. I was ecstatic to see it and Peggy & I posed for pictures with a local Masai chief with the volcanic mountain in the background. It was a dream come true.

We traveled on to Lake Manyara and then to the Ngorongoro

Crater – both places were beautiful. The crater was caused by a volcano which imploded many years ago and it holds teaming herds of cape buffalo, rhino and antelope. As we passed by one of the several lakes in the crater there was a beautiful flock of pink flamingos wading in the shallow waters. Again, it was right out of a picture book, and we loved every awesome part of it. We spent two nights in the Serengeti Plains of Tanzania where we saw the fabled migrating herds of zebra and wildebeest. Literally, there was a line of animals from one horizon to the other and as we passed the clear rivers and streams, we saw crocodiles basking in the warm sun along the banks.

We then drove to the town of Arusha, Tanzania for lunch to be followed by a flight to the Masai Mara plains of Kenya. After we finished eating, Cosmas walked us out to a tall obelisk located in a traffic roundabout in front of the hotel where we had just finished a nice buffet lunch. He pointed to it, and we read on the side that indicated it was the geographic half-way point between Cairo and Cape Town. We were in the middle of the "Great Rift Valley" which runs for 7,000 kilometers (4,000 miles) from Lebanon, through east Africa south to Mozambique, and creates a beautiful escarpment that looms over the Mara. Our lodge there was a lovely place, and our quarters were very well-appointed green tents. We did have running water for a hot shower and bathrooms, which was much fancier than what I had experienced in Botswana several years before. We were told to make sure we zipped our tents very tightly lest the pesky baboons run inside and take our possessions!

The next morning, we woke early and were driven about twenty minutes from the camp for a sunrise hot-air balloon ride over the Mara. Our balloon took flight as the sun began to break just over the horizon; the morning was clear and quite chilly as we drifted along literally hovering just a few feet above a herd of elephants & eland. Our pilot spotted a pride of lions and slowly let our balloon drop right over them; we were so quiet they had no idea we were only about 25 feet above them! When our pilot hit the burner to give our balloon some lift, the noise clearly surprised the lions below us and they quickly sprinted away.   After about an hour flight, we landed in a beautiful open field and were picked up by several vans and trucks from the lodge that had been following us. We loaded in and after a five-minute drive we arrived at a big white tent with a wonderful champagne breakfast waiting.   It was magical and we were completely overcome with the majesty and awe of this very special place.

One of the "side trips" was a fishing trip for Nile Perch on Lake Victoria, about an hour flight from our lodge. I was all over it, so we booked it and had the driver take us to the dirt runway just outside the lodge's high fence where we boarded a single engine Cessna for the flight over to the lake. Cosmas and one of our new friends from the trip (a young man named Kevin) joined us, which was a real treat.   Our pilot was a native Kenyan and told us "I'll keep us at tree top level for the first twenty minutes after we take off and then we will gain altitude and climb up over the edge of the escarpment".   And we did.   As we flew over the edge of the escarpment, with the Masai Mara disappearing behind us, our pilot pointed down to a large tree just below us: "that's where the final scene of 'Out of Africa' was filmed" he told us.   I had seen the movie several times and as we continued climbing over the vast coffee & tea plantations towards the lake the beautiful theme music from the movie, composed by John Williams, was playing in my ears.   I was pretty sure that this was the most inspiring and magical thing I had ever experienced!

Very soon we could see the lake appearing in front of us as our pilot lowered the nose of the plane and put us safely on the runway. Lake Victoria (named for England's Queen Victoria - as is Victoria Falls in Zimbabwe) is bordered by the countries of Uganda, Kenya & Tanzania and is a huge body of water; it also serves as the headwaters of the Nile River which flows north thru Uganda, South

Sudan, Sudan & Egypt and finally terminates into the Mediterranean Sea. It provides life and irrigation for many people who live along its banks in what would otherwise be an uninhabitable Saharan desert.

The airstrip ran along the edge of the lake and once we climbed out of the single engine Cessna, it was a short walk over to a very nice fishing boat which would take us out. Now, for reasons I didn't consider then and can't really explain now, my expectations for catching fish were pretty low. I mean, we were passing by vintage Ugandan fishing skiffs with tattered sails dragging very worn-out nets. These boats were overloaded with fishermen who appeared to spend more time bailing water than actually fishing. But I was told by some African friends that Nile Perch could get very large and were quite tasty – so even if we didn't catch anything it was very cool thinking about what we had seen on the flight over and to comprehend that we were on Lake Victoria in the scenic heart of East Africa. "Not many people can say they have seen and done this" I thought to myself as the boat captain and first mate unleashed the outriggers and started putting lures on the fishing lines. We had only been out about 20 minutes and already we had "bait" in the water trolling behind us.

A few minutes later we heard the high-pitched scream of the fishing line being pulled away from the boat and saw one of the fishing rod tips bending over. "Fish on!" yelled the first mate to the captain and pandemonium broke out. The first mate handed the rod to Peggy who took a seat in the chair as the rest of us grabbed another rod and reeled up the line – we needed to make sure Peggy's fish didn't get tangled in our other fishing lines which would surely mean we would lose the fish. She began a good fight and soon had the first Nile perch of the day at the back of the boat. The first mate pulled it into the boat and removed the hook from its mouth. (We had decided that we wanted to keep some fish so we could take it back to the camp with us; the cooks there had told us they would enjoy cooking it for our dinner that night.) It was a beautiful fish and Cosmas reckoned it weighed about twenty pounds, not bad for a bunch of rookies from the U.S.!

Over the next hour or so we caught three more perch, all about the same size as the first. It was time to head back to the dock, clean and filet our fish and board the plane for the sixty-minute flight back to our lodge. We had plenty of filets now to feed anyone who wanted Nile perch for dinner. The cooks at the lodge were very pleased when we walked into the kitchen with our catch and told us they would create a nice sauteed stew of curried fish filets over a bed of jasmine rice. We paired it with a nice Stellenbosch Chardonnay from the South African wine country. It was delicious and we all enjoyed telling our fishing stories and sharing our bounty from Lake Victoria with our new friends on the trip with us.

Like every wonderful trip, this one would end in a day or so after a quick flight on Kenya Air to Nairobi. We gave Cosmas a big hug and a heart-felt thank you (and a nice tip for seeing us so safely and capably through east Africa for ten days) and then boarded a British Air 747 for the overnight flight to London. We would arrive at Heathrow Airport early the next morning, short on sleep but filled with wonderful memories of our time together. The lodging, scenery, local people and herds of animals were spectacular and everything I could have imagined when we booked the trip. I found the countries of Kenya and Tanzania to be both beautiful and inspiring; and yes, while the roads might have been bumpy and narrow and the facilities a little aged, it didn't matter. They clearly had something very special here and the local people shared it with us with pride and enthusiasm. As the 747 pilots lifted our modern jet into the sunset sky of Kenya, I heard the landing gear lift into the belly of the plane and I thanked God for the opportunity to see this part of his wonderful creation and hoped, no prayed, to come back again one day.

"Peggy, what the hell are you doing here??" I heard a voice

exclaim. It woke me out of a deep sleep. After we landed in London, we had several hours before our flight on Continental departed for Houston. So, Peggy used her credentials to get us into the CAL crew room where we grabbed a light bite of breakfast and curled up on a couple of the sofas to get a little shut eye. The crews were beginning to arrive for the upcoming flights to Houston, Newark and Chicago and the large room, with adjacent kitchen, was beginning to get busy. It was about 9 am in the morning. "Oh my God" the same voice continued, "are you guys headed home from your honeymoon?!" Cathy Accardi was a flight attendant for Continental whom Peggy knew well; in fact, she had been at our wedding in Austin two weeks earlier and was excited and surprised to see us in the Heathrow crew room.

Peggy & I wiped the sleep from our eyes and shared some quick stories of Africa with Cathy over a fresh cup of coffee. Peggy told her "We are on the wait list for the 12-noon flight to Houston. Is that the one you are working?" she asked. Cathy said she was working that flight but then gave us a concerned look. "You're flying non-rev?" she asked. We confirmed that we were and asked why she seemed so worried. "Oh my gosh" Cathy continued, "do y'all not realize that this is Spring Break? All the flights are full, and most are over-booked." Now, I had become a seasoned non-rev flyer over the years of traveling with Peggy and I knew that, even in good conditions, trying to get on a flight as a non-revenue passenger could be a dice roll. And CAL only had two daily flights from London to Houston. Just then, a family of four walked into the crew room and overheard our conversation. The Dad was a CAL pilot traveling with his wife and two children who told us "We've been here three days trying to get on a plane" he said. "There's not an open flight until the day after tomorrow".

Peggy & I gave each other a worried look; we were already a little sleep deprived from the flight from Nairobi the night before; the thought of hanging out at Heathrow for three days sounded like absolute torture. Cathy saw our problem and had an idea: "there are two crew rest seats y'all could use" she offered. "Let me see if the crew would be ok with that" and went off to canvass them. This was beginning to sound a lot better until Peggy, who had flown the Houston – London flights many times and, unlike me, knew the intricacies of "crew rest rules" quite well, said "well, even if the crew agrees to let us use those seats, we can only sit there for the first and last hour of the flight. The crew, by rule, uses them to rest up the other eight hours". Ugg, I thought, this doesn't sound too good. "So, I asked, where do we sit for eight hours high over the Atlantic Ocean if we can't use the crew seats?" Peggy looked me squarely in the eye and said, "on the jump seats back in the rear galley". Which is exactly what we did. While the other passengers sat reclined in their cushy seats, drinking cocktails, watching movies and enjoying a hot lunch, Peggy & I shifted from one leg to the other sipping a soft drink trying not to fall off the jump seat when the plane hit bumpy air. And we didn't get one second of sleep.

When the plane finally landed in Houston we grabbed our gear off the turnstile, found my car in the parking lot and made the three-hour drive back to Austin. Fatigue had set in hours before and it was all we could do to stay awake, but we made it. As we dropped our luggage on the bedroom floor, darkened the windows and climbed into bed I couldn't help but calculate how many hours we had been awake. "Peggy, I said, "we left Nairobi forty-four hours ago. It's been almost two days since we've had more than a ten-minute nap". With that, we took the phone off the hook (no cell phones in 1998) and drifted into a deep, long, exhausted doze.

Chapter 32: A new light. A new point of view.

In July of that year, Mom & Dad were going to celebrate Mom's birthday in New York City, so Peggy & I flew out and joined them. Peggy got us a room at the Milford Plaza since she was able to get really good rates there from her airline connections. We decided to travel on to Wyoming from there and join her aunt & uncle on a fly-fishing trip on the Platte River. Since I was turning 38 that fall and Peggy was 33, we talked about starting a family pretty soon. Little did I know that we would hit the jackpot on that trip and nine months later Savannah was born. Fortunately, Peggy had a pretty easy pregnancy, and we turned the guest room in my small townhouse into a nursery. Peggy & I agreed that we did not want to know the gender of the baby until delivery, so we made sure the doctors didn't slip up & tell us. I was excited about becoming a father – I had been an uncle, at that point, for twenty-eight years so I had the benefit of watching my sisters raise their children, so I felt ready for the responsibility and looked forward to the joys and challenges of being a parent.

In September, with Peggy only about a month pregnant, we joined Mom & Dad on a golf trip to Scotland. Our good friends from South Padre, Doris & Rusty Bentley, had lived in Scotland for several years while Rusty was in the oil services business in Aberdeen. Rusty had created the "St. Andrews Society of South Texas" and organized an annual golf tournament that paired father & son teams together. Dad & I had played in the tournament together two years in a row at the Rancho Viejo resort between Brownsville & Harlingen. Both times we finished second and had a very good time playing together and enjoying the group. When Rusty announced that the St. Andrews Society of South Texas golf tournament would be held in Scotland the next year, we were all over it. The dream that Dad had planted in me many years before of playing golf together in Scotland would actually come true. The trip over was hard on Peggy; she was in her first trimester and really feeling poorly. When we finally arrived in our hotel room in Nairn, in the northern area of Scotland, she was exhausted. She skipped the dinner festivities that night and opted for a hot bath and room service in our suite. The next morning all of us golfers headed to the Royal Dornoch course for our first of three rounds.

The weather was typical Scotland in September (and it just happened to be my birthday): windy with a slight drizzle. Since there were no caddies, we dropped our golf bags onto "hand carts" and headed to the first tee. Dad & I played well, given the tough conditions, and all of us headed back to the hotel for dinner. Peggy had gone out and walked the town and was in good spirits when we got back to Nairn. We had a nice birthday dinner with the group and made plans for round two the next day at Royal Carnegie, named after American industrialist Andrew Carnegie.

When we arrived, we were introduced to the caddy who had been assigned to Dad and me. His name was David, and he instantly loved the fact that we were from Texas. Once he learned it was my birthday weekend, he went the extra mile to help us play well on a course we had never seen before. The day was perfect: not a cloud in the sky and no wind. It was as close to golf heaven as it gets. Dad & I were both hitting the ball pretty well and David was a big help. I hit my approach shot a little short of the third green and had a long way to the pin; I wanted to get up and down to save par. I turned to David, who by now had a pretty good feel for my strengths & weaknesses, and said "David, I am thinking I use my putter here. What do you think?" He looked at the pin, pulled a 9 iron out of the bag and while he handed it to me, he said in a deep Scottish accent "Oh no, Lad, this calls for a wee chip & run". I knew I couldn't let him down, so I hit the shot he called for and made my par. I went on to make two birdies and an eagle that day and it was magic. As

Dad and I walked off the 18th green, in solid position to win the tournament, I reached over and grabbed his hand. He looked over and gave me a quick wink. Dreams do come true. And that day, it happened on a beautiful golf course with Dad in northern Scotland, and a consummate caddy named David.

May 1999: Early one morning Peggy woke me up and said her water had broken. We were actually very calm about the whole thing; she called her doctor, a wonderful girl named Marty, who suggested we come on into the hospital quickly so they could monitor the situation and progress. I grabbed a quick shower and off we went to Seton Hospital on 35th street. It was about 5 am in the morning when we arrived; we checked in and made our way to our room on the maternity floor. We had been ready for about a month, and I had a Jimmy Buffett mix tape (yes, this was still the day of cassettes and boom boxes) so that my child would come into the world listening to "Come Monday, it'll be all right. Come Monday, I'll be holding you tight".

Peggy asked me to call her family (I reminded her it was two hours earlier in California, so we waited until later in the morning). I called Mom & then Shelley and gave them the news; they had already said they wanted to be there for the birth (still not knowing whether it was a boy or a girl) so they jumped in the car and headed for Austin. Peggy had said that she was ok with them being in the delivery room and I really appreciated that; Mom later said she had birthed 5 children but had never actually been a part of the delivery of another baby – she loved being so connected to the process and having her & Shelley there really calmed my nerves.

Peggy's contractions were pretty far apart, and she wasn't dilating very much, so after talking to our doctor we agreed to start a drip of Pitocin in her I.V. Well, that stuff works because within about thirty minutes Peggy was feeling some very sharp contraction pains. In fact, she grabbed my hand and said, "tell them to turn off the Pitocin!". I could tell she was in pretty severe pain as I kept an eye on the meter next to her bed measuring the start and end of her contractions – I could see the needle charting her contractions go up & up and knew it was really kicking in! Naturally, the doctor told us that they couldn't stop the drip and she would just have to bear it. After a couple of hours, they decided Peggy was sufficiently contracted that they could give her an epidural. Once the numbness took over, she fell fast asleep and I was amazed how she could now sleep through contractions that, just a few minutes before, were causing extreme pain.

Mom & Shelley arrived, and we briefed them on the situation. Not long after, our doctor said it was time to push and soon, I could see the baby's head crowning. Poor Peggy pushed & pushed and finally, after another hour or effort, Savannah was delivered around 5pm that evening. When she came out, I expected her to be kicking and screaming; instead, she looked lifeless, and I was very concerned. The nurse whisked her over to a table near the bed and I could see her, Mom & Shelley gathered over Savannah and looking at my newborn daughter. I was trying to comfort Peggy, but I was worried about things: "why isn't she crying" I asked with a tone of worry in my voice. "You want her to cry" the nurse asked? "Yes, I said, is she ok? Shouldn't she be crying?" With that, the nurse gave Savannah a hardy thump on her foot with her finger and Savannah let out a big, loud cry. I could tell her lungs were full of air and she was breathing just fine – it was the first time I heard my daughter's voice, and it was music to my ears. She is ok, I thought, and turned my attention back to Peggy. She assured me she was fine and feeling ok, so I got up from her bedside and walked over to see my new baby girl.

Savannah was lying on the table wrapped in a fresh towel and as I looked down at her for the first time, she was the most beautiful thing I had ever seen. "Love at first sight" is kind of trite, but in this case, it was so true. The nurses dressed her and put a little knit cap on her head, and I held her for the very first time. It was magic and

I walked her over to Peggy and laid her in Peggy's arms. What a beautiful sight to behold. I was a Dad and it felt great. Mom & Shelley dabbed tears and we all had a big hug. After a couple of hours, they drove back to their hotel, and I decided to walk back home leaving my car at the hospital. Life would never be the same and I was thrilled.

Chapter 33: Arlington National

Peggy had six months of maternity leave and we settled into life as new parents. I worked during the day and did as much as I could to help with the baby when I was home. As her maternity leave was coming to an end, she put in the paperwork to return flying in November 1999. We agreed that she would fly from Friday afternoon until Sunday night or Monday morning. Since all her trips began & ended in Houston, she had to bid trips each month that allowed her to commute to Houston in time to check in for her flight. Sometimes she would drive herself to the airport and sometimes Savannah & I would take her on Friday and pick her up when she came back home. At first, it was a little scary being responsible for a six-month-old baby, but soon we settled into a routine of feeding, naps, play time, another feeding, another nap, and plenty of diaper changes during the day. It was great to be a hands-on Daddy and I knew Peggy enjoyed getting away and helping bring home some income. All in all, it was pretty good times.

In late October, as Peggy was planning her work schedule for the next month, she got a phone call from a dear friend who was also a CAL flight attendant, Jan Colling. Jan's husband, Howard, was a CAL pilot and when they became empty-nesters Jan went to flight attendant school so she could fly with Howard and spend more time together. Jan & Peggy were classmates at CAL. Jan & Howard had been at our wedding the year before and were delightful people. I thought it was pretty cool that their son, Kevin, was in the Navy and a pilot for the Blue Angels. Howard told me some amazing stories about the places the Blue Angels went to perform and the red-carpet treatment they received while there. As Kevin described it to his Dad, "people act like we were the Rolling Stones or something" when they rolled into town for a weekend air show.

The Blue Angels were formed in 1946 by Admiral Chester

Nimitz, then Chief of Naval Operations, who had a vision to create a flight exhibition team to raise the public's interest in naval aviation and boost Navy morale. (Nimitz was born in Fredericksburg, TX. and his original home there is a National Historical site.) Between March and November of each year, the Blue Angels perform every weekend across the country (and even in Canada) culminating with a show at their home base, the Naval Air Station Pensacola, where they also trained constantly. The maneuvers they perform during their shows are incredibly precise and intricate. It takes exact timing and complete focus to pull off the stunts they demonstrate, all while going upwards of 500 miles per hour. If they weren't performing, they were training, and the schedule was demanding. Each pilot is on the team for only two years due to the stressful nature of the assignment; Kevin had been a part of this elite team for several months and had clearly found his stride. Until one morning, as he was riding in the back seat of one of the training jets, the pilot in command in the front seat failed to pull out of a g-force dive and slammed nose-first into the ground. Both were killed instantly, and the news was on every major cable network within minutes.

Peggy burst into tears when Jan called with the news. I had never met Kevin, but Peggy had, and she was crushed over the loss. "We have to go to the service" she told me once she composed herself; we said a quick prayer for Howard and Jan, who had just lost their naval aviator son. Over the next few days, we made plans to fly, with Savannah, to Norfolk, VA. for the memorial service there at the Norfolk Naval Air Station, which is just down the road from Virginia Beach, on the Atlantic Ocean. (Kevin and his wife lived in Virginia Beach when he wasn't on the road with the Angels.) The burial would be the next morning in Arlington National Cemetery several hours up the highway from Norfolk.

I had never been to a military funeral before, but I will never forget it. The pomp, the pageantry, the love of country and the outstanding young people in uniform were beyond impressive. As the service ended, after each of the Blue Angel pilots had said a few words about Kevin from the lectern, we all stood and sang the Navy Hymn:

Oh, Christ whose voice the waters heard, And hushed their raging at Thy word,Who walkest on the foamy deep, And how amidst the storm did sleep,O hear us when we cry to Thee, For those in Peril on the sea.

Eternal Father strong to save, Whose arm has bound the restless wave,Who bids the mighty ocean deep, It's own appointed limits keep,O hear us when we cry to Thee, For those in Peril on the sea.

Oh Christ, the Lord of hill and plain, O'er which our traffic runs amain,By mountain pass or valley low, Wherever, Lord our brethren go,Protect them by Thy guarding hand, From every peril on the land.

O Spirit, whom the Father sent, To spread abroad the firmament, Oh wind of heaven, by Thy might, Save all who dare the eagle's flight,And keep them by thy watchful care, From every peril in the air.

O Trinity of love and power, Our brethren shield in danger's hour, From rock and tempest, fire, and foe, Protect them wheresoe'er they go, That evermore shall rise to Thee, Glad praise from air and land and sea.

It was a moving and wonderful tribute to Kevin, and I was so proud to be an American and to know these young people put their lives in jeopardy every day so that the rest of us can sleep soundly at night.

After the service, we were all invited to join the Blue Angels at the officer's hall for a celebration of Kevin's life with cocktails and snacks. I moved up to the bar, wedged between two of the Blue Angel pilots, and noticed they had Shiner Bock beer available. I exclaimed loudly, to no one in particular, "wow, this place is awesome. You have Shiner Bock!" The two pilots both turned to me and asked, "what is Shiner Bock?" So, I proceeded to tell them all about the Spoetzl Brewery in little Shiner, Texas, just down the road from Austin, and how good their dark beer, Shiner Bock, was. Neither had ever tried it and began to canvass the other Blue Angel pilots if they had. Soon, all six pilots, in their crisp Navy whites, were gathered around me discussing this Texas beer they knew nothing about. "Well," I said, "it would be my honor to treat each one you Blue Angel pilots to your first Shiner Bock!" So, I ordered seven of them and, after loudly clinking our bottles together in a toast to Kevin and the United States of America, we downed a big drink of Texas beer. And they liked it as much as I did! For a Moment, I felt like I was part of the Navy and fully understood the magnetism of military service.

The next morning brought a clear, crisp, cool autumn sunrise as we drove along the Washington, D.C. turnpike towards Arlington National. Men and women in uniform were there to guide us past the rows and rows of white headstones that populated the grassy hills inside the cemetery. Peggy wore a nice dress, and I was in a dark suit and red tie; Savannah had a precious red jumper on with a black beret that framed her beautiful curls and sparkling blue eyes. She turned every head as we parked and walked towards Kevin's open gravesite with his flag-draped coffin perched over it. The gathering was smaller than the service the day before, but every bit ceremonial and beautiful. As the Navy Chaplain recited special words and bible verses, with birds chirping close by and a Marine Sargent playing *Taps* on his bugle, I couldn't help but fixate on Howard and Jan. The nation was honoring their son by receiving his body into its most treasured resting place, but I knew even that couldn't completely mend their grief. And I thought about my own brother; could he have been a Blue Angel pilot? Would he have one day been honored by his community and nation? He certainly brought pride to the Marines with his drill team performances in

New York and around the state of Texas. That's the hardest part of losing someone too soon in life: it's the things and times that are taken from you that you can never have. I was startled back to reality by a nice woman who was holding a very large walkie talkie as she walked up to me.

"Do you know the father, Mr. Colling?" she asked me. "Yes" I said, "that's him right there by the casket. Why?" "Well," she continued, "could you ask him if we can go ahead and do the flyover now? We have National Airport on hold and no airliners can land or take off." Wow, I thought, these military folks really know how to honor their own! "Um, sure" I said, "let me go see if he's ok with that". He was of course, and I could tell neither Howard nor Jan knew that the Navy was doing a flyover. I walked back over to "walkie talkie lady" and said "yes, Howard and Jan said, 'please go ahead'". She pressed the microphone button, held the unit near her mouth and mumbled a few words into it. Within what seemed like fifteen seconds the most tremendous roar started from the direction to my left. As I turned my head towards it, four F-18 Blue Angel jets were flying right towards us in a low-level, tight formation. I had to wonder if it was the same guys I had enjoyed a beer with the night before; I'm pretty sure it was. As they moved just past us, one of the jets peeled out of formation and climbed straight up into the beautiful Washington, D.C. morning sky leaving dual trails of white smoke behind it. "Missing man" one of the Navy pilots standing next to me muttered. "That was for Kevin".

Chapter 34: Our third President.

We gave hugs all around to the Colling family and headed back to our hotel to change into comfortable clothes.   Since it was just Friday and the weekend was upon us, I proposed to Peggy that we drive down to Charlottesville, VA. and get tickets to the Virginia vs Georgia Tech football game the next afternoon. She agreed and soon we were driving through the beautiful Virginia countryside with its hills adorned in the bright red, yellow and orange leaves of fall. I had been there before, fourteen years earlier in 1985, interviewing at U.V.A. for graduate business school. What I already knew, and began telling Peggy, was that U.V.A. was founded by three men, Thomas Jefferson, Joseph Cabell and General John Hartwell Cocke. "There's a Cocke Hall on campus, just down from the main Rotunda building" I told her. "Let's take Savannah there and get our picture taken".

****

Richard Cocke was born in England in 1597 at Pickthorn, Shropshire and baptized Dec. 13, 1597, at Sidbury. Richard's early education is not known, but he was both literate and educated enough to act as an attorney in court; in the early 1600's, he immigrated to the U.S. through Jamestown, VA. The first Virginia record of Richard Cocke is from December 24, 1627, when he appeared at the court in Jamestown to give testimony as the purser of the Thomas and John (I assume that is a ship) *that four men of Mr. Sharples (*I assume slaves*) had run away while being transported to Virginia.*

On March 6, 1636 Richard Cocke "Gentleman" patented 3,000 acres (*he brought sixty settlers over from England and received fifty acres for each of them*) in Henrico County and expanded his holdings further on March 10, 1639 with an additional 2,000 acres. On December 6, 1652 he added 2,842 more acres in Henrico County with his last acquisition on June 21, 1664 consisting of 2,974 acres on the south side of the Chickahominy River. By the time Richard Cocke died in 1665 he was in possession of 10,916 acres of land spread over three sites named, "Bremo" (his home site), "Malvern Hill' and "Curles".

He married Temperance Bailey, the widow of John Browne, on June 5, 1632, and settled Browne's estate for a fee of 6,397 pounds of tobacco. Richard and Temperance had two sons, Thomas and Richard, and a daughter Elizabeth. Thomas (c. 1639 – 1697) was the first child born in Colonial Virginia with the last name "Cocke". I am 10th in line as a direct descendant to Thomas Cocke. Gen. John Hartwell Cocke, born in Surry County, VA. in 1780 was Thomas Cocke's great-grandson, and would then be my great uncle about 8 times removed.

On Christmas day, in 1802, John Hartwell Cocke married Anne Blaws Barraud whom he met in Williamsburg where both were attending school. Around 1808, he moved his family permanently to Bremo Plantation on the north side of the James River, approximately twenty-five miles southeast of Monticello.

An officer in the Virginia Militia, Cocke rose to the rank of brigadier general in the War of 1812; his military record lead members of the General Assembly to recommend him for the office of governor. Said to exhibit a "keen sense of civic responsibility," but also "destitute of political aspirations," General Cocke declined to be considered. Farming practices, social reform, religion, public improvements, education, and architecture were foremost among his varied interests and areas in which he made significant contributions.

Cocke expressed "continual hostility to slavery" and sought to "elevate the Negro through education and skill training" views that apparently once led him to be violently attacked by someone who thought differently about the treatment of blacks. Appointed in

1835 to the board of directors of the James River and Kanawha Canal Company, he participated with his close friend, Joseph C. Cabell, in the development of water transportation along 200 miles of the James River.

John Hartwell Cocke was thirty-seven years younger than his neighbor, Thomas Jefferson, but these landed gentry shared numerous concerns and became close associates during the latter years of Jefferson's life. Cocke was "Jeffersonian" in his habits and views: both men attended William and Mary, led organized lives, owned large plantations, and were well-read, civic-minded, and restless in their inquiries into the world around them. Soon after arriving at Bremo, Cocke exchanged letters with Jefferson. Their early correspondence concerned sheep, plants, and a horse Jefferson wished to buy from Cocke.

General Cocke was a steadfast supporter of public education and efforts to establish a state university in Virginia. Consequently, at Jefferson's request, Governor Nicholas, in 1817, appointed Cocke to the Board of Visitors of Central College, from which would emerge the University of Virginia. Cocke served on the College and subsequent University Boards of Visitors for thirty-six years. In addition to Jefferson and Cocke, the first Board of Visitors included James Madison (4th President of the United States), James Monroe (the United States' 5th President), Joseph C. Cabell, and David Watson. In subsequent years the two neighbors communicated frequently when attending meetings of the Board of Visitors, during Cocke's frequent visits to Monticello, and on numerous other occasions. Their written correspondence during the years of university construction reveals the collaborators' preoccupation with the myriad details and problems of building the state university. The historian, Philip Alexander Bruce, suggests that Cocke's diligent work on the committee of superintendence "gives him a place in the University's early history second only to that of his close friend, Joseph Cabell," making him, in the words of another author of John Hartwell Cocke's history, "one of the three fathers of the University of Virginia."

Jefferson's last letter to Cocke, his neighbor and collaborator, was dated May 28, 1826. An ailing Jefferson invited Cocke to breakfast at Monticello, "tomorrow morning," to discuss business, explaining that he, Jefferson, was not well enough to travel to Charlottesville. Jefferson died five weeks later on July 4, 1826.

Both Jefferson and Cocke opposed the institution of slavery, yet neither advocated an immediate emancipation of those enslaved. They believed blacks could not survive if freed without education and skill training. In their view, the only solution lay with gradual emancipation with expatriation to another country. Unlike Jefferson, however, General Cocke made visible efforts to educate those he enslaved even when laws forbade it and worked publicly to advance the re-colonization of blacks to Africa, eventually emancipating and sending abroad some of those he enslaved.

Despite his opposition to the institution of slavery, General Cocke defended the Confederate cause during the American Civil war. Following the war, he was granted a Presidential pardon and died on July 1, 1866. He is buried in the family cemetery at Bremo, his home in Henrico County for many years, with its sweeping views down the rolling hills to the James River below.

****

After my interview at the U.V.A. business school in 1985, I jumped in my rental car and made the short drive out to Bremo. I wound my way up the hill to the beautiful home, parked in front and knocked on the large, wooden door. I even took my driver's license out and had it handy to prove I was "part of the family". A very nice, older gentleman answered the door and greeted me warmly. When I introduced myself, he said "Oh yes, we are well aware of all the family from Texas. We are about to sit down for lunch, would you like to join us?" He led me through the home, back towards the dining room where he introduced me to his wife. Her name escapes me now (let's call her "Lois") but her maiden name was "Cocke" and, as the Great (times nine) Granddaughter of Gen. John H. Cocke, she now owned Bremo. She, too, greeted me warmly and as we took our seats at the large, long dining table the aura of the place and its deep history began to sink in. They lived full-time in Birmingham, AL. but spent as much time as they could at Bremo, she told me. We had a nice lunch and shared stories about our backgrounds and experiences growing up in the Cocke family. Lois was keen to learn more about the "Texas Cockes" and what had brought me out to Virginia.

She knew that the family migrated from Virginia to Tennessee (there is a "Cocke" County in Tennessee) and eventually to Texas. I would later learn that my great-great grandfather, James Rogers Cocke, (who was born in Grainger, County Tennessee in 1838) would settle in Gonzales, County Texas where he would meet and marry Grace Elizabeth Bartlett. They had ten children together and are buried next to each other (they both died in 1919) in the Rancho Cemetery just north of Nixon, Texas in Gonzales County. I have visited their gravesite (and the Cocke family cemetery in Buda, just south of Austin) and even taken Dad, Savannah & Marshall there to see it.

As lunch was wrapping up, Lois asked me if I would like to join her in the library and see Gen. Cocke's handwritten diary. "Wow, would I ever" I exclaimed, and she led me down the hall to a beautiful, oak paneled library that was steeped in colonial design and history. She gently removed the diary from its shelf and opened it to a few pages she had bookmarked. She motioned me closer, pointed to a specific passage in Gen. Cocke's handwriting (it was, of course, quite faded over time) and said "I like to show this to family when they come visit. Here, read it for yourself". I stepped over to the desk where the diary now lain, leaned forward and read his words: "President Jefferson summoned me to Monticello several days ago and I was saddened that Anne (his wife) was too ill to make the trip with me. But, to my delight, when I arrived James & Dolly Madison were there and shared the weekend with us".   Dang, I thought, that is pretty cool, and it made me so glad I had driven out that day from Charlottesville. Gen. Cocke's diary now resides there at the University of Virginia Library.

****

Peggy, Savannah & I toured Monticello the morning before the football game and were so impressed with the history and colonial significance of it. We made our way across the well-manicured lawn, past some of the small buildings behind the main house and arrived at President Jefferson's grave. After the two days we had just spent in Norfolk and Arlington National, steeped in national pride and military pageantry, I was again reminded of what a wonderful country we live in.   The preamble to our Constitution, written primarily by Thomas Jefferson, James Madison, Thomas Paine, and John Adams, states:

> *We the People of the United States, in Order to form a more perfect Union, establish Justice, insure domestic Tranquility, provide for the common defence, promote the general Welfare, and secure the Blessings of Liberty to ourselves and our Posterity, do ordain and establish this Constitution for the United States of America.*

Their goal was to "form a more perfect union". Not a <u>perfect</u> one, just one better than what the colonials were forced to endure under the rule of King George. And even with all our problems and divisions, people from all over the globe risk their lives (and their families' lives) every day just to get here. We enjoy a freedom, even 236 years after the Constitution was adopted by the Continental Congress, that is the envy of the world.

"Smile!" the young U.V.A. student said as I held Savannah in my arms standing proudly in front of Cocke Hall, posing for pictures. The bright Virginia sun was shining into our eyes, and we had to squint a little, but it was so worth it. Peggy joined us for some photos, too, and several passers-by were curious enough to ask why we were there. "He is descended from Gen. Cocke" Peggy told them, and they were clearly impressed. I wasn't going to correct her that I wasn't "directly" descended from him, because in that moment, the most important thing was that he and I shared the same name, and so did this beautiful five-month-old baby girl I was holding. With that, we made our way to Scott Stadium for the football game to enjoy even more of what a colonial college campus has to offer. And by the way, Virginia upset #7 ranked Georgia Tech that day 45 - 38! Virginia was led by their star running back, Thomas Jones, who would be the 7th overall pick in the N.F.L draft in 2000. Georgia Tech's quarterback, Joe Hamilton, finished second in the Heisman Trophy race the next month in New York City.

Back home in Austin, about three weeks later, the doorbell rang. I opened it to see a FedEx delivery driver standing there with a large package under his arm. I signed for it, carried it inside and with Peggy's help, began to open the cardboard box. Inside was a beautiful, framed picture of the Blue Angels flying over the Golden Gate Bridge in San Francisco. And it was personally signed by each of the pilots just below a message written in calligraphy that said, "To Savannah, our Blue Angel". God bless America.

Chapter 35: One of each.

At this point I had been an independent commercial real estate guy for almost six years. I was meeting a lot of people and gaining a lot of traction in the office leasing market, focusing mostly on representing office tenants who were either renewing their lease or moving to newer, nicer, or larger offices. One day the phone rang, and it was Jerry Lumsden from CBRE. Jerry told me he was moving out of management and into straight-commissioned brokerage. Would I like to come join him as a two-man team and work for CB? I knew Jerry well; he was an outgoing and very likeable guy who, over the last 15 years running the Austin office of CBRE, had gotten to know pretty much every business heavyweight in town. CBRE has a vast, national (and even international) network of offices and a very strong brand platform in the industry. Since I knew almost all the brokers in that office, I jumped at the chance to be a part of that group, and quickly made the move.

Valentines was coming up and Savannah was almost nine months old. Peggy had a long layover in Boston for the holiday and asked me to come with her "We can get a babysitter at the hotel, the Copley Plaza, and go have a nice romantic dinner for Valentines" she said. She had checked the passenger loads of the flight going out and coming back and knew we could get on the plane as non-revs. I thought it sounded like a lot of fun, but I wanted to surprise her, so I told her I didn't want to do it. "It's just so much work flying with an infant, Peggy. You go enjoy yourself and we will see you when you get home". Imagine her surprise & delight when I walked up to her at her gate in Houston for the Boston flight with Savannah in a stroller.

We arrived at the Copley Plaza and checked into our room; since she was on a layover United Airlines paid for it, so we were able to really splurge on dinner. I had called ahead and arranged for a babysitter and when she arrived, we were pleased to learn that her son also worked for United. Off we went to dinner which was a short walk away; since it was early February it was pretty cold, and we bundled up against the winter wind. We had some very nice wine with our dinner and then walked back to the hotel. We went up to check on Savannah and the sitter said the baby was sound asleep and all was well. The sitter assured us she & Savannah were fine, so we went back down to the lobby bar for a couple more glasses of wine. When we returned both of us were in a festive, loving mood and Valentine's had set the appropriate mood. I reminded peggy that I had not brought any "protection" as we grew amorous and she almost laughed: "I haven't had a period in 18 months, there's no way I can get pregnant right now" she said. Well, she was wrong and about a month later she broke the news to me over dinner after work one day. "Are you sure?" I asked. "Yes, she said. I did a home pregnancy test, and it was positive. And, she continued, I can just feel my body already changing."

My male instincts immediately kicked in and I realized that my small townhouse was not going to be big enough for a family of four, so Peggy & I talked about selling it and moving to a more traditional neighborhood and a larger home. The problem was that this was early 2000, and the real estate market in Austin was very tight. Austin had become a beacon for "dot com" start-up companies and Wall Street was throwing hundreds of millions of dollars at them. If you had a new idea for a company to start a web site and grow rapidly, then money to finance it was easy. And Austin was a mecca for it. We listed my house with an agent and started driving neighborhoods looking for a "for sale" sign in the yard. Finally, as we drove through the Great Hills neighborhood (so named for the rolling hills in northwest Austin) we saw a nice home on the corner for sale. And we bought it. In fact, we celebrated Savannah's 1st birthday there in May of 2000 right after we moved in.

It was a nice home with good neighbors, and we settled in with much more room and amenities than we had back in my former "bachelor pad". Peggy was still flying, and Savannah & I shared many wonderful weekends as father & daughter with me managing her feeding & nap schedule. Mom & Dad helped us enroll her in pre-school at Good Shepherd Episcopal School where she made some very good friends. Naturally, she was invited to many birthday parties for her classmates so I would bundle her up, grab the gift Peggy had bought & wrapped before she went off on her weekend trip, and take her to the gathering of young children. Most of the time I was the only Dad there, but that was fine with me. The other Moms were very nice and even gave me some advice about parenting. I think they thought it was kind of refreshing to have a man there that they could talk to!

Peggy was going to fly until about three months before our second child was born. I was glad to have the extra income since the office real estate market had taken a big dive once the stock market finally realized that all of these darling high-tech start-ups were just a big idea and had no real prospects of ever making a profit. What was once a high flying, throwing money at anything related to a company with a new idea to capitalize on the burgeoning "tech boom" had become a bust. The stock market dropped dramatically and so did the real estate market. It was a tough time to be a commercial real estate jock – especially with a baby on the way. But we were positive and upbeat and sure we would be just fine – I was still doing ok in office leasing (and had a nice nest egg under me from the sale of my town house).

Peggy & I agreed that we did not want to know the gender of our second child (like we had with Savannah), so we told the doctors that's what we wanted. Peggy's OB/Gyn again was Marty, and we liked her very much. Marty told us she wanted to schedule a delivery for November 5th if Peggy didn't go into natural labor before that – that sounded like a good idea to us because we could plan ahead for someone to care for Savannah and help around the house for a few days. Sure enough, November 4th arrived, and Peggy wasn't showing any signs of delivery. So, the morning of November 5th we handed Savannah to our neighbor, Janice Norment, and headed to St. David's hospital. Shelley jumped in the car to drive up and help Janice at our house. Mom and Dad came with Shelley and drove to the hospital to be with Peggy & me. It was very similar to the first delivery: Marty broke Peggy's water and we waited for things to progress. Peggy had agreed to have Dad in the delivery room, and I was very glad. I was pretty sure we were having a boy and I thought it would be very cool for Dad to see his grandson born into the world; we told the nurses to station him over to the side and away from "home plate", and he was fine with that. Mom, on the other hand, stayed closer and provided loving care & support to me & Peggy.   (Since Peggy's folks lived in California, they had decided they would wait until the baby was born and come for a good visit in a few weeks.)

After consulting with Marty, we again agreed to start a Pitocin drop into Peggy's I.V. to get her contractions and dilation started. Just like with Savannah, once the medicine kicked in Peggy started having pretty severe labor pains. Mom & I were there holding her hand and dabbing her head with a warm washcloth; I was doing my best to be loving & supportive, and Mom was so wonderful; she knew just the right things to say to Peggy and could obviously relate to this much more personally than I could. Dad, on the other hand, was not ok seeing Peggy in such severe pain. He has such a huge heart and just cannot handle seeing anyone hurting, either emotionally or physically. And this was just more than he could take; I could tell he was ready to bolt for the door. Since I had seen this before, I was more at ease about it. I knew it was going to be ok and could see the beauty in the process, even though it hurt me to see Peggy fight through the contractions. "Dad, this is just a part of it" I told him. "Just believe in the process; Peggy is going to be ok and will probably get an epidural in an hour or so and that will ease her pain." When Dad realized he was going to have to watch this for an hour he knew he just couldn't; he excused himself down the hall to the waiting room.

After several hours of labor, Marty came in and Peggy started pushing. And pushing. And then more pushing. It was clear that our son (we would meet him very soon) was just not going to come out on his own. "Peggy, I think we need to do a caesarian" Marty said. I know Marty was trying to avoid it, but it was time, so they put me in a gown & mask, and we wheeled Peggy down the hall to O.R. I was told to wait in the hall as they got Peggy all prepared for the surgery; she would be numb from the waist down but totally awake and aware the whole time. I was excited to meet our new baby and learn its gender! It had been a long day, but our spirits were good. When I was allowed into O.R. Peggy was lying on the "gurney" with her head towards me and her feet pointed away from us. There was a "partition" placed right over her belly button so that neither she nor I could see what was going on on the other side. After a few minutes and lots of commotion, Marty lifted the baby up and exclaimed "it's a boy!".

Instinct kicked in – I wanted to see my SON! So, I stood up to get a look at this strapping newborn baby boy. Which meant I could see over the partition. Immediately I felt a very strong hand on my shoulder pushing me back down to my chair next to Peggy. Welcome to the world Marshall Staton Cocke. Like Savannah, he was pretty exhausted from the labor and didn't make much noise, but after a minute or two he also belted out a good cry and kicked his limbs into action. Ten toes and ten fingers – all good, I thought. It would take a little while for them to wheel us back to our room and bring Marshall to us, but he was every bit as beautiful as his sister. Wow, I thought we have one of each and both are healthy and strong. Very freaking cool.

Chapter 36: M.V.P.

Peggy would have a year of maternity leave this time and we settled into a regular routine. The holidays slipped by and then Spring arrived. I was working diligently at CBRE, and we were enjoying the Great Hills neighborhood and people there.

Since Jerry Lumsden had moved out of officially managing the Austin office, a new manager was brought in from the Houston CBRE office. Jerry Frey was a seasoned veteran of commercial real estate, knew all the upper management of the company well and was a U.T. graduate. We hit it off immediately. One day in the Spring of 2001, Jerry called me into his office. "Cinco" he asked, "do you know what CB 102 is?" I knew that the company did a lot of on-going training for its mid-level and even senior brokers and managers, and I had heard a little about CB 102, but I didn't know too much about it. Jerry went on to explain that it was an intensive, one-week training class (it started on Sunday afternoon and ended the next Saturday) held several times a year at the U.C.L.A. conference center at Lake Arrowhead, California. CBRE's headquarters were in Los Angeles and the guy who ran all their training, John Ollen, was a U.C.L.A. graduate, so that location was a natural fit. In fact, the only person from U.C.L.A. to ever win college football's Heisman trophy was a guy named Gary Beban, who played QB for them back in 1967. (He beat out O.J. Simpson that year; O.J. would win it the next year, 1968.) Gary worked for CBRE in L.A., and I had met him once or twice – he was a solid real estate executive and a heck of a nice guy.

So, I flew out to Orange County airport in Southern California and caught the shuttle for the one-hour drive up to Lake Arrowhead. The conference center is surrounded by tall, green pine trees with a view of the glimmering lake not far away. The setting was very nice and would be our home for the next six days; we started at breakfast, broke for lunch and dinner and our final training session was after dinner. It was intensive, exciting, and very rewarding. The topics ranged from negotiations to marketing and time management; most of the speakers and instructors were from outside CBRE and they were good. One topic on the agenda was Personal Financial Planning; I was anxious to hear what they covered because it was something that Dad had imparted to me since I first started working at the company and earning a regular paycheck. To my surprise, John Ollen taught it. And it flopped. As he struggled through the 60-minute presentation my disappointment grew; and I developed a keen appreciation for how hard he was trying. It was just not good content or delivery.

The week progressed and I developed some very good friends. There were a lot of "small group" breakouts and short presentations (which we wrote on the spot) to our entire class, which consisted of about fifty people from around the country. Some of the senior management people came up from the L.A. headquarters to give brief talks about the short- & long-term goals for the company. I was really feeling the energy and threw myself into every assignment and every conversation with the instructors. If the idea was to lead and inspire this group, then it certainly worked on me. Ollen had nailed it, as far as I was concerned, except for that one part he taught a few days before. Saturday arrived and we had one short session after breakfast that morning, after which everyone went back to our rooms to pack and then reconvene for lunch. During that final session, Ollen announced that our class would be voting for the "Most Valuable Participant" from the week. He did not have a vote, he told us. It was to be chosen from our classmates by our classmates and he would announce it at lunch before we all departed for home.

As we gathered for lunch and made our way through the buffet line, I grabbed a plate and looked for a place to sit. Ollen had an empty chair next to him and motioned for me to join him. I had gotten to know John well that week and felt a common bond with him. He is a dynamic fellow and a strong leader. So, I took my place next to him as the tables filled up. After everyone was seated John stood up and made some closing remarks. There were lots of "thank yous" to him for this great week and some scattered applause at his comments. He concluded by announcing that the most valuable participant in this session of CB102 was "Cinco Cocke". I was floored. John stuck out his hand and I stood up to shake it; he then gave me a warm hug and the group offered their applauding congratulations. I couldn't believe it. Me? I'm the most valuable participant?? Wow, I thought, this feels great to be recognized by these people this way. I knew Jerry Frey would be happy for me and proud that I represented the Austin office so well. I felt a bolt of confidence in that Moment and was grateful to my classmates for their recognition.

I sat back down, and John gave me a hearty "well done" and a pat on the back. He then asked me to critique the week, especially the topics and instructors. "John", I told him, "This week has been great. All of the topics were very useful and interesting. The instructors were all really good". "Yeah, ok" he replied, "but if you could change one thing here what would it be?" Ollen is a former Marine and still carried a little of the intense, Drill Sargent air about him. I was very hesitant to say anything negative and apparently, he sensed it. "Come on, Cinco" he pushed, "surely you have an idea for improving the class". So, I pushed my plate back, took a sip of my tea and told him I thought the personal financial planning segment was weak. To my surprise, he said "I know, damn it, it needs some improvement. What are your ideas?" I told John he should talk about basic topics, like having a budget, saving for college, saving for retirement and making sure everyone had a current Will. I told him "Most people don't have the foggiest clue about the power of compounded investment growth, John, and they should". He perked up instantly and asked me if I could e mail him a summary of my ideas when I got back to Austin. "Sure, John, I would be happy to" I told him, and we stood up to make our way out to the waiting shuttles for the trip down the mountain to the Orange County airport.

Peggy and the kids were waiting for me at her folk's house in Rocklin, CA, just outside of Sacramento, where they had lived for several years; she had flown there with the kids a few days earlier and I was going to join them for a couple of nights before we all flew back to Texas. As my flight landed, I was still sky high from the week in Lake Arrowhead and the surprise of being voted M.V.P. of the class. But when I walked to the curb where Peggy and the kids were waiting for me in a rental car, her mood was pretty crummy. My thoughts of filling her with all the wonderfully positive things that had happened to me the last six days flew out the proverbial window.

Peggy's folks, Bill & Mary, were nice people. They had worked hard and had good Midwestern values, as best I could tell. I usually enjoyed our time together though I could sense it always seemed to give Peggy angst. She had told me before how she felt like they had favored her three siblings over her growing up; she described her Mom as pretty emotionally distant. The more I observed it, the more I understood why she always needed a few days to "decompress" after visiting them. It was a regular thing that she would be in tears as we drove away from their house and headed home after another weekend visit. I guess the feelings of abandonment came flooding back to her; she would almost always say "I don't think my parents love me, because they have never said it". She told me that once in high school, she and her Mom had a fight, and she hid in the park across the street from their house all night. The next morning, she waited for her Mom & Dad to leave for work, dashed in for a quick shower and then made it off to school just in time. That night, when everyone was back home, her Mom never mentioned Peggy's absence the night before. When it was time for dinner, Peggy's usual place at the table was not set like everyone else's was. I guess that's how Mary decided to "handle" it but the clear message to Peggy was "you don't exist".

It broke my heart to hear that from her but after being around their interactions several times, I could see why she felt that way. Well, apparently, she was back in that emotional place, because I got an ear full of it from Peggy in the car. She had been staying with her parents, but we had decided to get a hotel room once I arrived. Marshall was six months old, and Savannah had just turned two, so traveling with them was tough even under the best of conditions. We thought some privacy and "only us" time for the four of us would be a good thing; turns out we were right. Peggy regaled me with all the subtle and not-so-subtle things that her parents had done to hurt her feelings the last few days. She said that when she gathered all of the kid's things (including diaper bags, car seats and the pack-and play) she expected her folks to offer some help. But they didn't, and it really upset her. She had to carry all the gear to the car by herself, schlep it over to the hotel, get checked in and then carry it (and the kids) into our room. Why her parents didn't see her need and offer to lighten the load, she had no idea. And neither did I, except it was sort of "par for the course" for them to tune her out like that. Especially her mother.

A couple of years later Bill would have a heart attack and was admitted to a hospital in San Francisco waiting on a transplant. We made plans to fly out with the kids (now maybe three & five years old) for Christmas. Mary had spent a lot of time in the bay area holding vigils for Bill and had gotten to know the hospital staff well. As we were settling into their house in Rocklin, Mary told us she was headed to San Francisco the next day and proceeded to make a huge batch of her homemade cinnamon rolls for Bill's nurses. I heard about these Christmas treats and was anxious to try them; I knew the kids would be, too, as we watched her painstakingly roll out the dough and add all the scratch ingredients, measuring each one with great precision. The wonderful smell of them baking in the oven made my mouth water.

The next morning, when I strolled into the kitchen to get a cup of coffee, Mary was gone.   And so were all the cinnamon rolls; not even one from a batch of two dozen was left for us.   I was shocked at her lack of thoughtfulness to us, but decided not to say anything about it; I figured she had a lot on her mind but still, "you couldn't leave just TWO cinnamon rolls for your grandchildren?" I thought to myself. Later that morning, as we took a day drive up to Lake Tahoe so the kids could play in the snow, Peggy got very teary. "Can you believe Mom took ALL the cinnamon rolls to San Francisco and didn't leave ANY for us?" she asked as she dabbed her tears.   I admitted it was very thoughtless; "well", Peggy said, "that's Mary for ya".   (She always called her "Mary"; she never referred to her as "Mom").   And it wasn't the last time Mary would let Peggy down like that.   Soon, it would be an issue for Peggy & me since my folks were so loving and so overly thoughtful, frequently inviting us on nice trips and sending generous gifts to her & the kids.   I could tell it created an emotional tug-of-war for Peggy to accept my parents' generosity when hers were so emotionally absent.

It wasn't the only source of trouble between Peggy & me at that time.   Her emotional ups & downs could be pretty severe; when it was good it was really good but when it was bad it was awful.   For example, she would often refuse to go out to dinner with my friends at the last minute, even though we had accepted the invitation weeks before.   There were other examples, and she eventually saw a psychiatrist about her inability to control her impulses and her mood swings.   She tried medications of various types, but nothing seemed to help.   I bought some books and tried to educate myself on the issues she was dealing with and her lack of emotional self-control. I was pretty sure her issues were rooted in the feelings of abandonment and disregard from her mother, but I also knew there was no way I could fix it.   We got into marriage counseling and tried to work through it, but Peggy would routinely get defensive and eventually refuse to keep going. The mood swings could be pretty severe, and it was taking a toll on me; three years after that fateful trip to California I moved out and filed for divorce. It absolutely broke my heart to do that to the kids, but it was a bad situation; I decided it was better for them to not grow up like that and I knew I would have them every weekend, which I was already doing anyway with Peggy flying so often. She moved down to the Circle C area of Austin and about a year later asked me to give her some money as the down payment to buy a house. I consented quickly, knowing it was best for her & the kids to have a home of their own in a nice neighborhood full of children their age. Eventually, I sold my house in Great Hills and moved to Circle C to live near the kids.

Chapter 37: You want me to do what?

When I got back to the CBRE office in Austin from the 102 class and subsequent time in Rocklin, I knew I owed Ollen an e mail. So, I scratched out my thoughts for personal financial planning on a notepad, organized them by topic and composed my message to John. I was glad to help him and still feeling pretty good about my time at Lake Arrowhead. A few days later, Ollen called and said "hey, I really like the outline you put together. You think you could put a power point presentation together around this outline?" Now, I didn't know squat about power point and had certainly never even used it, but that wasn't about to stop me. "Sure, John" I said, "give me a few days and I'll have something in your inbox". Ollen sat two doors down from the current C.E.O. of CBRE, Brett White, so I was feeling excited about plugging into the company's senior management structure and for the opportunity to help John improve his presentation at CB 102. I found one of the support staff in the office who had really good PPT skills and together we assembled the slides and graphics. Once I gave it a "real time" run through, it took right at 55 minutes to read. "Perfect" I thought, "this is just what Ollen needs" and e mailed it to him.

I really forgot about it after that, immersing myself in my pipeline of office leasing clients and business development. Several days later the phone at my desk rang and when I looked at the name of the caller, it read "John Ollen". "Hey, Ollen" I said into the mouthpiece, "what's going on?" "Cinco", he said, "I just looked through the PPT you sent, and it is really good stuff. It's exactly what I need". I told him I was glad he liked it and hoped it would make for a great improvement to the 102 curricula. As I started to say "goodbye" and hang up, John stopped me. "Cinco, I want you to come out to Lake Arrowhead and start teaching this for the 102 classes. We do it once a quarter, so you'll be my guy to teach personal financial planning". I was caught by surprise but managed to stutter an "oh wow, John, that sounds great" even though I was having doubts about my ability to pull it off. Writing the PPT was one thing; standing in front of some of the more successful CBRE brokers & managers from around the country and actually TEACHING was a giant leap for me. The world voice was now speaking straight at me through John Ollen. Before I could protest, he asked "do you know Ron Evans from the Dallas office?". Ron was on a team with a senior guy named Hunter Blanks; Hunter and I worked together on the CBRE law firm practice group and I knew him well. I had met Ron several times and knew him to be a smart, energetic real estate guy with strong connections in the Dallas office market, so I told John "Yeah, I know Ron pretty well. Why?"

John proceeded to tell me that he had just hired Ron to come teach Advanced Marketing at CB102 and wanted us to travel out there together and share the podium during class. "I want you guys to meet in Southern California and spend the night in and around the city and then spend half a day meeting CBRE brokers in the various offices throughout the area." We were to drive up to Lake Arrowhead after lunch and then teach that afternoon, Ron going on before dinner and me wrapping up the day after dinner; we would spend the night there after class, meet the 102 attendees and then fly back to Texas the next day. "Submit your expense reports to me and the company will cover your costs" he said. John knew this would greatly expand my (and Ron's) contacts and sphere of influence within the company and boy was he ever right. Twice we were awarded the Benjamin Arthur Banker Award for Educational Excellence and were recognized by CBRE people all over the country at various company gatherings, large & small. I discovered that teaching came naturally to me and the reviews and comments from the class were really strong. I had found a new outlet for my love of real estate and hit my stride quickly. Thank you, John, for believing in me and giving me the chance to discover something about myself I never knew existed. Ron & I became very good friends from our travels together and frequently visited each other's homes & families for fun and special events.

Chapter 38: The world changes forever.

Before Marshall was born, we had enrolled Savannah into pre-school for two-year-olds at Good Shepherd Episcopal for a few hours each morning so she could get a jump on social skills and give Peggy some one-on-one time with Marshall. I would drop her off on my way to work and Peggy (with Marshall riding along) would pick her up at lunchtime. As the fall 2001 approached, Peggy started to make plans to return to flying with United. Both kids were healthy, strong and growing quickly. Life felt good and safe. My 41st birthday, September 17th, was only six days away and it would be my third as a father.

That morning felt like every other morning; Marshall would turn one in about two months, and Peggy helped me get Savannah into the car so I could drive her to day school. I was about 10 minutes from the house when Peggy called me on my cell phone. "Hey", she said, "a plane just flew into the World Trade Center in New York City". Like most people I thought it must be some weekend student pilot who was out getting his "solo hours" and got disoriented. It had happened to me a few times when I was taking flying lessons back in Tyler, so I told Peggy I was sure that must be what happened. "No, Cinco" she said, "this was a commercial airliner that had just flown out of Newark airport." My first thought was "no way"; but then as I recalled the many times Peggy & I had flown in & out of Newark as non-revs on her trips I knew she had her facts straight. "Oh my God" I said, "how could a seasoned commercial pilot for a major airline make that kind of mistake?" Just then, Peggy told me a second commercial jet had hit Tower 2 of the World Trade Center! This was clearly no mistake – something very bad was happening. Peggy stayed on the phone with me as I dropped Savannah off at Good Shepherd and drove on to CBRE's offices. When I walked into the conference room everyone was glued to the television watching live T.V. of the twin towers engulfed in flames. It was truly surreal; we could see people jumping out of windows eighty - ninety floors up to escape the flames and heat from inside the buildings there.

CBRE had several offices in Manhattan, and we all had friends there; fortunately, we did not have an office in the World Trade Center so our thoughts turned to the people in those two towers who must be trapped and had nowhere to go. The flames were growing, and the situation was becoming very desperate; fire & rescue teams were arriving in masse, and we were watching live as teams of brave fire fighters mobilized in the lobby to head upstairs to bring the trapped people down. Many had already started up the stairways of the two 100-story buildings to help people down to safety. And then, unthinkably, the first tower collapsed onto itself. A few minutes later, the second tower collapsed, too.

My cell phone rang, and it was Peggy; like everyone, she was very concerned. Then the news reported that another hijacked airliner had crashed into the Pentagon! As we watched people in Manhattan run from the enormous dust cloud covering the island from the collapsed twin towers the news reported that a commercial airliner had crashed in a field in rural Pennsylvania – the early reports were that several passengers had called their families reporting that the plane was hijacked and had made a 180 degree turn back from its route towards the west. They had no idea where the terrorists who were in control were going but the passengers were determined to stop them. So, they stormed the flight deck and attacked the two terrorists sitting in the pilot's and co-pilot's seats. With no one in control, the plane nose-dived straight into the ground near Shanksville, PA. killing everyone on board. Those passengers on United Flight 91 would be the first Americans to fight the war on terror.

What started out as a nice, clear blue morning had turned into shock and outright panic. Clearly, our country was under attack: but who were the attackers? Would planes soon hit other notable buildings around the country? Was Chicago at risk since the Sears (now Willis) & John Hancock Towers were there? What about Austin? Our President, George W. Bush, had been our Governor for several years – would the terrorists try to send a message by "bombing" our city with hi-jacked airliners? Fortunately, the F.A.A. declared that all airborne commercial jets had to make an immediate landing at the closest commercial airport. The flight grid of our country, except for Air Force One, was closed. It would be a week or so before another passenger plane took to the air.

I remember my parents talking about December 7, 1941, when Japan bombed Pearl Harbor; Mom was thirteen and Dad was eleven when we went to war in the Pacific. Their stories of shock, disbelief and then anger stuck with me over the years. This felt very close. I drove back to Good Shepherd and picked Savannah up at noon; then we headed home and watched the news until late in the day. The early reports were that a terrorist group of extreme Islamists who called themselves "al Qaida" had claimed responsibility. How could a bunch of radicals hijack 4 commercial airliners from major airports in the northeast, we all wondered. Soon, it became clear that our airport security systems were weak and needed to be overhauled. But how could these people who openly hated America be allowed into our country in the first place? And who sponsored this and financed it?

As the weeks unfolded and the facts surfaced, we learned that al Qaida was centered in Afghanistan and had the financial backing of a Saudi national named 'Osama Bin Laden". President Bush, supported by his national security advisors General Collin Powell and Condoleezza Rice (Secretary Rice would later become the first female member of the Augusta National Golf Club in Georgia which hosts the annual Masters Golf tournament) went on a major counter-offensive against al Qaida and its supporters. The government of Afghanistan had turned a blind eye on Bin Laden and his henchmen and allowed them to organize and operate within its borders. Bush and our military started a major bombing operation in the Hindu Kush designed to destroy al Qaida and make sure they could never orchestrate another attack on our country, or any other, like 9/11.

Eventually, President Bush would decide that another major threat to our safety and our allies was Saddam Hussein, the dictatorial military leader of Iraq. Iraq, at that time, had one of the largest and most well-armed militaries in the world and Hussein made no secret of his nuclear ambitions. Once he used seron gas (a deadly biological weapon) on the Kurdish population of northern Iraq, killing thousands of innocent civilians, Bush and his advisors concluded that Hussein was a real & imminent danger to our safety (he was clearly an enemy of America and Bin Laden had showed us what our enemies were capable of doing) as well as our allies. He clearly had a biological weapon a had used it; what else might he have in his arsenal that he could unleash? It was an outcome too scary to comprehend and the U.S. had the means to stop him before he killed more people, and God forbid, somehow attacked us like Bin Laden had. With the bi-lateral support of Congress, Bush sent troops and arms into Iraq to capture Hussein and eliminate his "weapons of mass destruction" like seron gas. Eventually, Hussein was captured and executed after a trial in front of the Iraqi judicial system. While no nuclear weapons were ever discovered, the world felt better knowing a despot like Hussein was no longer in control of a major military with clear nuclear and terroristic intentions.

Chapter 39: They all borrowing? Then Lend, Lend, Lend!

Have you ever heard of "Collateralized Mortgage-Backed Securities"? No? What if I referred to them the way the brilliant (I'm not being sarcastic) boys on Wall Street did, as "C.M.B.S."? No help, huh? What about "Collateralized Mortgage Obligations"? Ring any bells? Well, welcome to the year 2007. Nobody had ever heard of C.M.B.S. back then, but we were about to learn all about them.

Back in 1977, Congress passed the Community Reinvestment Act which pushed banks to lend more to poor neighborhoods. In 1989, the Financial Institutions Reform, Recovery, and Enforcement Act (FIRREA) strengthened the CRA by publicizing banks' lending records. It prohibited them from expanding if they didn't comply with CRA standards. In 1995, President Clinton, very appropriately I might add, wanted more people in our country to own a home. And why not? A family's home usually represents most of their total net worth and has always been considered a safe way to gain security and financial independence. So, Clinton called on regulators to strengthen the CRA even more.

Mortgage lenders now had a ton of incentives to lend to borrowers who had, until now, not really been credit worthy. Those mortgages were called "subprime" since the borrowers had shaky credit. To produce more mortgages and more securities, mortgage qualification guidelines became progressively looser. First, "stated income, verified assets" (SIVA) loans replaced proof of income with a "statement" of it. Then, "no income, verified assets" (NIVA) loans eliminated proof of employment requirements. Borrowers needed only to show proof of money in their bank accounts. "No Income, No Assets" (NINA) or Ninja loans eliminated the need to prove, or even to state any owned assets. All that was required for a mortgage was a credit score.

Most banks and mortgage companies who make home loans don't keep them on their books; instead, they package a portfolio of loans together (thus diversifying the miniscule risk involved) and sell them. Sometimes the U.S. Government buys them thru the Federal Home Loan Mortgage Corporation ("Freddie Mac") or the Federal National Mortgage Association ("Fannie Mae"). So, what these mortgage companies needed, given the weak credit of the borrowers, was a place to package and sell these new loans. The Wall Street firms like Goldman Sachs & Merrill Lynch knew there was no way they could peddle these loans to conventional buyers, so they decided to create an "investment vehicle" and basically hide these loans within them. That way, the loans looked good "on paper" but if you looked closer (and no one did) you could see some real flaws.

Adding to the potential problems with all these new loans was the fact that most had floating interest rates. The mortgage companies and banks knew that more borrowers could qualify for a home loan if the payments were lower. The easiest way to lower the payment (and thus qualify more borrowers) was to artificially lower the interest rate. So, they did. But, after only a year or two, the interest rate on those loans "adjusted" to current market rates, or even higher. Which meant a big jump in the rate, and consequently, a big increase in the monthly payment. That was all clearly spelled out in the mortgage loan documents (insert universal laughter here) if these borrowers happened to actually read the damn loan documents. Which none of them did. All they cared about was they were first-time homeowners and a new member of the American Dream. With all this money available to homebuyers, home prices increased steadily until 2006. But then the Federal Reserve started raising interest rates to cool the market off.

Unbeknownst to these subprime borrowers, the loan they had

signed with the mortgage company wouldn't stay there very long. Their floating-rate loan, with all its flaws, was packaged with many others into an investment security "collateralized by mortgages". Hence the acronym "C.M.B.S." Goldman & Merrill & Lehman Brothers, among other Wall Street firms, peddled these products to all the big companies who had a lot of cash, like insurance companies and other investment banks. It got so hot that the commercial banks, like Bank of America and Citibank and Chase couldn't resist buying, too. (A.I.G. was a huge player in the market, too.) They were making mortgage loans in their branches, turning them over to Goldman et al who then packaged them with lots of other mortgages, and bought them back from Goldman! Or Lehman Brothers or Merrill Lynch or any of the other Wall Street firms who got in on the party. Sometimes, Goldman and the other brokerage houses would keep some CMBS for themselves. The fees from this and the profits made were obscene. In 2006 alone it was estimated that banks & other financial institutions made $600 Billion in subprime loans! Sorta reminds you of the L.B.O frenzy of the 1980s, doesn't it? They made a movie about this one, too, called "The Big Short" starring Brad Pitt, Christian Bale, Steve Carell & Ryan Gosling.

Anyway, everything was going ok until these borrowers, some who had bought multiple houses since the loans were so easy to get, started seeing their monthly payments go up. A lot. What was happening, they wondered. When they called the bank, they were reminded that the loan(s) they signed had an adjustable interest rate; most of these people didn't even know what that meant. What they did know was that they couldn't afford the new monthly payment. And the defaults on these mortgages started growing quickly and home prices tumbled. And, since they were the "collateral" for the C.M.B.S. investments held by all these financial institutions, the value of the C.M.B.S. holdings plummeted. It was the biggest financial disaster in our country since the Great Depression. Some economic experts thought it might eventually be worse. Total worldwide losses totaled in the Trillions of dollars for commercial banks, hedge funds & investment banks. The U.S. government bailed out the larger firms with capital infusions, at tremendous expense to taxpayers, and simply allowed others to fail.

By March of 2008, the debt & equity markets in the U.S. were in a literal freefall; the perfect time to start a development and construction business, right?

Chapter 40: Royale with Cheese

My cell phone rang and when I looked down the caller id said "Ron Evans". Ron had left CBRE for a marketing position with a general contractor in Dallas, but we remained good friends and talked often. I hit the "accept" button on my iPhone and said "hey, what's up?". Ron told me he was sitting in the Starbucks parking lot on Preston Rd in Plano and had just had coffee with a guy named Jerry Huffman. "Jerry is a neighbor of mine" Ron told me "and he is a successful developer here in the north Dallas area. I think you guys should meet". Ron went on to tell me that Jerry explained his business model, which was to build offices, usually through a condominium structure, for doctors and business owners. I had heard a little bit about office condos and most of it was not great: lots of developers had thrown up speculative buildings and saw them fail.   When I mentioned this to Ron he said, "that's the beauty of Jerry's model: he doesn't even buy the dirt until he has a project at least 50% pre-sold". Hmmm, I thought, that does sound a lot safer and less speculative. Ron went on to tell me that Jerry had operations in San Antonio and Denton, TX and was so busy he was turning down work in Austin. Since he acted as his own general contractor, there was immediate cash flow from the project; the trick was to price the offices with enough mark-up to make a profit. And by all appearances, Jerry was doing very well. "I mentioned you to Jerry and told him that you would be a great guy to open a Huffman office in Austin" Ron told me. "When can you get up here?"

We scheduled a meeting in Jerry's office, a beautiful two-story brick and stone building on Plano Parkway he had developed several years before. Jerry was a very likeable, low-key guy. He had built many office parks around north Dallas over the past 25 years and had the system down. "We find good sites and pair them with doctors and professionals who want to own their offices and not lease them" Jerry explained. "Starting out, our banks wanted us to have our projects at least 50% pre-sold to provide the financing to buy the site and develop the project" he continued. "So, that is still the model". He explained that it took some time to get to that level of pre-sales, which meant the seller of the land site had to be willing to grant a four-to-six-month feasibility period in the contract. "Some will do that, and others won't" Jerry said. "But we have been able to find enough sellers who will work with us that it has been successful". "How do you find the buyers?" I asked. Jerry explained that they do a ton of "cold calling"; literally, he told us, "We just walk into their offices and ask if the doctor has ever talked about owning his or her own office. Ninety percent of the time the answer is yes" he said. Since we would be a true start-up, I knew that marketing, especially early on, was going to be very crucial. Jerry suggested we sign a License Agreement with him so we could use the Huffman branding and, once we got a project going, we could call him anytime a question came up. (And plenty of them did.) We would pay him a royalty of each office sold and share in the cost of the many trade shows he attended around the state.

It sounded like a really good opportunity; about a year before, Jerry had set up another new Huffman operation in Denton, TX with a guy named Bill Pantuso. Bill had a solid background in business operations and paired up with a girl named Dee Dee Hunt whom he knew from his most recent company. So, Ron and I went to see Bill & Dee Dee and asked a lot of questions. They were about halfway into their first project and confirmed that everything Jerry had told them was true. Bill also confirmed that cold calling was the best way to find leads. Ron was as excited as I was, and we talked about being partners in this new endeavor. Ron is a master at business development and I'm pretty good, too. But I knew that once we got going, I would be the one to handle documents, finances & legal issues. In other words, Ron would sell the tickets and I would make sure the trains ran on time. It was a really good combination of strengths and experience. We signed the license agreement and leased a small executive suite near the Arboretum in Austin. Ron pitched the whole idea to his wife, and they agreed to move to Austin as soon as the school year ended.   We were off and running.

We met with a local attorney to set up our company and file the appropriate documents with the I.R.S. and Secretary of State. "What is the name of this new endeavor?" he asked. Hmmm, Ron & I hadn't even discussed it. "Well," he said, "give me something creative so that we can be pretty sure the name isn't already taken. That saves me a lot of time not having to make multiple calls to finally find a name available". Ron & I walked out to the car, and while we were driving back to our tiny little executive suite, he had an idea. We were both big movie fans and often quoted our favorite lines from our favorite movies to each other. One of our favorites was a line from the Quintin Tarantino movie *Pulp Fiction,* where John Travolta is explaining to Samuel L. Jackson why the McDonalds in Paris doesn't have a Quarter Pounder. "They have the metric system over there, so no one would know what a 'pound' means" Travolta says. Jackson asks, "what do they call it, then?" and Travolta says "they call it a Royale With Cheese". Jackson is very amused and keeps repeating the words. So, Ron & I decided to name our new venture "Royale with Cheese"; over the ensuing years we would get a lot of laughs, and even some confused stares from bankers, when we would explain the origin of our company's name. Eventually, we would organize many new limited liability companies as our operations grew and we started new development projects, using names like *Charlie Don't Surf, The Sheriff Is Near, Fightin' in A Basement* (a line from another great Tarantino movie) and *Tabloid Conjecture.*

Chapter 41: What have we done?

In addition to cold calling doctors & professionals, Jerry suggested we meet with bankers around town since they often had bank customers who fit our buyer profile. It was the summer of 2008, and the financial news was terrible. I recall one banker we met with, a guy I had known for several years, looked very tired and haggard. "Guys" he told us, "I like your model. It makes a lot of sense. But the FDIC has told us we cannot, under any circumstances, make any construction loans". I was almost stunned. "What do you mean?" I asked, still trying to absorb this news. What if all the banks told us that? I wondered. We would be screwed if we couldn't get financing for our development projects! "The bank regulators have clamped down on us, even though all our construction loans have performed, and we have had no write-offs. Even if you guys could secure the loan with a C.D. in our bank, I can't do it" he told us. On the car ride back to our offices I was disconsolate. This was really discouraging; both Ron & I left pretty lucrative and successful jobs to start this up, and I was wondering if we had made a mistake. There was no way we were going to give up; we just had to keep plugging and find a financing source for our first project, still not sure what that would be or where we might find it.

We were burning through our savings and needed to take a regular paycheck to support our households. I was still single but had two young children to support and other bills to pay. Ron's wife had a good job teaching, but they had three sons and household overhead to cover like me. So, Ron approached his parents about a start-up loan, and I called Dad. Fortunately, both agreed to kick in some money which bought us some precious time. We lived like hermits and didn't spend a dime if we could avoid it. We found one site we liked on Parmer Lane in Round Rock and negotiated a contract on it; now, we needed to order & install a sign on it advertising "medical offices coming soon". The sign company fabricated the sign and it looked great; the only problem was they wanted $50 to install it. Ron & I agreed that was ridiculous, so we bought a posthole digger at the hardware store and drove the sign over to our site. We were forgetting that it hadn't rained in several months and the ground there was as hard as concrete. We wore ourselves out for about an hour and had only dug down about six inches. And it was hot as hell. Finally, we looked at each other and said, almost simultaneously, "let's pay the sign company $50 to install this thing!" We would laugh about that story for years to come.

We continued to make cold calls and go to every real estate networking function we could think of. Like the banks, everyone liked the model and promised to give us a call if they knew anyone who wanted to own their own office. Early in 2009, the phone rang. It was a financial advisor who had a young dentist as a client. The dentist, Dr. Gentry, owned about three-quarters of an acre in Pflugerville and wanted to put her new clinic there. She had tried to put it all together herself but realized that her scope of knowledge in real estate development was weak. "Could we help?" the financial advisor asked. After a brief conversation, followed by an introductory meeting with Gentry, we learned that she only needed about 3,000 square feet, and her site could accommodate 7,500 square feet. So, we proposed that we buy the site from her (that took a little convincing, but Ron walked her through it in his smooth and solid way) and develop a 7,500 square foot building. Eventually, we found a dermatologist, Dr. Ted Lain, down the street who wanted 3,000 square feet and signed a contract with him to buy it from us once it was built. Ron & I would take the remaining 1,500 square feet for our offices. We were 100% pre-sold on our first project! Now, we needed to find a bank to finance it.

First Texas Bank in Round Rock was run by two savvy, conservative bankers named John Sloan and Landy Warren. I was introduced to Landy by a mutual contact, and we set an appointment with him. We briefly met John (later we would learn that he had earned the nickname "no loan Sloan") and gathered in Landy's office. We needed a loan to buy the land from Dr. Gentry, do the sitework and build the building; all in all, we were asking for $1,000,000. Even though we had never built anything before, we had Jerry Huffman as a resource, and he had vetted our loan request. "Everything looks fine" Jerry said, "good luck on your meeting". So, we laid the whole thing out for Landy, showed him our contracts with the two doctors and went over our development proforma. After about an hour, Landy said "I think we can do this loan for you guys". I was thrilled and it was the beginning of a good banking relationship that lasted for several years. Landy pitched it to the loan committee later that week (we found out later that the loan committee was basically him & John Sloan) and we had our first project financed. Jerry introduced us to a good construction project manager he had used before, and we were soon under construction.

The project was completed on time, even though we had a bear from the city who did all the inspections and caused our poor project manager, Mark, all kinds of heartburn. It became a running joke that Mark would be fighting mad for several hours after each inspection. It got so bad that we called the city manager and shared some of the issues we were having. I didn't expect any results but apparently, we weren't the first people to complain about this guy, because the city manager asked us to meet with him and walk him though the ridiculous things this guy was making us do. Eventually, they reassigned him, and we had another inspector on the job. Things went smoothly from there and both Dr. Gentry & Dr. Lain were very happy with their offices. Ron & I moved into ours and hired a part-time assistant to help us. We already had our second project in the planning stages: a two-building project in Round Rock each about 6,500 square feet. First Texas Bank did the loan on that one, too.

Chapter 42: Admit what you don't know.

The first building in Round Rock was under contract to a pair of Nigerian women, Rosemary & Cecilia, who co-owned and ran a successful home health care business called "Apicon"; they wanted to move out of leased space and own their office, so we designed and built it for them. The second building would have three offices (each an office condo) owned by a financial planner, a residential real estate company and an investor who leased his space to a hair salon. Quite an eclectic mix of owner-occupants, to say the least. Since almost 50% of the project was being built for Apicon, First Texas needed more security on this loan than the first. And we understood why they felt that way: half the proceeds to repay the construction loan was tied to Apicon, so the bank wanted them tied, in some way, to the loan. We got the owners of Apicon to agree to guarantee a portion of our loan with the bank; after all, this was a pure build-to-suit project suiting their floor plan and finish-out selections. We closed on the construction loan, built the building and everything was going smoothly. We did not hire a project manager for this one: I told Ron I thought I could handle it and he agreed.

Turns out, I was wrong. We stubbed our toe on several issues and the job of managing the construction while also running the day-to-day operations of our business was more than I could handle effectively. We were already putting our next development together, which also consumed a lot of time. The stress of it all was taking a toll. I did not, at that time, have good stress-management skills. I was more of a bull in the china closet and was letting every problem, big and small, raise my ire and blood pressure. Ron talked me off the ledge several times and did a good job of refocusing me on the bigger picture. It took a little time, but eventually I was able to do a better job and handling the stress and frustrations that come from running a company and wrapping up the construction of these two buildings.

And then, about six weeks before we were ready to finish both buildings, I got a call from Apicon's broker, a very nice Nigerian fellow named Jacob Iloka. Jacob stood to make a nice commission once the city issued a Certificate of Occupancy on the building, meaning we had passed all final inspections and the owners could close on the purchase and take occupancy. "Cinco" Jacob said, "the owners of Apicon have decided they don't want to buy this building. They are just going to renew their lease where they are now. How do they get their deposit back?". I was floored. After catching my breath and practicing some stress-management techniques Ron had taught me, I was able to respond. "Jacob, what's going on here?" I asked. He then told me that the two owners, Cecilia & Rosemary, were having some internal "struggles" and their business plans were "changing". Could we just refund their deposit (roughly $100,000 which we had applied to their design costs, per the contract we had with them) and move on? Jacob asked.

I would soon learn that Cecilia and Rosemary were having more than a few "struggles"; apparently, they were having a serious disagreement about how to run their business and were no longer operating as partners. I explained to Jacob that he and his clients needed to re-read the contract: "the deposit is non-refundable at this point" I reminded him. "And" I continued, "they have co-signed our construction loan, so the only way out of this for them is to buy the building and then re-sell it". Otherwise, the bank would call their guaranty and they would be in a serious bind. And we would too, since our contract price with them was right at $1.75 million and we needed that badly to pay down our development note with First Texas Bank. It was time to call Landy and let him know we had a potential problem on our hands.

Landy was a cool, level-headed guy with a ton of banking experience. I laid it all out for him and he agreed that the best, easiest resolution was for Apicon to buy the building and then either occupy or sell it. But I wasn't sure Apicon would do either. "You want me to call Cecilia and talk her through the options?" Landy asked. I thought that was a good idea and told him to give it a try. Several weeks went by and we were days away from a Certificate of Occupancy and a closing with Apicon; at least, that's what we hoped for. Apparently, Cecilia and Rosemary were going to split up and Cecilia was going to buy her out of the company. Cecilia still wanted out of the contract we had with them but soon realized that was not possible. To her credit, she applied for a loan with First Texas to buy the building without Rosemary and they approved her. That meant the contract had to be assigned from Apicon to an LLC owned solely by Cecilia, which also meant Rosemary had to approve it. Ultimately, Rosemary agreed, and we executed a contract transfer to Cecilia's company. It took several months to get it all worked out, which meant Ron & I had to absorb the interest expense on our development note, but Cecilia did buy the building and the closing went off smoothly. I give Cecilia a lot of credit for stepping up and doing the right thing. We are good friends to this day. (Sidebar: We did not have a clause in our contract with Apicon that triggered penalties or damages if they caused a delay in closing, but we soon wrote one and it was in every contract we ever executed after that. Lesson learned.)

With all the problems we faced on the second project, and with the pipeline filling up, we soon decided that we needed to find a seasoned construction guy who could oversee our day-to-day contracting projects so Ron could focus on biz dev, and I could handle overall operations. After asking around, we found a savvy guy, a Texas A & M grad who was born in Lebanon, named Charbel Dahdah. He and his family had immigrated to the U.S. when he was about six years old and eventually settled in Alvin, TX. just south of Houston. Charbel was working for a regional general contracting company in Austin but yearned to own a piece of the company for himself, which is what we offered him. He onboarded quickly and really improved our construction operations. On his first anniversary with us, we kept our promise when we hired him and gave him 20% of the general contracting business (that created some income tax he had to pay but he was cool with that). Additionally, he was a 20% partner in every development project we did going forward. It was a good fit and our general contracting revenues (we were doing a good bit of work for third parties in addition to our own development projects) soon hit $20 million annually. In 2017 we were named by the Austin Business Journal as one of the *Fifty Fastest Growing Companies in Austin.*

Chapter 43: If I could turn back time.

Burleson, Texas is a quiet town of about 50,000 people roughly forty-five minutes south of Fort Worth. I had never heard of the place until 1977 when some Harlingen friends of Mom & Dad's called to tell me their niece "Shelly" was visiting for the week, and would I like to have dinner with them? "Sure" I said. I wasn't dating anyone at the time, and I enjoyed Jim and Betty Cason's company. I figured their niece must be a pretty "cool chick" (it was 1977, remember?). Anyway, they dropped by the house to pick me up and we went to Arturo's restaurant in Nuevo Progresso, a tiny little outpost across the Rio Grande River about twenty-five minutes from our house on Bass Blvd. We had a delightful time and I really enjoyed Shelly's company. Over the next week we saw each other several times and by the time she left to fly back home we were almost inseparable. Talk about a summertime crush! Man, I was smitten, and I sensed that Shelly was, too. So, as soon as I could, I dashed a letter off to her and mailed it to Burleson. And waited for a response. Which never came. I was very disappointed.

Shelly was a year older than me and about to enter her senior year of high school. She was a very serious student and would graduate second in her high school class. Texas Tech offered her a full scholarship and she jumped on it. Good things happen to good people, and she deserved it. But bad things happen to good people, too. During Shelly's freshman year at Texas Tech her Mom, Janie Cason Southall, was in a bad car wreck and was a quadriplegic the rest of her life. I remember being in Fort Worth for a Key Club event and going with Shelly to see her Mom about two weeks after the accident. Shelly was then and has been ever since, eternally optimistic. Whatever pain or fear she must have been feeling, she never showed it. I had never actually met her Mom, so I was determined to be very positive and show a confident air. And then

I saw that Janie was in traction. Her head was held absolutely fixed by two pegs inserted into her temples; from there, a circular bar rounded over the top of her head which was connected to a long "chain" down over the top of the bed. At the end of the chain hung about four five-pound weights. They dangled in the air, and I could tell that they were preventing Janie from moving her head and neck in any possible way. My heart jumped as I saw it, but I was trying to be nice and kind to this lady I was meeting for the first time. I could only imagine how Shelly must be feeling. From that Moment on, I wanted to keep her close to my heart and be a solid, loving friend. And I have. And so has she.

The situation was even more difficult because Shelly had a younger brother, Cason, who was still home. Their father, John Southall, was an aspiring actor and a WWII pilot and suffered from severe P.T.S.D. and depression. Like Mom's first husband, Cmdr. Southall developed a drinking problem and had died of health issues before I met Shelly. So, she was the oldest child and the leader of the family. Especially now. A couple of years later, after they were able to get Janie home and had constant care for her, Shelly's younger brother, Michael, was killed in a car accident. Now we had another significant shared experience: the loss of a brother. I consoled Shelly as best I could.

Shelly's Dad had been married before to a very pretty lady named Georgia Sarkisian, an aspiring actress. Georgia had a very young daughter from her first marriage, a dark-haired girl named Cherilyn. Together, John & Georgia had another daughter, Cherilyn's half-sister, Georganne, and settled into John's modest home in Burleson. Early on, Cherilyn showed an interest in singing and acting, so Georgia enrolled her in voice classes and supported her desire to enter local talent shows. When Cherilyn was just nine, John & Georgia divorced, so Georgia moved the girls to Los Angeles so they all could pursue show business there. Later, when John married a lady named Janie Cason, they had three children together, Shelly & her two brothers. The three girls, Cherilyn, Georganne and Shelly remained close growing up despite the geographical distance between them. I heard Shelly talk of her sisters often and was happy for her that she maintained that relationship. It wasn't until we were in college that Shelly finally revealed to me that her half-sister Cherilyn, was Cher Bono.

Naturally, Shelly was very protective of this relationship and knew she could only share it with her most intimate & trusted friends. I respected Shelly and certainly wasn't going to spread this around; it was her relationship and she needed to check who knew about it. But over time Shelly shared some "Cher" stories with me that made me respect & admire Cher. Once Janie was able to move back home from the hospital, Cher remodeled the entire house so that it was A.D.A. compatible. And Janie wasn't her biological mother; Cher did it out of the goodness of her heart. And when Cher would be on tour and was playing the Dallas/Fort Worth area, she always made a point of visiting Janie in her home in Burleson. Shelly said it was quite the scene in the neighborhood when Cher's limo and tour bus would roll down the street! Apparently, all the neighbors would come out onto their lawns hoping to get a sight of Cher and maybe even meet her. Shelly told me other stories about Cher hosting them at her home in Malibu, CA. for a week-long summer visit, and how Cher could immediately secure box seats to a Dodgers game (in Tommy Lasorda's box, no less) or reservations at the best restaurants in town. Cher hosted Shelly's entire family with hotel suites and backstage passes at her concert at Madison Square Garden in New York. As Shelly told me, "we had to remind the kids that this is a world that only a few people can understand or experience. At times, it was hard to comprehend". On one of the summer visits to Malibu, Shelly recalled how she & Cher were having coffee by the pool one morning in their plush bathrobes when they saw a man whom Cher recognized running along the beach. Cher called out to him, and he stopped to say hello; Shelly instantly recognized the man as Stephen Spielberg.

Shelly offered many times to get me "really good tickets" to see Cher live, so when Cher signed with Caesar's Palace in Las Vegas to a series of shows there in 2010 I was in. Shelly asked if I would like to meet Cher after the show and I really thought she was joking. But she wasn't. I was dating a girl seriously at the time and set the trip up; I told her we had tickets to see Cher but didn't tell her anything else. We arrived at the will call window at Caesar's and were quickly introduced to a white-jacketed usher who showed us to our seats in the center of the auditorium, four rows back from the stage. "Wow" my date said, "how long ago did you get these tickets? Our seats are awesome". A few minutes later, as the arena was filling and the energy was growing, a nice fellow in a suit with a walkie-talkie in his hand came over and introduced himself. "Mr. Cocke?" he asked. (I don't remember his name; let's call him "Julius", get it?) "Yes", I said, "I am Mr. Cocke". "Welcome to the show, Sir. Cher is looking forward to meeting you. When the final encore is done, please make your way over to that elevator. I will be waiting there for you, and we will make our way down to the backstage area". My date nearly flipped out of her seat. "We're meeting Cher??" she asked. I explained how Shelly had set it all up for us and that "yes, we are" going to meet Cher after the show.

Shelly & Cher's sister, Georganne, was married to a guy named Ed Bartlack, and Ed was the head of Cher's security detail. It was, as one can imagine, a huge job. Cher was and will always be, one of the most successful icons in the entertainment business. Besides her phenomenal voice (it's even better live) and her seven Grammy Award nominations, she had become a huge success in movies, acting alongside Susan Sarandon, Michelle Pfeiffer and Jack Nicholson in *Witches of Eastwick*, as well as playing the leading role in *Mask* with Sam Shepherd. Her star adorns the Hollywood Walk of Fame and her song with Sonny, "I Got You, Babe" was #1 in the U.S. and Britain and is sung in every karaoke bar in the world. It's even quoted in Kenny Chesney's song *We Went Out Last Night*. But undoubtedly, her biggest movie success came in 1987 when, playing the Italian daughter of a cheating plumber in Brooklyn, N.Y., she was cast as Loretta Castorini with Olympia Dukakis, Danny Aiello & Nicolas Cage in *Moonstruck*. Shelly told me that Cher's Academy Award for Best Actress in *Moonstruck* sits on her mantel in Malibu. Surely everyone remembers the "morning after" scene where Loretta is making Tommy Camareri (Nichols Cage) swear never to tell anyone that they had spent the past night together. But Tommy is now deeply in love with Loretta and wants to proclaim his love to everyone, including his brother to whom Loretta is engaged! With a huge slap to the face, Cher screams "snap out of it!", and then slaps him again. It is cinematic genius.

So, it was with all of this in mind that we made our way to the elevator after the show to find Julius waiting for us, walkie talkie in hand. And about 10 of Caesars Palace's highest high rollers were joining us on the elevator! Julius looked at a bag I was carrying and immediately stopped me. "What's in the plastic bag?" he asked forcefully. I could feel all eyes on me as the elevator doors froze and another security guard immediately appeared right behind me. "Um", I said, "we're sorta family." I could sense all the high rollers were very perturbed by this delay as I nervously explained that "I was told by Cher's sister that Ed Bartalack (Shelly always called him "Ebar") was a big U.T. football fan. So, I had brought him some U.T gear from the Co-Op on the Drag in Austin". Julius rifled through my bag, complete with U.T. logo mouse pad, pencils and bumper sticker, decided I was no threat and let the elevator doors close. Now, all the high rollers had instant respect for us since they realized we actually <u>knew</u> Cher. We were hammered with questions like "how do you know her?" and "what is she really like?". I glanced over at my date who, as nervous as she was an hour or so ago, was now totally petrified. And then with a loud "ding" the elevator doors opened, and we were led down a long hallway to a reception room.

Cher was "in residence" then at Caesar's with Celine Deon and Bett Midler, and the three of them rotated in and out doing constant shows for adoring fans and invited guests of the casino. As we made our way down the long hall, each dressing room door on both sides of the hall was adorned with a photo of either Celine or Bett with the name "Ms. Deon" or "Miss Midler" next to it. I was starting to feel a little intimidated. My date's knees were shaking, so I slid my arm under hers and tried to act like we were very comfortable in this star-studded environment. Julius led us all into a very nice reception room; brightly lit on the far side was the photo backdrop wall festooned with the familiar "Caesar's Palace" logo. And Cher was standing there gleaming.

Chapter 44: I'm the lead singer, you're just the drummer.

Every year, usually in January, Ron, Charbel and I would take a weekend off and have a "partner's retreat". Usually, we would rent a house in the Texas hill country. The purpose was to review our company's performance the year before, critique ourselves as partners and managers, agree to our operating budget for the coming year and generally discuss areas of weakness or room for improvement. And it usually went pretty well, but as the company grew larger things began to be a little testy at times. Ron is admittedly very ADHD, which was fine except that he would regularly forget important meetings and often make mistakes with documents or spreadsheets. When we were just starting out, it wasn't really an issue; but now that we were really doing well, he started taking offense to my comments and corrections to his work. "You catch 'em" I told him often, "Charbel will clean and cook 'em and I will make sure the fuel bill gets paid and the insurance coverage doesn't lapse". It seemed to work before, but Ron became very reluctant to turn loose of what he considered "his" projects. It created confusion with our buyers, attorneys and lenders and I spent a lot of time cleaning up his errors and oversights, which frustrated him even more. I had to choose my words very carefully around him, lest he feel I was being critical or micro-managing him.

Another issue was the commissions we earned when we bought our development sites: because Ron & I were licensed real estate agents we split the buyer's (us in this case) commission 50/50. Since he was our business development guy, he naturally sourced most of our development projects and contracting jobs. That was his role and title, after all. But Ron wanted to start keeping all of those commissions for himself and not share them with me. Not only was I not in favor of that, Charbel had recently gotten his real estate license renewed, so I proposed that we split the buyer's commission one-third each.   Ron pushed back vigorously, telling us "It's me who brings in the projects so I shouldn't have to share the commissions with anyone".   So, in one of our weekly partners lunches, when we discussed current topics of importance, I forced the issue by making a formal motion on it and called for a vote. Ron was the lone dissenter, so my motion to share commissions one-third each passed. Not only was he not going from a fifty percent share in commissions to one hundred percent (which is what he wanted) his share was being reduced to thirty-three percent. It was the fair way to handle it, in my opinion, and Charbel clearly agreed. But it started a rift in my relationship with Ron that only grew from there.

Soon after that, Ron wanted to make other fundamental changes in our work structures, titles, and responsibilities. He thought all of us should be focused on business development first and said so. He even said, in front of Charbel, that the real reason he called me in the first place (from the Starbucks parking lot in Plano) was because I was "such a great real estate marketing guy". It was bullshit and he knew it and I reminded him that soon after we got ramped up (10 years earlier) with development projects I moved out of business development and into day-to-day operations management. It had been a good combination of skills and still was, in my opinion. We had grown to 16 full-time employees with hundreds of subcontractors & suppliers; the H.R., legal and finance issues were cumbersome at best and often daunting. "If everyone is selling tickets who is going to make sure the trains run on time?" I asked him. I didn't get a good answer and eventually Ron & I hired a business coach to help improve our communication. That really didn't work either.

The whole thing came to a head, for me at least, on a partner's trip to Las Vegas one long weekend in June 2018. We were rewarding ourselves for our hard work and success and booked nice rooms at the Wynn hotel, complete with nightly dinner reservations and show tickets. Ron & I had done the trip several times before Charbel came on board and had a blast. I was expecting a nice, relaxing trip and for the first day it was. Day two found us at the Wynn "European" pool where tops were optional. We had a nice poolside sunbathing pad with a big sunshade and lounge chairs in the water; we even had a private waitress. We were ordering pitchers full of mojitos and snacks, so naturally we attracted lots of people who wanted to meet us and share general poolside Vegas banter. It was all good fun, but I could tell Ron was especially interested in a couple of the young girls who were there. As the day was ending (it was time to hit the showers and meet at the Wynn steakhouse for our dinner reservation) we started gathering up our gear to move inside. So, I turned to Ron and without anyone else able to hear me told him "Do not bring those girls to dinner". He just smiled and shrugged it off, but I felt sure he understood my discomfort with it (all three of us were married at the time) and would comply with my request. I was wrong. He walked into the restaurant about an hour later with one of the girls on his arm and told the maître de that we were a "table of four now". I was pissed that he flatly ignored my request and showed such disregard for my feelings.

The next day we flew back home with a layover in Phoenix. Waiting for our flight to Austin, Ron asked that the three of us move to a quiet area where we could "discuss some things". I was sure he was going to apologize for his behavior the evening before (and maybe also for his inappropriate sexual references at our most recent company dinner) and set it straight in front of Charbel. Instead, he gave me a lecture about "leaving the office early" on certain days during the weeks I had Marshall at home. And, he had the nerve to tell me it was "setting a bad example" for our employees. I was floored – Ron's whereabouts were often a subject of conversation in the office and several times customers and prospects would arrive for a scheduled meeting with him and we had no idea where he was or when we might see him. This was over the top and gave me the final push I needed to get out. Our working relationship had dissolved into a "yes you did, no I didn't" argument and I was done with it. When we got back to Austin, I asked him for the specific dates he was referring to so that I could check my calendar and give him a response; at first, I refused to tell me, but finally, after much cajoling and expressing my right to respond with real data, he agreed. And there were six days over the last six months that were in question! So, I pulled my calendar and e mail log and created a spreadsheet showing the time (on each of those days) I sent my first e mail and/or had my first meeting and likewise, how and when my day ended. On average, I was working before 7 am each of those six days and finished sending & responding to e mails after 10 pm, long after Marshall had been fed and put to bed. When I shared this with Ron & Charbel, complete with a fully noted calendar and supported by e mail printouts and a chronological spreadsheet, they both seemed unimpressed; if I expected any kind of retraction or contrition from them, it sure didn't come. I wasn't really surprised and had already made up my mind I wanted to sell my forty percent shares back to them anyway. This just confirmed for me that the working relationship was seriously flawed.

My first task in getting out was to meet with an attorney who could advise me. Through some good friends, I was introduced to a guy named Ed McHorse with McGinnis, Lochridge. I called Ed and was soon sitting in his conference room in downtown Austin with the company agreement Ron, Charbel & I signed several years before. Ed read through the section that addressed how a partner's shares would be repurchased; and he complimented me on having good documentation. "The process for buying a partner's shares is very clear" Ed told me. "There is a 10% down payment and then the balance is paid at eight percent interest monthly over the next five years". That was what I understood, too, I told him. "So, what's the company worth?" he asked. I think he expected a vague "I don't really know" kind of response, but what I told him clearly surprised and impressed him:

"Well, the three of us take an owners retreat every year in January" I told him. "We always discuss and approve the operating budget for the next twelve months (it was something I spent a lot of time preparing and presenting to them) and then we agree on a value of the company at that particular time." I consulted several bankers, business brokers & CPAs on the mechanics of valuing an owner-managed, tightly controlled "small" business and the three of us agreed to the metrics we used. Mostly, we did this so that we would make sure we had plenty of life insurance on each of us in case something tragic happened and we needed to buy a partner's shares from his estate. And I did not want a grieving widow to come in and make claims that she was "told by him" that the company was worth much more than it was. It was good business management and I had learned the lesson well watching Dad navigate the process of buying out his parents and siblings at Varmicon. As I laid all of this out for Ed, he noted that "it is June now" and asked what the value was we had agreed to six months earlier. I reached into my laptop bag and handed him the corporate memo each of us had signed in January 2018 confirming the value of $1,000,000. "Ok," Ed continued, "do you think the value of the company is increasing this year?" he asked. I was sure it was and told him I expected it to double; my shares would then be worth $800,000. "Well, then it serves your interests to stay on, work hard, play nice and make it to January 2019. Can you do that?" he asked. I told him I was certain that I could, and we scheduled a follow up meeting in December to check on the progress of the company and the status of my working relationship there.

Over the next six months I did my best to stay focused and continue to make a valuable contribution to the company. We were enjoying another good year and the revenues of our general contracting company that year surpassed $25 million. While we were getting a nice salary, we still had well over $600,000 in start-up debt to repay and were determined to put our obligations to those debts first. Which is why I was so shocked when Ron showed me plans for a huge 6,000 square foot house he was going to build in Georgetown, TX. I said "Ron, most people downsize when they become empty nesters. Have you lost your mind?" He was clearly offended at my lack of enthusiasm for his grandiose temple.

January 2019 arrived, and I prepared the year-end financials for us to review on the retreat. And, after a good conversation and applying the valuation metrics we had used successfully in prior years, we agreed unanimously that the company was indeed worth $2,000,000. I wrote up the memo, printed it out and we each signed it. Several days later, I e mailed it to Ed at his office in downtown Austin and set up a meeting with him in a few weeks to put the "share redemption plan" in motion.

Ed drafted a letter for me to present to Ron & Charbel referencing the buyout terms of the company agreement and the valuation we had recently signed in Fredericksburg. Ed's letter was brief but succinct and reflected my thanks for the wonderful personal & working friendship we had enjoyed over the years. At this point, Ron and I had known each other almost twenty years and had shared some wonderful times together.   I felt like it was in his best interest for me to move on so that he could be free to operate the company as he saw fit without my "scrutiny and questions" as to his oversights and whereabouts. Especially at company functions and executive getaways. I wanted this to be a smooth transition and expected them to be relieved that I had decided to get out. But, like lots of life's expectations, they were not so happy or relieved. In fact, a week later they fired me and gave me 24 hours to remove my belongings from my office. (I wasn't given the chance to say "goodbye" to the people I had hired and groomed over the years and who had helped us build this wonderful enterprise; I thought that was very unfortunate.) Since Ron and I together owned the office in a separate LLC, I asked Ed if they could really force me out of it. He wisely advised that I comply with their request and keep my eye on the "bigger prize". So, I did. (About a year later Ron & I sold the office to a physician and split the proceeds 50/50 as per our written agreement).

Ron & Charbel hired their own lawyer, and we began the work of writing a share redemption agreement. Between the three of us, we had several other LLCs (some actively developing real estate and some not) in addition to the operating general contracting business that I was selling out of. And there was the start-up debt that we had to include in the negotiations. After several months, and one successful mediation session downtown, we had the terms all ironed out. In June of 2019 I agreed to take the ten percent down payment over six months (instead of in a lump sum) and to continue paying my fifty percent share of the start-up debt to the debt holders (mostly Ron's parents and in-laws at this point) each month. I also agreed to a clause saying I would not compete with them in Central Texas in contracting or development until they had fully redeemed my shares. We shook hands and several days later I signed the agreement and got my first check. With interest, they were going to pay me just over $1,000,000 over the next five years; now, I just had to go find another job or start another business.

Chapter 45: A mother, a son, and a sunrise.

A lot was going on in my life in the Summer of 2019: I had signed papers to sell my interest in the business but had also agreed I wouldn't compete with my former business partners in the Austin area; Marshall had just graduated from Bowie High School in Austin and would be joining Savannah at O.U. in Norman, OK. After twenty years of hands-on fatherhood, I was now an empty nester. And I was living in a house that was bigger than I really needed.

Fortunately, I had been spending a good bit of time in the Houston area doing business development for the Huffman development model: custom build-to-suit office condominiums for doctors and professionals. And I was having some success: I had two sites under contract: a 2.25-acre site in Pearland and a 1.5-acre site in a well-developed office park in Katy. (Katy is famously known as the place where the actress, Rene Zellweger, grew up.) Both cities are growing, well-established suburbs of Houston. So, I listed my house in the Circle C area of Austin and quickly sold it. I went townhouse shopping in the Heights area of Houston, and I found a really nice three-story townhome in a great area that suited me well. Two months later I moved into my new townhouse, after selling a lot of my household furniture (the townhouse was about 30% smaller than my house in Austin) and downsizing. I would work out of the house and continue expanding my contacts and sphere of influence in the Houston real estate market.

In October, I had several doctors interested in potentially buying offices in both Pearland & Katy and they were reviewing my purchase documents and talking in detail about how much space they thought they wanted. Soon the holidays arrived and honestly, I wanted to slow the pace of my life down; I had been working 60-

hour weeks for almost 12 years and needed some time to recharge. The doctors interested in my potential offices were moving slowly and I was ok with that. I vowed to work less and relax more and get through Christmas (a nice few days with Mom and Dad in the hill country) and the New Year of 2020. I did my best to spool up my energy and get focused on real estate development, but it wasn't easy. I just wasn't sure I wanted to keep on doing office condo development. As February arrived, I was asking myself if the potential profits were worth the tremendous effort and capital required.   And then one morning the phone rang.

Mom had been in declining health for several years and had been diagnosed with vascular dementia. Dad did his best to care for her and strongly objected to the idea of them moving into a retirement community; my sisters and I discussed it but decided that we should honor Dad's and Mom's wishes. We even sent a social worker to their house just to do a "needs assessment" on the care Dad was providing. After she made a house visit and evaluated the situation, she assured the girls and me that she thought Mom was getting adequate care at home and there was no need to move her. But as I answered the call on my cell phone and seeing that it was my sister "Shelley" I had a feeling this was not good news. And it wasn't. Mom had been suffering from severe back pain for several months and an ultrasound confirmed that she had two or three compressed disks in her back; the doctor explained that there was very little he could do besides the frequent cortisone injections she was already getting.   And they weren't providing much relief. Mom's mental faculties had also diminished quickly the past few months; I noticed a big decline in her at Christmas. She even said "Cinco, I know I am dying. And I am at peace with it. Just please take care of your Dad when I am gone". I guess none of us but Mom really understood how much her body was failing her. On the phone, Shelley explained that "Mom's pain meds are making her very drowsy, and she is refusing to eat." I knew that was a bad sign, so I packed a bag and drove quickly to Ingram, just outside the quaint hill country town of Kerrville nestled along the scenic banks of the Guadalupe River, covered in places by large lily pads, with tall Cypress trees on both sides.

By the time I arrived all three of my sisters were there. Mom's pain was, for the Moment, regulated but it was clear that Tylenol was not enough for her. With her doctor's support, we called Hospice and convinced Dad that Mom needed full-time care in a treatment facility or hospital. To our surprise, he agreed, and we quickly "booked" her into Hilltop Village, a care center in town that Cindy found and liked. By the end of the next day, Thursday, Mom was moved there and started receiving stronger pain meds through an IV. Friday morning her doctor arrived, and after a thorough examination of her vitals and brain activity, told Dad, the girls and me that Mom was nearing death. I think we all knew it, but still the news hit hard. I was, at this point, more worried about Dad than Mom. But as the five of us, now joined by Mom's sister, Jean, sat with Mom and told her goodbye that Friday afternoon I sensed that Dad was starting to accept the reality. Her doctor said it might be a "few days, or a week at the most" before she would die. That night, Dad, the girls and I went to dinner with Aunt Jean and the next morning, Saturday, I ran by Hilltop Village before sunrise to see Mom once more before driving back to Houston. (It was pretty clear that we were going to have a funeral the next weekend and I needed to make travel plans for my kids, several family friends, and find a house big enough for us to stay in for three nights. I had let everyone know what the doctor had told us and asked them to start making plans for the following weekend in Kerrville.) Shelley had spent the night in Mom's room and as I walked down the hall towards them the nurse stopped me. "How did Mom do last night?" I asked. She gave me a very caring glance and said, "it will be tonight".

I woke Shelley up as I walked into Mom's room, but I had a Vente coffee from Starbucks and poured her some as she stirred out of her sleep. "The nurse said Mom will probably die tonight" I was

273

finally able to say. As I looked past Shelley, the most gorgeous Texas sunrise was breaking over the hilly horizon through the full, mature oak trees just outside Mom's window. She noticed it too, and simultaneously we both realized that this was likely Mom's last sunrise on earth! "Mom needs to 'see' this" Shelley exclaimed. And I agreed. So, we swung her bed 90 degrees so that she was now facing the window and said "Mom, here is the world waking up just for you". It was bittersweet and poignant and about an hour after sunrise I knew that I needed to get on the road for my four-hour drive back to Houston. With a kiss on her cheek and one more "thank you for everything" I headed out to my car and left Mom there with Shelley, arriving home right at twelve noon. At just after midnight, early Sunday morning, Mom passed peacefully into god's arms. My first thought when Shelley called with the news was how thrilled Mom must have been to hug State again after almost forty-five years. But I also knew that I would miss her terribly.

Chapter 46: What is a Pandemic?

The second week of February 2020 brought beautiful weather to the hill country: warm days and cold nights with very low humidity. Many family & friends came in for the service Saturday morning, and as I glanced across the church to begin giving Mom's eulogy from the front pulpit, I was pleased to see Ron & Charbel walking through the door. After Mom's funeral service that day, the kids and I retreated to our nice, rented home with outdoor fireplace and beautiful family room. We opened several bottles of red Cabernet, grilled some thick ribeye's and sat down to a beautiful dinner. The conversation eventually turned to news out of China about a virus that had somehow started in an open "live meat & vegetable market" in the large city of Wuhan. No one knew much about it, but we did know that it was starting to spread around the middle east. My kids said the rumors on most college campuses was that the Chinese had intentionally released it on Iran in hopes that it would sicken many people and potentially stop their nuclear weapons program. I'm not much for conspiracy theories and shrugged it off as nothing more than conjecture. Besides, it had been a grueling eleven days since I first drove to Kerrville, and we admitted Mom to Hilltop Village. And since we had just had her service that day, I wanted to try to relax and stay happy. Dinner wrapped up and after some light conversation we all headed to bed.

The following weekend we had Mom's service in Harlingen and interred her ashes at St. Alban's Episcopal church there. I drove Dad back to Ingram and helped him settle into the house. Dad was struggling with neuropathy in his feet & ankles and needed a walker with wheels to move around. As I drove away, headed to Austin, I knew it would be really tough for him facing the future without the woman he had loved for almost 65 years. I decided to listen to the news on the radio and it was blowing up about the virus, now called

"Covid 19" since it started in 2019. The Chinese were refusing to admit they were responsible, but our government was sure they were. President Trump, not a person for subtle speeches or soft approaches, told the American people that we were sure the Chinese had fabricated the virus in a medical lab in Wuhan and that the "live market" story was B.S. Everyday another country was announcing that someone there had tested positive for the virus and was very sick. And it was very contagious. "What if it comes to the U.S."? we all wondered, and Trump declared that all inbound flights from China were cancelled and anyone traveling from or thru China would not be allowed into our country. The liberal media, who hated Trump and still couldn't accept the fact that he had beaten Hillary Clinton in the Presidential election, called him every name in the book: "China hater" and "anti-immigration" to name a few. And then a man in Washington state, who had visited China just a few weeks earlier, tested positive. Covid 19 was officially in the United States; the bigger question was "what exactly does that mean?".

As the weeks unfolded and we learned more about this respiratory illness, it became clear that it was very contagious and could be deadly, especially to older people and those with pre-existing health conditions. Since the U.S. was about two or three months behind the rest of the world in facing the arrival of the virus and its repercussions, we had to look at what was going on in other civilized and third-world countries, and it wasn't pretty. The rate of spread was rapid and there was no vaccine available yet. The White House would hold daily briefings with Trump quickly yielding the podium to our most-trusted medical officials, namely Dr. Anthony Fauci who was the Director of the Centers for Disease Control. I don't think anyone in charge really had any idea what the near- or long-term future really looked like, but they did their best to sound positive. Trump even claimed that this virus "would be under control by Easter". I have no idea where that information came from, and knowing Trump, he probably made it up on the spot thinking he needed to prevent mass hysteria. While we weren't quite to that point, the media took it upon themselves to scare the crap out of people and give us daily updates on how many people in our country were infected. Very soon, there would be confirmed cases in all 50 states, and the deaths were starting to mount.

One of the most common phrases to come out of the crisis was "social distancing" which meant if you were out in public, you should stay at least six feet away from anyone else, lest they be an unconfirmed carrier and sneeze the viral particles into the air! Businesses would place stickers on the floor indicating where and how people should "que up" in order to maintain a good social distance from each other. Restaurants began operating at half capacity so that their customers could be spread out while dining. Grocery stores and other big stores would only allow a certain number of people inside at any given time, which caused long lines of people trying to get inside and buy essentials. For whatever reason, there was a "run" on toilet paper and eventually bottled water and hand sanitizer; grocery stores had to limit the number of each that customers could buy, but the shortage was acute and would last several months.

By mid-March, Covid 19 was THE story and companies were telling their employees to work from home and not come to the office, another attempt to reduce human interaction and potential spread. Hospitals were quickly filling up and doctors, especially in the densely populated cities like New York, were stretched very thin. And while it was encouraged that people wear a "mask" while in public, no one seemed to agree how effective they were. And there was a run on them, too, so anyone who wanted to wear one while in public probably couldn't buy one. Airline bookings dropped; people bought groceries and gas but otherwise stayed at home. And while the FDA was working on a vaccine, there was a big shortage of testing kits, so if someone thought they had symptoms they couldn't get a test anyway! Some would be positive but not show any symptoms; others would get very sick and literally die within days of becoming symptomatic. And the news around the world was even worse: China was absolutely covered in Covid cases given their very dense populations centers. Italy was hit very hard and countries without good medical facilities and doctors were overwhelmed.

And it had only been forty-five days since the first confirmed case in the U.S.! I was certainly worried but not ready to panic. The lines at the stores were a nuisance, for sure, but I really thought this was going to pass. Until it was announced that the Houston Livestock Show & Rodeo, which had just started its annual three-week run at NRG Stadium, was being cancelled. The vendors, city and any people involved would lose millions. That's when it hit me that this was going to have a major impact on our daily lives. No one knew for sure how long the impact would last, though. And very soon the "doubters" and "conspiracy theorists" came out with their own interpretation of what was going on: some thought that China did this intentionally to take over our country; others said the Democrats saw it as an easy way to ruin our economy so that they could win back the White House; some thought Fauci was a liar and stood to profit from the money that the pharma companies would soon earn once the F.D.A. approved (with warp speed) a vaccine. And the hospitals were calling any death of someone with Covid a "Covid death" since they could charge the insurance companies way more money that way, even though the person who "died from Covid" was probably very immune-compromised anyway and died from pre-existing conditions made fatal by Covid. The world was definitely talking, but who knew what to believe?

Marshall & Savannah were both in college with Spring Break coming up in a few weeks. Marshall had made plans to go to Destin, Florida with a group of his friends, which was a tradition for O.U. freshmen. But even they started having doubts about whether it was a good idea to expose themselves that way. And again, the biggest fear was that someone would have symptoms and couldn't find a hospital with any empty beds to treat them. To my surprise, but also to my relief, his group cancelled their plans, and he went home to Austin for the week. Colleges were trying to figure out what to do with all of their students, who were packed tightly into on-campus housing and crowded into classrooms and lecture halls. At first, they told all their students to take two weeks off for spring break (instead of the one-week break that was scheduled) apparently to give everyone more time to assess the best route forward. But before the first week was over, O.U. and every other college in the country announced they were closing the campus and all further instruction would be online via Zoom or one of the other video-conferencing applications we would all learn to know very well. That meant Savannah could choose to go back to the house she lived in (she did) or stay home the rest of the semester. But Marshall lived in a freshmen dorm on campus, and they were given two weeks to move out. He & I loaded boxes and empty luggage crates from summer camp into my Expedition and headed to Norman, OK to gather his things and move him out of the dorm.

We would all learn about "Zoom" meetings and virtual classrooms. The idea was to eliminate as much interpersonal contact as possible to slow the spread of the virus until a vaccine could be approved. The economy did, in fact, slow way down; except online "e commerce" boomed. Since people couldn't easily go to the store for the things they needed, it was easier to order online and have it delivered. Amazon, UPS & FedEx saw their sales skyrocket; to compete, major retailers had to dedicate parking spots in their lots for people who would order online and then drive over to the store, pop their trunk open and the store employees would load their groceries or whatever into their trunk. It was and still is called "contactless" delivery and it is here to stay. With so many people, and their children, staying home social interaction was extremely curtailed which began to cause mental health issues: people were scared and depressed. Special events, like birthdays & weddings, were either postponed or cancelled completely. The N.B.A.

cancelled its season; high school and college graduation ceremonies were cancelled. Major U.S. cities with dense populations were becoming ghost towns. Every day the news channels were a constant stream of horrible news about the rates of infection and malaise. You just couldn't escape it. 2020 would become a year that everyone had to endure, and no one wants to go through anything like it again. By the end of 2022, worldwide Covid 19 cases totaled over 670,000,000. Worldwide deaths were almost 6.9 million. In the U.S., total Covid cases were almost 105,000,000. Total U.S. deaths were 1,142,380 including my wonderful cousin, Rory Thomas, who died in Lubbock in the fall of 2020 after her breathing machine was removed.

As bad as it was, we have had pandemics before (in fact there have been nineteen pandemics in recorded time that have each killed more than 1.0 million people worldwide; AIDS alone has killed 40 million according to Wikipedia) and will likely have them again. The major difference between now & then is that we have social media and a system of broadcast news that is instant and worldwide. And the news media feeds on bad news. Covid gave it plenty.

Chapter 47: A teacher is reborn.

As the spring of 2020 turned to summer and the world waded through the challenges of this pandemic, the two development projects I was working on to build offices for doctors in Pearland and Katy fizzled out. No one, least of all doctors, was going to sign a contract to buy a building in fifteen months and borrow $1.0 million to do it. At times, I found myself battling my own issues with depression and hopelessness. Since I was already working from home my daily routine hadn't changed much, but my sources of interaction, namely church, the gym, restaurants and grocery shopping were all significantly reduced. I found solace and metal health riding my bike on White Oak trail near the house. I could jump on it, be away from traffic, and ride a 25-mile loop in just under two hours. That summer, I was riding 75 – 100 miles a week and lost about fifteen pounds. But what did all of this mean? Physically, I felt great; psychologically, I wasn't so sure. Did I really want to build small office buildings for doctors & professionals, I wondered? I wasn't sure that I did.

But then an idea occurred to me: I felt the itch to teach coming at me. I remembered how great it felt to connect with the CB 102 students at Lake Arrowhead, CA. and I wanted to get that feeling back. So, I submitted an application to the Texas Realtors Association as an instructor in continuing education. A few weeks later, I received a letter telling me I had been approved. My first move was to call the guy at TRA who supported the instructor field, Jon Houser, and pick his brain. "So, Jon" I began, "what courses can I teach?". Jon explained that I could teach the mandatory courses because TRA together with the Texas Real Estate Commission created the material and would share it with me. "But, what about these cool elective courses?" I asked. "Can I teach some of these, too?" Jon then told me that those courses were written by the instructors who taught them, and it was very doubtful they would share it with me, lest I take their work and get paid to teach it. The world was speaking to me through Jon, and almost instantly I thought about the many times I had called on a "For Sale" sign on a tract of land that looked like a good site we could develop. Once I was able to get the listing agent on the phone and ask some questions, it became clear that they didn't know much about the site. It was clear, as I thought more about it, that the licensed real estate agents in Texas who were working land listings (and almost all of them either are or want to) needed help understanding the land due diligence process. I told Jon I had some ideas and would call him back.

Now, this was a big pivot point: I hadn't taught a live class in twenty years, so I was taking a pretty big leap thinking that I could not only teach a class on real estate but actually write the course material. But something inside me told me I could. The world was talking to me again. And I decided to listen to the sound of my soul saying, "do it".

My pulse was quick as I listened to the phone ringing on the other end. With Covid in full attack and most people not working in their offices, it had become very difficult to reach people by phone. Hell, it had become hard to reach them at all! But then I heard Jon answer and say "hello, Cinco, what's up?" "Jon" I asked, "how do I get T.R.E.C. to approve my continuing ed class?" "You have a continuing ed class you want to submit to T.R.E.C.?" Jon asked. I explained that I did not have a c.e. class "yet" but assured him I would soon. He walked me through the process and basically said I had to submit an outline of the course to T.R.E.C. that showed how much time the course would take. I was sure it would be a three-hour elective and went to work writing the timed outline and "course objectives" as Jon had explained on the T.R.E.C. form. I submitted it online, as per T.R.E.C. rules, and waited for a response. To pass the time, I rode my bike more. I found a new trail that basically ran east from Buffalo Speedway along Braes Bayou through the Texas Medical Center and Hermann Park to the Houston Ship Channel. I could see the massive Sidney Sherman Bridge spanning the channel right in front of me, which was my turnaround spot. Round trip, it was 25 miles. (By the way, from the top of that bridge, if you look carefully to the east, you can see the famed San Jacinto Monument (which is taller than the Washington Monument – we Texans like size) marking the spot where Santa Anna, Mexico's Commander of the Army, surrendered to Gen. Sam Houston on March 2, 1888. In that Moment, Texas was born.)

A month or two later, a letter arrived from T.R.E.C. saying my *Development 101* class had been approved; I decided it needed a catchy subtitle so that licensed agents would want to take the class, so I came up with *"Sell Land to Developers and Make Big Commissions"*. Now I just had to get people to hire and pay me to teach it, but I wasn't really sure how. After another call to Jon Houser and several other seasoned instructors, I learned that I had to market my class to local Realtors Associations across the state of Texas. Most of them had their proven stable of repeat instructors so it was difficult to get through to them and extol the virtues of my new class! No one seemed very interested in some new instructor who had some new class that had never been taught. I was discouraged but I had been a member of the Central Texas Commercial Association of Realtors for several years and knew the Association Executive, Amy Ables, well. So, I called her up, explained my new class and then e mailed her the course marketing flyer. Well, I guess the world was talking to Amy that day and telling her to take a chance on me, because a week or so later she called and booked me to come teach it for C.T.C.A.R. in October 2020. I quickly hired a newly minted graduate of the University of Houston and had her create a Power Point presentation of the course that I could use to teach.

Naturally, I was nervous when I arrived at the private dining room at Che Zee restaurant in Austin that day. But I was more excited than nervous and anxious to see how the class material would be received and whether my confidence in my teaching skills was justified. Twenty-five people had registered for the class and were filing in and filling the seats around the nice round tables covered in white tablecloths. An instructor is always nervous about any technological glitches in a new venue, and this was my first venue of any kind! As I powered up my laptop and connected it by HDMI cable to the large screen behind me, the first slide of my power point came to life. I tried using the remote control which would advance the PPT from slide to slide and it worked! One quick "testing, testing" spoken into the microphone pinned to my shirt (it sounded great) and I was set. For the next three hours, with breaks every fifty minutes per T.R.E.C. rules, I walked everyone through the process of how I, as a developer, evaluate land sites for a potential development. I gave them two real-time case histories of the site evaluation process and walked them through how one turned out to be great and the other was a total mess. As I say in the class, "as I go through the due diligence process, I simply trying to determine if I am about to kiss a Frog or a Princess." And I tell them they should do the same thing before going on listing pitches with potential land sellers, because most landowners really don't know much about their land and many have unrealistic notions of its true market value. As I wrapped up, I reminded everyone how important it is to fill out the course and instructor evaluations on the Texas Realtors website. (As instructors, we have to consistently achieve a 4 out of 5 rating to maintain our T.R.A. certification.)

As people began gathering their materials and getting ready to leave, I turned around and saw about 6 people in line wanting to talk to me! A couple of them just wanted to say that they really enjoyed the class and had a couple of quick questions. But several more had real time listings they needed help with or knew someone who owned land, wanted to develop it, had no clue how and wondered if I could do it for them! I was overwhelmed with the reaction, and it proved to me that my instincts about the need for this type of course was spot on. The evaluation links are open for four days after the class at which time I can log in and read them. It was a resounding success. I got a 5 on every question regarding the course material <u>and</u> me as an instructor.   The written comments were very positive, and several people said they "wanted more" courses like this one! I was blown away – the world was right again, and I was being rewarded for listening to it. A few days later my first check arrived in the mail for a whopping $500 – I was officially a paid real estate instructor (and writer!) and feeling very gratified.   Now, I just had to keep calling members of T.R.A., finding the person in the office who handled education for the local agents and sell them my class. It was slow at first but like anything else, persistence began to pay off. It took me two years to finally get to teach for the Houston Association of Realtors (and its 48,000 members) and for the Austin Board. Soon, I was teaching all over the state and something funny was happening: everyone kept asking me for "more" on the topic! Frequently, someone would ask "when are you teaching Development 102?". At first, I sorta laughed it off – "there isn't a 102" I would reply. But then, the message became clear: I needed to write Development 102 as a follow-up to the first course. People were speaking – I decided to listen. So, in the summer of 2022, I submitted the timed outline for Dev 102 to T.R.E.C. and it was quickly approved! I was soon teaching the classes back-to-back around the state, with Development 101 in the morning and Development 102 in the afternoon.

Chapter 48: Go north, the rush is on.

(Note: in compliance with an N.D.A. I executed, the names in this chapter have been changed. Any resemblance to actual companies or people is purely coincidental.)

With Covid raging in the summer of 2020 and my teaching endeavors not yet started, I was bored. And like most people, the unknown ultimate effects of Covid 19 had me unsettled. Then one day in August I got a random call from a guy who introduced himself as an "executive recruiter". He told me that he found my information and credentials on LinkedIn and had been hired by "a large oil & gas company here in Houston" to find them a seasoned real estate consultant. Would I have any interest he wanted to know? My first thought was it sounded too cumbersome – me, work for a big oil & gas conglomerate? I didn't know anything about oil & gas and hadn't worked for a big company for almost fifteen years – but as he explained the specific needs of this company and gave me an idea of the comp package, I decided to hear him out. The company was (and still is) one of the largest privately-owned oil & gas companies in the country, called White Oak. I had never heard of them, but he told me they had recently purchased the production and assets (real estate and otherwise) of Yukon Oil & Gas in Alaska. I would later learn that the purchase price of the deal was north of five billion dollars. This was a scale and scope that I had never been involved with, but it certainly sounded intriguing – he kept talking and I kept listening.

As the call wound up, he told me he wanted to arrange a zoom introduction with the company's Chief Financial Officer, Jane Murphy. A few days later, I was logged into zoom and talking to her from her office in downtown Houston. Jane explained that White Oak, by virtue of its Yukon purchase, now owned and/or leased quite a bit of commercial real estate in Anchorage, the Kenai

Peninsula and the North Slope. She said they had a good idea of what they now had but weren't really sure what fit into their long-term needs and strategy. "Do you think you can help us?" she asked. After explaining that I had grown up in construction and over the past twenty years had leased, sold, developed and constructed almost 2 million square feet of commercial real estate, she was clearly comfortable with my skills. The next step, Jane said, was to interview with several more White Oak people, including Larry Gregory, White Oak's C.E.O. I told Jane my schedule was fairly flexible, and I could be available to accommodate Larry's schedule. As we were wrapping up, she asked one more question: "Have you ever been to Alaska?" she wanted to know. "Yes, as a matter of fact I have" I replied and told her about a great fishing trip that I had taken there with family several years before. Jane was a warm and very affable woman and I immediately felt comfortable talking to her. "That's good" she said, "then you know how beautiful it is". As we ended the zoom meeting and she told me to expect an e mail or call from her office to set up the next round of interviews, I thought to myself: wow, this sounds like a great fit. They needed me for about a year (at which time they would scale back to a property manager overseeing their real estate) so the timing was good. I could never have imagined myself coordinating the real estate portfolio of a major oil & gas company, but here I was talking to one about doing that very thing. I'm glad I listened to the recruiter when he called even though my first instinct was to decline.

****

It was a cold, cloudy day in early November as my United Airlines flight from Denver descended into Anchorage. As we finally broke out of the clouds, I could see the snow-covered mountains and Cook Inlet below us; it was frozen solid. Covid was in full force and Alaska had been hit particularly hard; in order to travel to the 49th state you had to have proof of a negative Covid test that was no more than 72 hours old. Which meant you had to get tested (Covid tests were finally in adequate supply) and get your results back quickly to even board the plane. Every traveler had to create a "traveler portal" on the state's website and upload your negative results once you had them. As we deplaned into the terminal it was a little surreal; this was a Sunday afternoon which is typically a busy travel day. But the terminal, much like my flight, was half-empty. Stores and restaurants that would normally be open were closed and as I walked down the concourse towards baggage claim I looked up and saw two rows of long tables flanking my path. On each side sat people in full hazmat outfits with a laptop in front of them. Each of us was directed to an open table where we presented our I.D. and boarding pass. The person at the laptop, fully covered from head-to-toe in what looked like surgical gear, checked our traveler portal to confirm we had tested negative as per the state's rules. The young female in front of me handed my driver's license back to me with blue latex glues on her hands and said, "welcome to Alaska". I found my bag and walked outside to a waiting White Oak vehicle driven by one of the Anchorage employees. It was probably about 20 degrees F outside.

I was joined in Anchorage by Mary & Kent, two White Oak people from the lower 48 who had good knowledge of the company's real estate & facility operations. We were there primarily to coordinate moving about 50 former YUKON people (who now worked for White Oak) into White Oak's offices across town. This was the first of three moves to occur. The first day was consumed with meeting the White Oak people in Anchorage and touring their offices, warehouses and raw land. Yukon had built a 14-story office building, the Yukon Tower, with an adjacent day care facility across the parking lot for its employees. But Yukon had sold the building to a REIT in Chicago several years before and signed a master lease with them; that lease still had ten years of term remaining, so it represented a large obligation to White Oak. I read the lease and operating reports on the flight up and was familiar with its terms, so it was at the top of my priority list to create some recommendations for Jane about how to minimize costs. Mary, Kent and I set ourselves up in the Yukon Tower command center on the ground floor of the building and walked every floor of it so that I could get a feel for its layout and amenities. While a little dated (it was built in the mid-1980s) Yukon had maintained it well and furnished it with some impressive Alaskan artworks. Other than the first-floor lobby, second floor data center and the top floor executive offices (with some very impressive views of the Kenai Range, by the way), every floor was full of cubicles from one end to the other. And all but about four floors had no one on them. The Yukon employees who weren't staying on with White Oak either took other jobs or early retirement; the empty floors and cubes and chairs were an eerie ghost town. Boxes of books and office supplies were everywhere, as well as laptops and monitors. It was clear that the clean-up job was going to be daunting. And finding other tenants to take a full floor (22,000 square feet) of cubicle space in a soft Anchorage market (I read the Costar office report on the flight up, as well) was gonna be even tougher.

We went over to the management office and met six (yep, six!) men who worked there; they had been with Yukon since the building had been built. These were good, knowledgeable building engineers with strong skills; the challenges of maintaining a 14-story office building in a harsh Alaskan winter had to be tough I thought to myself as we shook hands. I was anxious to talk to them and find out what they did on a day-to-day basis. "So, where is the day care building?" I asked. They walked me out the back door (over heated sidewalks to prevent ice from building up) towards a quaint building that looked very similar to a home in a Thomas Kinkade painting. We walked through the facility, and I met the staff; Yukon had leased the facility to a day care operator from Portland, Oregon but was subsidizing the rent dramatically so that their employees could get daycare at a discount. I had been told before going up to Anchorage that it was time to renegotiate the rent "at market rates".

As we walked through the building, with classrooms full of very young children flanking the hallway, I learned that there were close to seventy children enrolled there.   And most were from Yukon/White Oak families. At the end of the hallway was a door leading outside to the playground; imagine my surprise as we walked out to see 20 small 3- and 4-year-olds running and playing all over the place in the 20-degree temperature. The snow and ice didn't seem to bother them at all! But immediately, I saw potential liability, and lots of it. What if one of these children were to slip and fall? Or lose their handle climbing on the icy jungle gym and suffer a serious injury?? I took my cell phone out of my coat pocket, stripped the gloves off my hands and dialed Jane's direct office line back in Houston. She answered quickly and I said "Jane, White Oak is selling the day care" and showed her what I was looking at via Facetime.   She quickly agreed that the day care didn't align with White Oak's core business and gave me the green light to find a listing agent and get it sold. Six months later, after a lot of coordination and effort (day care operations are licensed and regulated by the state, which meant we had to find someone already in the business there) we closed the sale of the day care building.

****

As my second day in Anchorage was drawing to a close, after a tour of a 50,000-sf warehouse building that White Oak was moving out of (also a very big logistical project headed by White Oak's director of Information Management, Meredith Cameron) Mary, Kent & I were getting hungry. They had driven over from the hotel that morning together and I had my own White Oak SUV, a nice Ford Expedition with snow tires and 4-wheel drive. I would learn quickly why every vehicle in the state had remote starting features: so that you could get the heat going 10 minutes before walking out of the office and getting in it! Mary suggested dinner at one of her favorite local places, a pizza joint called "Mouse's Tooth" with a vast array of craft beers. "Sounds good to me" I said and told them

I would meet them there after wrapping up some summary e mails for the day. As they headed out the door I walked over to the window, pressed the "start" button on my remote and watched as the lights of the Expedition came on indicating that the engine was running, and the heat was engaged. This Texas boy was learning Alaskan ways and enjoying it very much.

Walking out to the Expedition, it was 6 pm local time so it had been dark for well over an hour. Snowplows kept the parking lots fairly free of snow and ice, but the footing was still pretty tricky. And the streets were just as slick. As I climbed into the warm driver's seat and started the navigation system to Moose's Tooth, I could hear and feel the crunch of snow under the tires as I made my way out of the parking lot and onto the busy, two-lane thoroughfare running along the front of the Yukon Tower. All of a sudden, a pickup truck sped past me on my left and was throwing snow in all directions; he was clearly driving way too fast for the conditions and as his vehicle passed mine, I heard a very loud "wham". I knew he had sideswiped me, but I had no idea how bad it was. My head was spinning. As I eased my foot onto the brake and began to slow down, I looked at the driver's side rear-view mirror: it was busted to pieces. It was clear that his side mirror had impacted mine, but I still wasn't sure if there was body damage. Thoughts raced through my head; mostly I was concerned about being very new to White Oak and already involved in a car "accident" even though it was clearly not my fault. And then I looked up to see this guy had stopped in the middle of the street at an angle that blocked both lanes.

I eased the Expedition closer and could see him pointing to our left as though he wanted me to drive down the side street. He had absolute rage on his face, and I was sure there was no way I was following this guy anywhere! Cars were beginning to pile up behind us when he climbed out of his truck and began walking towards me. I quickly checked his hands to see if he was carrying any kind of weapon; fortunately, he wasn't. I rolled my window down about halfway, engine still running, as he walked up to my SUV and shouted at me, "hey, assh—e, you hit my car!" "Whoa" I replied, "I think you hit mine when you passed me so fast". He was clearly very angry and looking for a fight. "Oh yeah" he shot back at me, "so now you're gonna argue with me?". I explained I wasn't arguing but that it was clear that he had caused this accident, not me. I was trying to maintain a calm demeanor and get the hell out of there. At which point he put his hands on his hips and said "Well, my kid is having open-heart surgery. What the f—k are you going to do about that??"   And in that Moment, I heard a voice say "this guy is scared to death about his child. And he is struggling to handle it. Go gentle with him." "I'm so sorry about your child, is it your daughter or your son?" I asked. "Her name is Annie, and she is nine years old" he told me. His voice was a little calmer and his posture a little less threatening. "Well," I said, "I will say a prayer for Annie tonight that she is strong and recovers quickly". With that, the guy muttered a "whatever, man" and walked back to his truck. As I pulled into the parking lot at Moose's Tooth my heart was still racing; there was no body damage done so I was relieved about that. I knew I would have to report this to Kelly Davis, White Oak's office manager and liaison to Human Resources, the next day. She was very understanding, said that "fender benders" are pretty common in Anchorage in the winter, and not to worry about it.   I wanted to hug her neck.

****

Over the next four months I would make two more trips to Anchorage, each for about 10 days. My last trip was in March 2021 and while it was still pretty cold some of the snow was beginning to melt and the blue skies appeared. I took one day off, a Sunday, and drove up to the Alyeska ski resort about an hour's drive from Anchorage to do some snow skiing. I told myself "Not many people can say they have skied in Alaska" and I wanted to do it. I even

292

passed a heard of moose grazing along the highway on my drive up there. The views of Cook Inlet (still frozen) from the mountains along the Kenai Peninsula there in Alyeska were beautiful. After a day of solo skiing, I enjoyed a cold beer back at the resort, spent the night and then drove back to Anchorage the next morning in time to get to the office by 8am.

I met and worked with many wonderful people in Anchorage, including Kelly and many commercial real estate agents and attorneys. My goal was to help craft a real estate strategy for the newly acquired Yukon assets, streamline real estate decisions and implement the plans that had been agreed to. Mostly, I worked with White Oak's in-house general counsel, Susan Singer. Susan was a smart, polished, savvy attorney who had been the de facto real estate director since the Yukon acquisition. (Her office window faced Mount Denali, the tallest point in North America at just over 20,000 feet above sea level, and offered an awesome view of the peak on a clear day). I could tell she was very ready to offload most of those duties and responsibilities. Over the eight months between November 2021 and June 2022, Suan and I would talk almost daily and work together on a vast array of assignments and tasks. Together, we oversaw three moves of Yukon people from the Yukon Tower into White Oak's offices, including the relocation of the Yukon artwork, and coordinated the reduction of many operating costs of the Yukon Tower by hiring a new management company and negotiating a significant reduction in the building's appraised value and related ad valorem taxes. Together, we saved White Oak millions of dollars in operating expenses related to the Yukon Tower and its Anchorage properties. I know she is as proud of it as I am.

As June 2022 arrived, I signed my exit agreement with White Oak and quickly took off for a long weekend with Robert Fowler in a house we rented in Lake Tahoe. My buddy from Austin, Judd Olson, rode up on his new Ducati motorcycle, so Robert & I rented a couple of Harleys and the three of us took a day riding around the lake area of Nevada and California. We hit the casinos, grilled some steaks and poured some nice red wines that Robert brought from one of his frequent visits to Napa Valley. The scenery was beautiful and reminded me of certain parts of Alaska. Judd left a day earlier so Robert and I grabbed a tee time at Edgewood Golf Club and played a round of golf together. I was feeling the stress of the White Oak pace lifting and began to set my sights on what might lie ahead. Would the world talk to me again? I wondered. Would that familiar world voice be there guiding me along to the next phase of my life & career? Boy, would it ever.

Chapter 49: La Frontera

I have been keenly aware of the cross-border trade between Mexico and the U.S. since I was a young boy. Often, we would drive to Matamoros for dinner so that Mom & Dad could buy a couple bottles of their favorite scotch at steep discounts. Apparently, Mexico didn't have the liquor taxes that we do here in the U.S. I also recall back in the early 80's when diesel fuel was way cheaper in Mexico than the U.S. Anyone who had a diesel vehicle would drive over the Rio Grande and fill their car. The savings, again, were significant. As U.S. citizens, we could travel freely into Mexico and drive all the way across it if we wanted. I had spent many family vacations in Mexico over the years and spoke Spanish fluently (another advantage of growing up in South Texas).

In fact, during my college years and after I would frequently grab Dad's Suburban (I lived in Harlingen for about two years after we sold Varmicon), load it with friends and frat brothers and drive three or four hours south of the border to our favorite small towns for bird hunting. This was, of course, well before the turf wars broke out between the "Sinaloa" and "Gulf" drug cartels. We would stay in Jiménez, or Soto La Marina or even Ciudad Victoria, the capital city of Tamaulipas state with a population of 400,000 people. All three towns were nestled in the foothills of the Sierra Madre Mountain range and very scenic. During hunting season, we made the trip almost every weekend and would often leave our shotguns under the bed of our motel rooms when we checked out! The motel owner knew about it and assured us not to worry; and our guns were always there when we went back the next Friday for a weekend hunt.

From Dad and his business ties all over the Valley, I heard about the maquiladora "twin plant" program that fueled a growth of industrial development on both sides of the river and created lots of jobs, too. So, when my friend Wynn Searle told me about a speculative warehouse building, roughly 135,000 sf, he was developing in Laredo for a wealthy group of Ft. Worth investors, I was intrigued. The idea of building one very large building, instead of ten small ones and all the minute details of medical finish-out for several, if not many, very challenging customers, sounded really good to me.

Wynn had already leased his first building and was well along on the planning of the second one, a 330,000-sf concrete tilt-wall distribution warehouse in Pinnacle Industrial Park. Laredo has two commercial bridges crossing the Rio Grande, and the 18-wheeler traffic there is "vibrant" to say the least. Pinnacle Industrial Park is located on Mines Road, between the two bridges. Wynn agreed to drive down to Laredo with me and introduce me to his general contractor, Park Avenue Construction. While there, we would meet several bankers and a couple of commercial real estate leasing agents. I also wanted to meet the guy who was developing Pinnacle Park (in phases, by the way) and talk about any lots he had for sale. But first, before making the trip, I needed to do some homework on Laredo to understand why it was such a busy border crossing point for commercial trucking.

After much web searching and research, it basically came down to this: Laredo prospers because of its geographic location. It is only two hours north of Monterrey, Mexico, the capital of Nuevo Leon state and a metropolitan area of over six million people. And it is the commercial juggernaut of northern Mexico; hell, it might be the commercial juggernaut of the entire country! Many Mexican and U.S. companies have significant manufacturing and assembly operations there; the list of U.S. firms with major operations in Northern Mexico includes just about every one of the companies listed in Standard & Poor's 500 stock market index. And once their products are brought over the river into Laredo, it is then only two hours farther north to San Antonio; and San Antonio sits at the confluence of IH 10 & IH 35! IH 10 runs east/west from

Jacksonville, FL to San Diego, CA. And IH 35 runs from Laredo, TX. to Duluth, MN on the Great Lakes. Talk about a geographic logistical advantage! Laredo has it in spades.

As I was doing my research, I found a website listing the busiest ports in the U.S. measured by combined total of imports and exports annually. Number one was the port of Los Angeles/Long Beach; second was Chicago O'Hare Airport; and third was good ole Laredo, Texas. And it was a close race between them. Not only that, but L.A. was also declining, O'Hare was stable, and Laredo was growing at a steady pace. I was hearing the world again, and it was telling me that this makes sense. I went to Costar and to CBRE's website and dug around for their most recent market reports: the vacancy rates for industrial warehouses there was around 2%! A "stable" market, meaning neither the landlord nor the tenant has a particular negotiating advantage, is typically considered 10%. This was a strong landlord's market if ever I saw one! When I searched Costar for "industrial buildings for lease" the only thing that popped up were some older, metal buildings that had low ceilings and crummy truck courts. Wynn had leased his first building before it was even finished (you need a Certificate of Occupancy from the city to allow a tenant to move in, hence we refer to it as we "C.O.d" the building). And he wasn't the only one; buildings started out as speculative projects only to be leased before a C.O. was issued.

And the news about cross-border trade was good, too. By the fall of 2021 Covid was waning and the world economies were picking back up. But some odd things were happening: many workers around the world decided they didn't want to go back to work. Businesses were trying to hire but had few applications. And China was a long way from solving their Covid pandemic problem; many of its plants and ports were either completely shut down or operating at half capacity. Some Chinese companies set up dormitories for their factory workers so that they could spend every night there and never go home after the workday ended. Many essential products in the U.S. come from China, including medicines, computer chips, essential raw materials and products. But China couldn't get it to us because of the significant reduction in manufacturing capacity there. Many people believed it was intentional to weaken our economy and exert control over us.

China was also making threats about bringing Taiwan under Chinese control. Taiwan is an independent, sovereign nation and a close ally of the U.S. Many essential products and parts come from them, too, and the U.S. has a compelling interest in maintaining a free and democratic Taiwan. Everyone in the world knew that the coronavirus started in Wuhan, China and most were pretty convinced China did it on purpose. Whether or not they did, it was very clear that the U.S. needed to wean itself away from the "C.C.P." (Chinese Communist Party) and bring the sources of essential products & materials closer to home. And what place is closer than Mexico? The buzzword being used was "onshoring" and it meant we needed to lessen our dependence on the C.C.P. and bring manufacturing/assembly onto the shores of North America where we could depend on it. That manufacturing/assembly would most likely be in Northern Mexico, and its most likely port of entry into the U.S. was Laredo, TX. The demand for industrial buildings, especially new ones with modern facilities, high ceilings and ample trailer parking wasn't likely to slow down for the foreseeable future.

****

I was introduced to the listing agents for Pinnacle Industrial Park and began looking at their inventory of lots for sale. Since Wynn's group was now developing larger buildings (over 300,000 sf) I told him I would look for lots where I could develop something smaller, in the 100,000-sf size; we agreed that we would not compete with each other in Laredo. After several months of negotiations with the Pinnacle Park people, and a couple of restarts on which lot I was going to buy, I executed a contract to buy 6 acres on the north side of the park. I wrote a personal check for the earnest money and had ninety days to find an equity partner. With the help of Park Avenue Construction, I had some very good preliminary plans (after several iterations we agreed that I could put almost 104,000 sf on the site) and they gave me an idea of what the construction costs for the site & building would be. After factoring in the cost of the land and additional costs for project management, marketing/commissions and financing costs, I assembled a development proforma and was ready to show it to a bank and apply for the construction loan. The total project cost was just over $10 million which equated to roughly $100 per square foot.

I called three local Laredo banks and set an appointment to sit down with them and go over the figures I had put together. All three of them knew the people at Park Avenue Construction, including their owner and C.E.O. John Valle. By this point I had gotten to know John well and felt very comfortable with him and his team. P.A.C. had been one of the largest industrial construction firms in Laredo for many years and had an excellent reputation, so now I needed a construction loan so that I could hire P.A.C. to design the building and give me a fixed price to construct it. After meeting all three banks and their chief lending officers, I felt most comfortable with Texas Community Bank, which was run by a bunch of people from the former Laredo National Bank. We discussed what percent of the total project they were willing to loan and kicked around different scenarios for personal guarantees from me and my equity partners. T.C.B. agreed to limit the partner guarantees if I could bring $2.5 million in equity, which meant they were willing to loan this yet -to-be-named enterprise $7.5 million. Even though I was a rookie at this kind of development, they clearly felt confident in my ability to pull it off. With a loan in hand, now all I had to do was go find $2.5 million.

I put together a projection of cash flows based on current leasing rates in the market and calculated the potential IRR if we sold the occupied building at current cap rates. It was essential that the IRR on this completely speculative project be at least 20% and 25% would be even better; using some spreadsheets that I got from a CCIM class, I plugged in all the variables of the project and solved for IRR. We would definitely hit the 25% target, and with a little luck (a higher lease rate or lower construction costs, or both) I could get the IRR closer to 30%. I spent hours writing the *Private Placement Memorandum* that I would soon send out to equity investors I knew; the plan was to buy the land, construct the building, lease it and then sell it for a nice profit. I was committed to putting $200,000 of my own money in the project (roughly 8% of the total equity) which I was sure would give investors' confidence that I believed in this enough to put my own money at risk. And, like most development projects like this, once it was sold and the original cash investors got their money back (plus accrued, preferred interest) I wanted to share in a greater percentage of the profit than my own eight percent investment. In other words, I would be "promoted" to a bigger piece of the pie once the building sold.

I started calling people who I knew had invested in developments like this to see if they would have an interest. I canvassed friends and colleagues in commercial real estate for equity leads; it was time consuming and cumbersome, but I was sure it was going to bear fruit. Two seasoned real estate veterans in Austin, Doug and Charlie, were high on my list of potential partners. They were smart and experienced, and I knew they had the resources to do this deal; it would mean only three partners in it, them and me, and that sounded very appealing. Doug was receptive when I called him and agreed to have a look at my P.P.M., which I quickly e-mailed him with a copy to Charlie. After a few days, Doug called and said they were going to turn it down. Naturally, I was disappointed but vowed to stay in touch with him and update him on any news that I thought was positive. And I did. There was frequent news about the volume of trade across the border at Laredo and how it was growing. Anytime I saw an updated market report, showing an absolute dearth of industrial property for lease, I sent it to Doug

& Charlie via e mail.   And again, they turned it down.

My best prospect at this point was a fraternity brother, Rusty Tamlyn, who had been very successful in industrial real estate leasing & sales all over the country. Rusty and I had reconnected thru the men's bible study group at St. John Episcopal and I gave him a very brief idea on what I was doing. He asked me to send him the P.P.M. and said he thought he knew some people who might have an interest.   I was an absolute sponge for any data or contacts that might help me better pitch my development.   Rusty thought he could help. After reviewing the program, he called and told me he & a colleague wanted to come to Laredo and do some "fact finding" on the market. I was very pleased to hear this since Rusty has influence and contacts all over the U.S. When he learned I was putting a significant portion of my own money in the deal, he was even more positive he could help. One day my cell phone rang, and I saw it was Rusty; "Cinco" he started out, "there aren't many commercial flights to and from Laredo. We are trying to make it a day trip but that is looking impossible". So, I said "Rusty, if you really want to do this easily, you should consider chartering an airplane". Rusty agreed that was a good idea and the next day called me with his travel plans; I agreed to meet them at the Laredo airport at Signature Flight Services.   All I knew was the "N" number of the plane and the time they would arrive. Imagine my surprise when a beautiful Learjet taxied up to the parking area and Rusty climbed out.

We had a great day driving the market and touring many industrial parks. Rusty was very positive about the dynamics of the market and the prospects for raising equity. As Rusty's beautiful, chartered jet climbed into the blue south Texas sky, I was feeling good about my project. As I drove away from the airport and navigated my way towards my hotel, my cell phone rang loudly. And when I looked at the caller I.D., I saw Doug's name on the screen. "Hey, Doug" I said, "what's up with you and Charlie?"

Doug and Charlie were thinking seriously about being my equity partners, but there was one thing Doug wanted to know: would I consider holding the building once it was leased rather than selling it? My first thought was that I didn't really think so, because it was the sale of the building that would really put a nice jingle in my pocket. But I listened as Doug explained why they wanted to hold it: "we like the deal, and we think the returns are good, but if we put our equity in and then pull it back out 24 months later, we then have to find another place to put the equity". That made sense to me, but what about my big "kiss" from the sale proceeds, I asked him. "Cinco, you're prepared to put in 8% of the cash needed, right?" I confirmed that he had the math correct. "Well, how about this: we will agree that you get more than 8% ownership in the deal. Would that work?" As we talked through more details and agreed, verbally anyway, how much of the partnership I would actually own, I was excited. I had known Doug for many years and always enjoyed meeting with him and hearing his wisdom. He and I clicked. So, we agreed to have his attorney form a brand-new partnership and draw up the company agreement.

There was just one more thing I wanted to kick around with Doug: "you and Charlie, together, will be majority owners. Which means my vote may not carry much weight. What if I want to one day sell some or part of my shares at some point? Would you two buy me out?" Doug said that they would certainly be willing to put language in the company agreement which described the mechanism for me to sell my interests to them. Soon, we had finalized the company agreement and everything I wanted (and they wanted) was in it. We executed the agreement and each of us wired our equity funds to Texas Community Bank in Laredo. Overnight, our account balance went from $0 to over $2.5 million. Now, we just needed to close on the land and get our plans drawn up and approved by the city. Park Ave Construction was ready to sign a Fixed Price contract with us and coordinate the civil site plans and building drawings. We were off to the races, so to speak.

In May 2022, we bought the land and were making good progress. Our new company, CCD Laredo #1, hired me as the project manager (we signed the P.M. Agreement at the same time as the Company Agreement) so I now had a new, full-time job. But there were some clouds on the horizon: as the world economy awoke from its Covid slumber demand was sky high for goods & products. But many people who had been laid off or lost their jobs during the pandemic decided they didn't want to go back to work. I guess all the stimulus checks the U.S. government had been sending out made lots of people flush with cash. So, a serious labor shortage existed. Which meant companies had to pay higher and higher wages to attract people. And the wait times for construction materials like lumber, steel, plastic, concrete and fixtures grew longer and longer. Since contractors needed these materials to keep projects on schedule, they were willing to pay more to get them. Commodities markets sensed the inflation that was going on and futures prices for oil, natural gas, gold and silver shot up, adding to the inflationary pressures of world economies.

Very soon, the Federal Reserve knew they had to stem the growing inflation that was pinching working people's buying power. Grocery prices were going up quickly, especially meat and eggs. Gasoline at the pump went from less than $2 per gallon to more than $6 a gallon in some markets in the span of six months! So, Fed Chairman Jerome Powell announced that the Fed would start raising interest rates. Their goal was to make borrowing more expensive which would serve as a disincentive for people to buy and borrow. It had worked in the past, and Powell was sure it would work this time. Between March and December 2022, the Fed raised interest rates seven times, taking the prime rate from 3.5.% to 7.5%. But such action has a lagging effect, so anyone who had seen this before knew it would take time for the inflation factor, which had been 2.3% in February 2020 before Covid to 8.3% in April 2022, to ease.

John Valle called me. "Cinco, we're having problems, like everyone else, in getting construction materials". I was very nervous that John and Park Ave were going to renegotiate our contract for a higher price, but to their credit, they didn't. And I will always respect them for it. They went to work, locking in prices on materials and scheduling well in advance of delivery to keep their costs, and mine, within our contract prices. But I knew the higher interest rates would mean our interest payments on our construction loan would be higher than I had budgeted. I had a decent contingency amount – let's hope it is enough to cover it. Such is the life and risks of real estate development!

But the rumblings from China were still loud. Because of their densely populated cities (there are thirty cities in China with more than 10 million people!) they had not solved their Covid problem. The C.C.P. issued lockdown orders which meant no one could leave their home. Cities, factories and ocean ports were totally shut down. And the growing call for onshoring and lessening our dependence on China was growing ever louder. Which meant more demand for assembly and manufacturing in North America, especially Mexico. Clearly, our timing on our first building was good: land prices were increasing and lease rates for industrial property were, too. I didn't know how long this mini boom would last, but I was feeling good about our early position. We were even offered a $500,000 profit on our lot in Pinnacle Park just six months after we bought it. Was our timing a little lucky? Yeah, it definitely was. But like the Roman philosopher Seneca once said, "luck is what happens when opportunity meets preparation". Or as Lee Trevino (a wonderful, outgoing Hispanic golfer who was born on the rough streets of El Paso, Texas and rose to golf's highest heights in the 1970s) once said: "the more I practice the luckier I get". How true.

Once again, I had perked my ears up twelve months before when I heard about what was going on in Laredo. Having grown up in a predominantly Hispanic area, I understood the culture and traditions of the border region. And having a Hispanic nickname didn't hurt, either. I was in a good place, personally and professionally, and was enjoying the opportunities and challenges of industrial development. It had been a very challenging three years: I became an empty nester, sold my business, lost my Mom, moved to a new city and started my career all over due to a killer pandemic. And all of it combined to take me places I never could have imagined, dealing in development projects in the tens of millions of dollars, and making new and wonderful friends along the way.

Chapter 50: A gentle giant moves on.

Christmas 2022 was fast approaching, and I was anxious to get on the road from Laredo for the five-hour drive back home to Houston. I had been there twice during the last two weeks, once for our new building's groundbreaking and the second trip was for Park Avenue Construction's wonderful Christmas lunch. Both were very special events, and I was so pleased that my friend Stacy Locke attended the groundbreaking, together with my sister Gayle. At the P.A.C. Christmas lunch, many Laredo businesspeople whom I had gotten to know well were there and it was a fun and festive time. But as I drove into my garage back in Houston on the night of December 22nd, I was glad to be home for a while and ready to celebrate a calm and meaningful Christmas at home. I quickly unpacked, poured a glass of red wine, grabbed a shower and hit the rack for some much-needed sleep. No alarm clock for me in the morning, I declared.

Except that I forgot to silence my cell phone, so when my sister Cindy called at 6:30am I was startled out of a deep REM sleep. "Hey, what's up?" I mumbled, still very groggy. I knew this was probably a call about Dad; we had moved him to an assisted living center, Menger Springs in Boerne, TX, earlier in the year near Cindy's home. I had spent Thanksgiving with him and noticed further deterioration in his mental and motor skills. At 92 years old, he told my sisters and me often he was "ready to go and be with your mother". Watching him struggle to move around, and even eat his Thanksgiving dinner, I fully understood.

"Dad is in E.R. here in Boerne" she told me. "The nurse at Menger Springs checked on him early this morning and he was barley responsive, so she called E.M.S. I am here with him now." He had apparently had a stroke and was still mostly unresponsive. The doctor there had run some tests and found several things they wanted to treat, but that meant moving him to a hospital in San Antonio. Cindy quickly conferenced Gayle & Shelley onto the call and put the doctor on speaker phone. The four of us quickly agreed that Dad would resist going to a hospital; earlier in the year, when his G.P. found a spot on one of his lungs during a routine x-ray Dad refused to have it biopsied or treated. "Why would I do that?" he asked us when we told him about the spot and the treatment plan. He was beyond trying to "fix" anything wrong and frankly, I think he hoped it would eventually be the thing that took him down.

I asked the doctor "so what happens if Dad doesn't go to the hospital and get treated?" She said his organs would fail and he would die but was reticent about giving us any timeline on that. "Cindy, is Dad awake? Can we talk to him?" Shelley asked. Cindy walked over to Dad, and he could hear us. We explained his options and asked him what he wanted to do. I heard his feeble voice say, "I want god to take care of it". "So" Shelley asked, "no doctors and no hospital?" Again, Dad simply mumbled a weak but audible "no." Cindy volunteered to call Hospice and begin the process needed to get Dad back to his little apartment at Menger Springs. As the person appointed with his medical power of attorney and also holding his original "do not resuscitate" orders, I knew I needed to hit the road for Boerne, a good four-hour drive away.

The next day was Christmas Eve (I had plans to join my good friend, Gay Wickham, and her family in her home for dinner, with church services Christmas morning) but it was looking like I would be in Boerne for several days, so I packed a full suitcase, grabbed Dad's documents and headed out the door. Gayle arrived there about the same time I did, and we got Dad's room ready for his return. About twenty minutes later, E.M.S. rolled him into his apartment and moved him onto the hospital bed we had hastily installed with the help of Hospice. His color was good, but his mouth was open, and his breathing was already short and shallow. By this point, he was totally unresponsive. The nurses suggested we give him supplemental oxygen through a narrow tube placed under each nostril. There was conversation about giving him pain meds, but the nurses assured us he looked like he was pain free and resting well. "Patients like this, when they are in pain, usually show signs of it. We can tell your Dad is feeling ok" they told us. So, now it was just a waiting game. Cindy went home to rest up and Gayle and I sat in Dad's apartment chatting and holding vigil. At one point, I heard a light snore coming from him. It made me smile.

And then, about four hours later Gayle and I noticed that his breathing had become quite slow. We could see his chin rise and fall, but it was clear that his breathing had diminished dramatically. Gayle walked to one side of the bed, and I stood at the other, flanking this big man who was living his last few moments on earth. Gayle's cell phone rang, so she stepped out to take the call but said "I'll come back with the nurse". "Ok" I told her, not taking my eyes off Dad and his very infrequent breaths. Could this be it? I wondered. Is this the end for him here and the beginning in heaven? And with that, he fell silent. No breaths. No sound. No life. I rubbed the top of his hand, those big bear claws that had kept me in check for so many years, and said "well done, Dad. You made the trip just like you always wanted: just peacefully fall asleep and not wake up".

The silence was startled by Gayle and the nurse coming through the door. I gently put my hand up to them and said, "he's gone". I looked at the clock at it read 6:12pm. It only took four hours for him to be reborn into his eternal life. What a blessing. The nurse checked his wrist and neck for a pulse, and they even brought in a blood pressure machine on wheels just to be sure. But they did not need to. He was with Mom now, sharing their first Christmas together in three years. More blessings. Hospice arrived and officially declared his death at around 8 pm. We had called the funeral home that handled Mom's service in Kerrville, and they were there to take his body. Before they wheeled him out, I gave him a quick kiss on the forehead and said "thanks again, Dad, for everything. I hope to be half the father you were." Gayle and I turned, followed the stretcher out to the van, watched them load him into it and gave each other a big hug. It was time to check into our hotel and grab some dinner. I was famished and exhausted.

****

Saturday January 7, 2023 was a bright, clear, cool day in South Texas. I rented a nice three-bedroom condo at South Padre for the weekend; Marshall and Savannah were both coming for Dad's service, and they brought their significant others, Colaney and Jordan. We arrived at St. Alban's Episcopal in Harlingen with plenty of time to spare and gathered with all the family; given that Dad had seven grandchildren and eleven great-grandchildren, we were a big group. I had written and edited my notes for the eulogy several times and was ready to honor this man that had showed me and my family the world. In a quiet moment before the service, my world voice spoke again and lifted me up. "Your Dad was not a perfect man" it said. "But you chose to focus on the good, forgive the shortcomings, and enjoy a very special relationship with him for many years". And, you know what? That was a conscious choice I made.

After the service we gathered with many friends from over the years who had been a part of Dad's life and ours. It was an odd feeling not having a living parent, and as the kids, Colaney, Jordan and I loaded into the van for the one-hour drive back to South Padre I filled my Yeti tumbler with my favorite red wine (Saldo Zinfandel by Orin Swift) and climbed into a seat alone, next to the window. As we rolled past the places I had known for sixty-two years the memories flooded back. There was the football stadium where Eddie Casas cracked his arm on my head. There was the park where we had our Key Club flag football games and BBQ fundraisers. Down that street was where my first high school girlfriend, Sharon Haynes, once lived. Over there was the Sonic where we would all hang out on weekend nights (when we weren't in Reynosa, anyway). The tall palm trees, neatly flanking the highway, zoomed past. Soon we were driving through Bayview and the orange groves that had been there for many years. Shortly, I could see the blue waters of the Laguna Madre Bay appearing on the horizon. And just a little further, the beautiful causeway bridge that stretched from the mainland to South Padre Island; at 2.5 miles long, it is the longest bridge in the state of Texas. Our company supplied the concrete for it forty-five years ago, and I smiled thinking about the pride I knew Dad took in that. Yes, growing up in South Texas was special.

"Hey Dad, are we really taking some of Missy & Daddy Jim's ashes to Africa?" I was startled back to reality by Savannah's voice. All my parents' grandchildren called them Missy and Daddy Jim, and they had heard that my parents requested that a small part of their ashes be taken to Africa and spread there in the Masai Mara of Kenya. I was going to make that happen (I gathered some of their ashes into small plastic bottles before the service that day) and planned on taking Marshall & Savannah with me. During their years, Mom and Dad had taken every one of their children and grandchildren to Africa with them. Except for my kids, who were still too young then.

"Yeah, we are" I replied. "It is one of Mom and Dad's deepest wishes to be together again in Africa" I told them. So, the kids all whipped out their cell phones and began looking at pictures of Kenya and Mt. Kilimanjaro. Someone asked, "how long is the flight?" and "do we really stay in green tents?" The four of them were a beehive of energy and conversation about the trip and didn't wait for me to answer. Which was fine. At that point, we were passing the historic lighthouse in Port Isabel and climbing up to the peak of the causeway. From there, I could see the vast expanse of the Gulf of Mexico and mentally pictured Africa way beyond it. The herds of animals and the beauty of the rift valley are waiting. We will find the perfect spot, probably under an Acacia tree at the top of a rolling hill overlooking the vast plains and leave Mom and Dad there forever. Their hearts are already there; soon a part of their bodies will be, too.

Epilogue

State's body was cremated, and his ashes were spread in a nice, manicured area of our property on Bass Blvd between Harlingen and La Feria. Mature mesquite trees and some of mom's favorite lantana plants surrounded him. For several months after the service there, I would feel pensive and sad thinking about his untimely death. So, I would walk down the narrow lane that led from behind mom's greenhouse (she and I built it together from plans she pulled out of *Better Homes & Gardens* magazine) and walk to the spot where his ashes lain. Somehow, it gave me some peace just being there and feeling close to him. I imagined him looking down and knowing how much I missed him. And I could also hear his voice, or maybe it was my world voice for the first time, telling me to be strong and go make him proud. It was a pivotal point in my life, whether I knew it or not. I could choose to be sad and withdrawn and act like a victim, or I could get on with life in a way that showed I learned something from this tragedy. I chose the latter, and I chose to listen to the words I was hearing. I chose to listen and, as you now know, that has carried me along in life ever since. Have I stumbled and fallen at times? Sure, I have; haven't we all? Would I do certain things over in my life? Maybe. But I also realize that those failures and mistakes helped mold me into who I am. Like the PKA house poker games at U.T., I learned a lot more from the hands I lost than the ones I won. And I eventually parlayed that experience into more & more winning hands, and fewer losing ones. Life is very much like that, isn't it?

State's loss also taught me how precious life is and to appreciate more-fully what we have. It took many years to fully grasp it, and I am sure there were times I let stress or conflict move my anger more than it should have. But with more experience and maturity came a deeper faith in God. And a sincere desire to be Godlier; it's a daily effort for sure, but I have come to a place where I refuse to let other people's actions or impressions of me steal my personal peace. There are many things I don't understand: as I write this a war rages in Ukraine: Russia's autocratic leader, Vladimir Putin, ordered the invasion one year ago in February 2022. The death and war crimes he and the Russian army have unleashed on a peaceful, sovereign people is unspeakable. But I trust that God has a plan in everything, and I prayerfully ask him to help these innocent people. In the meantime, I draw from Philippians 4:6 which says, "the peace that passes all understanding will guard your hearts and minds". I may not understand it, but through scripture I can be at peace knowing a higher power is in charge.

A few weeks after I returned to Texas from my first trip to Anchorage for White Oak, I made plans to celebrate Christmas 2020 with dad at his home in the beautiful Texas hill country. I took a small tree to decorate and pre-ordered a full, traditional Christmas dinner for us. My sisters would all be with their grandchildren and Marshall and Savannah were with their mom, so it was just dad and me. It was our first Christmas without mom, and though we didn't talk too much about that, I knew we were both feeling her absence.

Christmas morning, we opened some presents and celebrated with a nice glass of champagne. I kept a warm fire going in the fireplace and dad played Christmas carols from the *Sounds of the Season* music channel on his cable TV lineup. As I tore open Shelley's gift to me (she is and has always been a world class gift giver and card writer) and opened the box, it was a book. And not just any book. It was *Alaska* by James Michener. All 1,125 pages of it! I had never read any Michener (even though he donated his entire collection of manuscripts and work to the Harry Ransom Center at U.T. Austin) probably because the sheer volume of his novels intimidated me. But I decided right then I was going to read this if only to tell Shelley that I did. In the opening chapter Michener describes how one million years ago, prior to the continental drift that occurred on our globe, Alaska was physically located on the equator! Now, having just flown seven hours to the north to get to Anchorage, and knowing that the North Slope of Alaska was only 325 miles from the North Pole (I googled it) that boggled my mind. But then that familiar world voice spoke to me and said:

"I am reading about something that happened one million years ago. Which means that one million years from now someone will be reading about what is happening today. And we are only here on mother earth for eighty or ninety years if we are lucky. Some, like my brother, get far fewer years than that."

And in that moment, I once again committed myself to spend the next thirty years of my life being as peaceful as I possibly could. And to sew peace in other people's lives, as well.

So, the next time someone cuts you off on the highway, or sideswipes you on a snowy, dark boulevard, give them the road. Maybe whoever is driving is trying to make it to the hospital before their nine-year-old daughter is wheeled into open heart surgery. Maybe their wife or sister is in labor on the back seat, and they are just trying to get her to medical care to ease her pain. It's called giving them the benefit of doubt and being empathetic. It's treating our neighbors the way we would want them to treat us. After all, in this short stint we have here on earth, we are all in it together. And if you happen to get to heaven before me, tell my brother I will see him soon. He and I have a lot to catch up on.